ELEMENTARY ARABIC
A GRAMMAR

ELEMENTARY ARABIC
A GRAMMAR

BY

FREDERIC DU PRE THORNTON

being an abridgement of
WRIGHT'S ARABIC GRAMMAR
to which it will serve as a table of contents

Edited by

REYNOLD A. NICHOLSON, M.A.
Lecturer in Persian in the University of Cambridge, and some time
Fellow of Trinity College

GYAN

Published by

GYAN

Gyan Publishing House
5, Ansari Road
Daryaganj, New Delhi-110002
Phone: 011-47034999, 9811692060
E-mail: books@gyanbooks.com

Distribution Network
gyanbooks.com
India, USA, Canada, UK, Australia, France

ISBN : 978-81-212-4305-6 (PB)
First Published, 1919

2nd Impression 2020

Printed at: Gyan Press, Delhi.

Elementary Arabic A Grammar
Author: Frederic Du Pre thornton

ELEMENTARY ARABIC
A GRAMMAR

BY

FREDERIC DU PRE THORNTON

being an abridgement of

WRIGHT'S ARABIC GRAMMAR

to which it will serve as a table of contents

EDITED BY

REYNOLD A. NICHOLSON, M.A.

Lecturer in Persian in the University of Cambridge, and some time Fellow of Trinity College

CAMBRIDGE:

At the University Press

1919

PREFACE.

FREDERIC DU PRE THORNTON was born in 1841 at Wendover in Buckinghamshire, where his father, the Rev. Spencer Thornton, was Vicar, and received his education at Brighton College. He commenced the study of Arabic in 1880, when he first visited Egypt and Palestine, following the method which he recommends in his *First Reading-Book*, namely, "to begin by reading aloud, from a book fully pointed, with a Moslem who is accustomed to recite the Qur'ân (Corân) in public prayer." From 1880 to 1892 he was almost continually in the East. As Mrs Thornton, who accompanied her husband on all his journeys, writes to me:—"He was very quick at languages and thought much of correct pronunciation, so that during several visits to Egypt he had one of the students from the University Mosque al Azhar, Cairo, to read Arabic with him. His whole thoughts and time were given up to his projected Series, and especially to the Arabic Grammar, as he found so many in Egypt, Army officers and missionaries, who did not care to go to the expense or labour of learning the larger and more difficult Grammars. We visited twice the Jebel Haurân, the ancient Bashan of the Bible, and found it a most interesting country to travel in, and the Druse people very hospitable, especially to the English. My husband's idea in visiting India was to find out about the Moslems there, and whether they spoke Arabic much amongst themselves, which does not seem to be the case. It is only used there as the Sacred Language." Mr Thornton was acquainted with most of the leading Arabists in this country—Professor William Wright, a portion of whose *Arabic Reading-Book* (Williams and Norgate, 1870) he read with the author; Professor W. Robertson Smith, Professor Ion Keith-Falconer, Sir Charles Lyall, Professor D. S. Margoliouth, and others. My friendship with him began, I think, in 1895 or a little afterwards, and we corresponded pretty regularly until his death, which took place in January 1903, besides meeting now and then to talk over the work on which he was engaged. I have pleasant recollections of the hospitality shown to me by Mr and Mrs Thornton on several occasions when I stayed with them at Westgate-on-Sea, as well as of the enthusiasm with which Mr Thornton would discourse on his favourite topics. Few can have known Wright's Grammar so perfectly as he did, and though the present volume bears witness to his minute accuracy and to the systematic thoroughness with which he entered into the smallest details of exposition, only those whom he consulted or who helped him in his work can have any conception how much thought and labour it cost him to produce. He was trying to improve it almost to the last day of his life.

This volume, however, does not stand by itself. It was Mr Thornton's intention to compile and publish an Arabic Series, based on the Corân, which should enable the learner to get a good working knowledge of the language without the necessity of constantly referring to other books. Of this projected Series he left two volumes already printed and in private circulation, *viz.* the present abridgement of Wright's Grammar and a First Reading-Book consisting of certain extracts from the Corân together with a Grammatical Analysis and Glossary. Subsequently he determined to enlarge the latter volume by adding to it some fifty pages of Wright's *Arabic Reading-Book*, which had nearly run out of print; and at his request I compiled a Glossary for this additional matter. It was passing through the press when its progress was interrupted by Mr Thornton's untimely death.

Fortunately, the scheme which he had so deeply at heart is to be carried out in its entirety, as far as another hand may be capable of executing his design; and since Mrs Thornton has entrusted me with the task of editing and completing the Series, I will briefly indicate the plan of the whole before proceeding to speak of the first volume in particular.

Thornton's Arabic Series will be published by the Cambridge University Press and will consist of four (or possibly five) volumes entitled as follows.

I. *Elementary Arabic: a Grammar.*

II. *Elementary Arabic: First Reading-Book.* This will contain selected passages from the Corân, *viz.* Ch. I, Ch. II 256, Ch. VII 52 to 62 and 101 to 170 inclusive, also Ch. LXIV; the text of a portion of Wright's *Arabic Reading-Book*, namely, pp. 13 to 64, beginning with "Stories of Arab Warriors" and ending with "The Escape of 'Abd al Raḥmân the Umaiyad from Syria into Spain"; a Grammatical Analysis of the above-mentioned Corânic texts; and finally a full Glossary.

III. *Elementary Arabic: Second Reading-Book*, containing passages from unpublished MSS. (or, at least, such as have not been previously edited in Europe).

IV *Elementary Arabic: Third Reading-Book*, which will probably comprise the whole of Wright's *Arabic Reading-Book* from p. 64 to the end.

The plan thus sketched departs from Mr Thornton's only in one comparatively trivial point. Instead of providing each volume with its own glossary, he contemplated a single Dictionary giving all the Arabic words contained in the three Reading-Books. There is indeed much to be said for this arrangement, by which a good deal of repetition would be avoided, but practical considerations seem to require that the First Reading-Book at any rate should be self-sufficing. With regard to the Second and Third Reading-Books the case is different, and I am inclined to think that they should not have separate glossaries. In this event a Dictionary such as Mr Thornton contemplated will form the fifth volume of the Series. Any suggestions as to the course which should be followed in this matter and also as to the scope of the Second Reading-Book, that is to say, what principle of selection would be most advantageous, will be gratefully received.

I now come to *Elementary Arabic: a Grammar*.

Concerning its origin I may quote Mr Thornton's own words appended by way of conclusion to the edition which was printed in 1900 by Messrs Stephen Austin of Hertford for private circulation.

"In the year 1885 I consulted Professor W. Robertson Smith about the possibility of there being written an elementary Grammar of Arabic capable of serving as introduction to Wright's masterly, but to beginners somewhat perplexing, book*; to which enquiry he made reply, 'There are two difficulties: to know what to put in, and to know what to leave out.' Ten years later I determined to make the attempt, 'putting in' all required by the grammatical analysis (then as now in manuscript) of my *First Reading-Book* and, so far as could be, 'leaving out' everything else; for I supposed that a rule would only be needed, if the Reading-Book's Arabic text afford an example in illustration; and I hoped by retaining Wright's section numbers that my abridgement might become a table of contents to his Grammar. I had supplied lists of omissions to Professors W. R. Smith and de Goeje with a view to their being remedied in the forthcoming 3rd edition; and such omissions as I subsequently discovered have been placed in this book under the heading of 'Note,' so that my trivial additions stand markedly apart from (my abridgement of) the scholarly text."

Mr Thornton then goes on to speak of his *Elementary Arabic: First Reading-Book*, to which reference has been made above, calling attention to the fact that all its words appear singly in Parts I and II of the Grammar, and all recur later in phrases to illustrate syntax. As he observes, "it may be said to supply almost without exception my Grammar's examples." The remainder of his Conclusion I will quote entire.

* A Grammar of the Arabic Language translated from the German of Caspari and edited with numerous additions and corrections by W. Wright, LL.D., late Professor of Arabic in the University of Cambridge. Third edition revised by W. Robertson Smith, late Professor of Arabic in the University of Cambridge, and M. J. de Goeje, Professor of Arabic in the University of Leyden. Cambridge: at the University Press, 1896.

"From a biographical sketch of M. S. de Sacy written in October 1895 by Professor Hartwig Derenbourg, Titulaire de la chaire de Silvestre de Sacy à l'École spéciale des langues orientales vivantes, I borrow the following:

La grammaire arabe de Caspari, le livre de classe qui, depuis 1848, n'a pas cessé d'être mis entre les mains des élèves dans des rédactions latine (1848), allemande (1859, 1866, 1876, et 1887), anglaise (1862 et 1874) et française (1880), tient le milieu entre les tendances des deux rivaux. "Elle s'appuie, dit M. Fleischer, sur Sacy et Ewald, et cherche seulement, avec quelques rectifications et additions que j'ai fournies, à réunir les qualités de l'un et de l'autre.... La grammaire de l'ancien arabe ne progressera vraiment d'une manière sensible que le jour où, d'un côté, on comparera et appréciera avec une balance de précision les philologues orientaux répartis dans les diverses écoles, et où, d'autre part, l'on soumettra les matériaux accumulés dans leurs plus excellents traités à une enquête approfondie dirigée dans le sens de notre linguistique."

Dans cette dernière direction, c'est à peine si nous avons dépassé la première étape, franchie d'un seul bond par le jeune Ewald, alors presque à ses débuts. L'édition anglaise de Caspari, par M. William Wright, ouvre seule quelques échappées sur l'horizon encore incertain de la philologie sémitique comparée. La *Grammaire de la langue arabe* qui, dans ses diverses transformations, continue à porter le nom de Caspari, se recommande et a réussi surtout à cause de son ordonnance harmonieuse: point de dérogations au plan général, chaque règle à sa place, pas de redites, pas de doubles emplois, une sobriété dans les tours de phrase n'excluant pas la clarté, une clarté obtenue sans redondances oiseuses et sans vaines amplifications. C'est un peu terre à terre, et cela manque d'essor; mais si l'imagination n'y trouve pas son compte, la raison est pleinement satisfaite par ce Lhomond de la langue arabe.

"Charles François Lhomond died in 1794 at the age of 67, having been maltreated by Parisian revolutionists, perhaps because of his writing in defence of Catholic faith as understood by him. His chief claim to posthumous fame lies in his devotion to the work of compiling elementary books and it is in this respect that his name may be conferred on those who do likewise. My readers will thank me for putting before them Professor Derenbourg's eloquent appreciation of the Grammar still called by Caspari's name, to the praise of which I heartily subscribe. Wright has, however, carried matters further, for the glimpses of Semitic philology mentioned above, together with much more, have been published by Robertson Smith in Wright's *Comparative Grammar*; and since 1895 Professor de Goeje has bestowed upon the world of Semitic letters a boon, for which we cannot be too thankful, by devoting his valuable time and known scholarship to the work of enabling Cambridge University Press to issue a 3rd Edition of Wright's *Arabic Grammar*: it is this which I have abridged.

"Much thanks are due from me to kind helpers more numerous than can be mentioned, but I must especially single out the Rev. G. W. Thatcher of Mansfield College, Oxford, without whose efficient assistance I might well have found it impossible to thread the mazes of Arabic syntax."

In preparing this new edition of Mr Thornton's Grammar I have incorporated some additions and corrections which I found in his interleaved copy of the last edition, and have added an abstract of §§ 191 to 230 in Wright's Grammar, which treat of Prosody. Mr Thornton omitted these sections on the ground that they were not needed for his *Elementary Arabic: First Reading-Book*, but he would undoubtedly have supplied the deficiency in view of the enlarged issue of that book, which has been described above and which will shortly be published as the second volume of this Series. I have also removed some references in the Grammar to the original edition of the First Reading-Book, giving the corresponding references to the Corân instead. In other respects I have made as few alterations as possible, since I know that Mr Thornton had pondered every word of his work over and over again and that he took infinite pains to secure the clearest and most concise expression.

It must be borne in mind that the author of this work intended it to be used side by side with his First Reading-Book, for which it is specially adapted and from which nearly all its examples are drawn. He regarded the one book as the complement of the other and even, I think, disliked the idea of their being sold separately. I hope, therefore, to bring out the enlarged First Reading-Book with as little delay as my other engagements permit, and I would strongly recommend all students of the Grammar to acquire the companion volume. At the same time it would, in my opinion, have been a mistake to limit the use of the Grammar to purchasers of the Reading-Book. The Corân, whence most of its examples are derived, is accessible to everyone, and the Grammar itself has the peculiar merit of serving as an introduction to Wright's masterly work. The reader will note that Wright's second volume begins at § 1, which corresponds with § 401 in Mr Thornton's abridgement.

It only remains to thank Mrs Thornton and Sir Charles Lyall, whom I consulted before writing this Preface, for the kind help which they have given me.

REYNOLD A. NICHOLSON.

CAMBRIDGE,
July, 1905.

CONTENTS.

PART I. ORTHOGRAPHY AND ORTHOEPY.

PART II. ETYMOLOGY OR THE PARTS OF SPEECH.

PART III. SYNTAX.

ADDENDA ET CORRIGENDA.

§ 27. لَهُ ٱلْمُلْكُ وَلَهُ ٱلْحَمْدُ. The reference is to Corân, Sûrah lxiv. verse 1.

§ 28. يُسَبِّحُ. The reference is to Corân, Sûrah lxiv. verse 1.

§ 43, Rem. *c.* جَاوَزْنَا بِ. The reference is to Corân, Sûrah vii. verse 134.

§ 45. Dele سَلِمَ *to be safe*, أَسْلَمَ *to preserve.*

§ 45, Rem. *c.* For أَسْلَمَ *to turn Moslem* from إِسْلَامٌ *Islâm* read أَسْلَمَ *to obtain peace, to surrender one's self* (*to God*) from سِلْمٌ *peace.*

§ 444, Rem. *g.* For Koran read Corân.

§ 456. For أَجِيهِ (p. 169, l. 11) read أَخِيهِ.

§ 470. Add, Rem. *f.* مَا is often inserted after عَنْ, مِنْ, and بِ without affecting their regimen and is then called مَا ٱلزَّائِدَةُ *the superfluous mâ* (see § 353*).

PART I.

ORTHOGRAPHY AND ORTHOËPY.

1. Arabic is written from right to left with twenty-eight letters, all consonants; three of which, however, are also used as vowels. In modern alphabetical order they range as follows, each with the equivalent employed by Wright's *Arabic Grammar*: the second equivalent (if any) is from *Elementary Arabic: First reading book*; being easier for beginners, as Dr Wright discards digraphs, i.e. two letters for the representation of one sound.

NAME	EQUIVALENT	SEPARATE	CONNECTED		
			INITIAL	MEDIAL	FINAL
أَلِفٌ		ا		ـا	ـا
بَآءٌ	b	ب	بـ	ـبـ	ـب
تَآءٌ	t	ت	تـ	ـتـ	ـت
ثَآءٌ	ṯ, th	ث	ثـ	ـثـ	ـث
جِيمٌ	ǵ, j	ج	جـ	ـجـ	ـج
حَآءٌ	ḥ	ح	حـ	ـحـ	ـح
خَآءٌ	ḫ, kh	خ	خـ	ـخـ	ـخ
دَالٌ	d	د		ـد	ـد
ذَالٌ	ḏ, dh	ذ		ـذ	ـذ
رَآءٌ	r	ر		ـر	ـر

NAME	EQUIVALENT	SEPARATE	CONNECTED		
			INITIAL	MEDIAL	FINAL
زَايْ	z	ز		ـز	ـز
سِينْ	s	س	سـ	ـسـ	ـس
شِينْ	ś, sh	ش	شـ	ـشـ	ـش
صَادْ	ṣ, ç	ص	صـ	ـصـ	ـص
ضَادْ	ḍ	ض	ضـ	ـضـ	ـض
طَآءْ	ṭ	ط	طـ	ـطـ	ـط
ظَآءْ	ẓ	ظ	ظـ	ـظـ	ـظ
عَيْنْ	ʻ	ع	عـ	ـعـ	ـع
غَيْنْ	ġ, gh	غ	غـ	ـغـ	ـغ
فَآءْ	f	ف	فـ	ـفـ	ـف
قَافْ	ḳ, q	ق	قـ	ـقـ	ـق
كَافْ	k	ك	كـ	ـكـ	ـك
لَامْ	l	ل	لـ	ـلـ	ـل
مِيمْ	m	م	مـ	ـمـ	ـم
نُونْ	n	ن	نـ	ـنـ	ـن
هَآءْ	h	ه	هـ	ـهـ	ـه
وَاوْ	w	و		ـو	ـو
يَآءْ	y	ي	يـ	ـيـ	ـي

REM. *a.* ا following ل forms لا lâm 'alif which is sometimes reckoned as a letter.

REM. *e.* ا, و, ي, are called حُرُوفُ ٱلْعِلَّةِ *the weak letters.*

2. The orthoëpy, i.e. correct pronunciation, of Arabic consonants is most easily acquired by learning from a Moslem to read the Corân aloud. With the exception of minute and insignificant divergencies this Corânic pronunciation is in theory identical nearly* everywhere, though in India, and probably in countries still more remote from Arabia, its distinctness has fallen off, and the sound of some letters, notably ع and ح, is lost. Further, the Corân's vowelling is beyond dispute; and this is of more advantage to beginners than they are at first capable of recognizing; vowel-signs exist, and are used, for purposes of grammar rather than to aid colloquial pronunciation. Slight indications only as to Corânic pronunciation can here be given, together with an explanation of the transliteration to be employed.

b, r, f, l, m, h	are pronounced as in English, but r must be trilled and h distinctly uttered, however placed: thus مَهْدِيّ mahdîy *one led aright* almost mahĭdiy, and وَجْه wajh *face* like wajhĭ.
t, d	sharper than in English, and with the tongue's tip, to distinguish them from
ṭ, ḍ	pronounced with broad of tongue, the tip being held against the lower teeth.

* A Turkish 'imâm will pronounce certain letters as in Turkish; thus kyâmil for كَامِل kâmil *one who is perfect.*

th̲ as in thorn, thump; but th as in goatherd, lighthouse.

j is pronounced (i) ĵ as in John Jim Jack at al Azhar (the famous Cairo University), but (ii) at the mosques of Damascus, Tunis and Algiers ǰ as s in usual, measure, vision, and as z in azure, and j in adjoin, adjective, adjacent, bijou, and g in lodge, prestige, singe. The former sound is represented by Frenchmen with dj and by Germans with dsch; if now we double ج thus سَجَّادَةٌ *a prayer-carpet,* it is easy to say saǰǰâdah̄ or saĵĵâdah̄, but not saĵĵâdah̄: the French ǰ of bijou is therefore more convenient. Turks however pronounce this letter as ĵ, and (iii) most Egyptians colloquially as the g of go, which last is the sound given in Hebrew.

ḥ can only be learned by ear: beginners must use h until they catch the sound.

kh̲ has long been employed by Anglo-Indians for the final sound, harshly said, of lough, loch; gh̲ being required for غَيْن gh̲ain, and ch̲ wanted in Persian etc. for the final consonant of beach, which were best transcribed bîc, i.e. with the Italian c in dolce: kh must sound as in blockhouse, thickheaded. Be it observed that خ is not a k but an h, which cannot in Hebrew writing be distinguished from ح.

dh̲ is as th in though, thee, this; being as δ of modern Greece: but dh as in bedhangings, adhesion.

ẓ is strictly th̲ said far back: but usually as z pronounced with the tongue's tip pressed against the lower teeth; then

z must be sounded sharply to make a distinction.

s sounds as in kiss: مُسْلِم *Moslem* (quasi-mosslem) is muslim the first syllable of which resembles that of muzzle -im neither in vowel nor consonant. If hissed with the tongue's tip s contrasts with

ç which must be pronounced further back, and with broad of tongue.

sh as in shore, wash; but sh as in mishap. For sh the French use ch and Germans sch, which last represents in Dutch سخ skh.

ع must be learnt by ear. The arrangement of throat is the same as that required for ḥ, but without aspirate. To mimic baby camels is best of all; otherwise one must repeat words in which عَيْن 'ain occurs between two vowels, as فَعَلَ fa'ala, *he did*, فَعَلْتُ فَعَلْتِ فَعَلْتَ فَعَلَتْ, etc. (see § 369, Table 1).

gh is the sound of gargling; but gh as in foghorn with the Persian گ gâf, thus گه gh.

q in Arabia is commonly pronounced as g in go, and so may be said at first; but the student will learn to harden g in the direction of k, and must sound

k very sharply in contrast. No one who can recite the Corân like a Moslem at mosque will confuse ك and ق as do uninstructed Europeans.

n as in English, نك nk being as in sank, sink; but نب nb sounds mb, thus مِنْبَر, *a pulpit*, called mimbar.

w, y are always consonants, as وَزِير wazîr *burden bearer*, سَوَاكِن sawâkin (*Souakim*) *female inhabitants*, يُوسُف yûsuf *Joseph*; but, as these three examples show, ا و ي are frequently letters of prolongation (see § 6).

ħ representing ـة and ة is sounded as h when final, and as t when followed by a vowel: it is called تَآءٌ مَرْبُوطَةٌ tâ' marbûṭaħ *tied*, as distinguished from ت t, تَآءٌ مَمْدُودَةٌ tâ' mamdûdaħ *stretched* (see § 294 rem. *b*)

---

4. The vowels and diphthongs are as follows :—

فَتْحَةٌ	ـَ	a	as vowel sound in aunt, wan, thumb, hat.
كَسْرَةٌ	ـِ	i	„ „ pin, bit, gift.
ضَمَّةٌ	ـُ	u	„ „ push, bull, mustache.
	ـَا	â	„ „ father, hard.
	ـِي	î	„ „ keep, beach, chief, seize.
	ـُو	û	„ „ moon, rule, blue, you.
	ـَي	ai	„ „ aisle, my, buy, sigh, die, I.
	ـَو	au	„ „ thou, how, bough.
	ـَى	a	is as â.
	ـً	an	tanwîn of fathaħ (see § 8).
	ـٍ	in	„ kasraħ (see § 8).
	ـٌ	un	„ dammaħ (see § 8).
	ـًى	an	as an, but in pause as â (see § 27).
	ـًا	ân	as an, but in pause as â (see § 27).

Rem. *a*. The three Arabic words above are names of the vowel-marks, the corresponding sounds being called فَتْحٌ, كَسْرٌ and ضَمٌّ.

Rem. *b*. A vowel is called حَرَكَةٌ *a motion*, its mark being termed شَكْلٌ *form* or *figure*, plural أَشْكَالٌ and شُكُولٌ. Hence a consonant when followed by a vowel is said to be مُتَحَرِّكٌ *in motion*.

5. When the Corân is recited, each letter, whatever its relative position, in theory represents the same sound; but in practice certain consonants somewhat modify adjacent vowels, for instance ق ظ ط ض ص cause â, following one of them, to be sounded like the Scandinavian å, which we represent variously in nor, saw, war, hall, wrath, ought, caught. As to the many jargons which constitute colloquial Arabic, they show divergencies too material to be learnt from any book: pronunciation of each of these spoken dialects (they are unwritten) is easy to an Englishman who can read aloud the Corânic extracts of *Elementary Arabic: First reading book* uttering the consonants like a Moslem at mosque; but it must be acquired by ear at the particular locality simultaneously with all eccentricities of vocabulary and grammar*.

6. The long vowels â, î, û are indicated (see § 4) by marking the corresponding short vowels before ا, و, and ي respectively, which are then called حُرُوفُ ٱلْمَدِّ *letters of prolongation.*

Rem. *a*. In certain common words â is indicated merely by fatḥah; as أَللّٰه, etc., which should properly be written with the perpendicular fatḥah, thus أللّٰه *God*, هٰرُونُ *Aaron*, أَلرَّحْمٰنُ *the merciful*, أَلسَّمٰوَاتُ *the heavens*, أَلْقِيٰمَةُ *the resurrection*, لٰكِنْ *but*, ذٰلِكَ *that*, هٰذَا *this* etc.: the words ثَلٰاثٌ *three*, ثَلٰاثُونَ *thirty*,

* Attempts have been made to print the Maltese dialect of Arabic in Roman character at Valetta, and by the Bible Society in London, but in neither case does the work betray a knowledge of philology. Far more scholarly is the following book, which will be found most useful on the Lower Nile;—"The Modern Egyptian Dialect of Arabic. A Grammar, with Exercises, Reading-Lessons and Glossaries, from the German of Dr K. Vollers. With numerous additions by the Author. Translated by F. C. Burkitt, M.A., Trinity College. Cambridge: at the University Press, 1895."

ثَمَانِيَةٌ *eight*, ثَمَانُونَ *eighty* and إِسْرَائِيلُ *Israel* are also written defectively, thus ثَلٰثٌ, ثَلٰثُونَ, ثَمٰنِيَةٌ, ثَمٰنُونَ and إِسْرَائِلُ.

7. Fatḥah before ي and و forms the diphthongs ai and au (see § 4). Colloquial pronunciation, however, frequently gives ai as ei in vein, reign, neighbour, thus شَيْخ as sheikh *elder, chief*, بَيْت as beit *house, family, verse*, اِثْنَيْنِ (oblique case of اِثْنَانِ) as ithnein *two*.

Note. The vowel sound in vein were better represented by ê, whereas ـَي ai should remain a diphthong as in the French word pays (nearly) pêî in contrast to the French letter p (nearly) pê.

Rem. *a*. A superfluous ا is written after و at the end of certain verbal forms: it is useful in manuscript to prevent the و seeming separate and so being mistaken for وَ *and*.

Rem. *b*. At the end of a word ى following upon fatḥah (i.e. a see § 4) is pronounced as ـَا â, so that عَلَى 'ala *upon* and عَلَا 'alâ *to be high* scan the same. When in this position ا and ى are called اَلْأَلِفُ ٱلْمَقْصُورَةُ *the 'alif that can be abbreviated*, because they are shortened in pronunciation if followed by a connective 'alif (see § 18); thus عَلَى ٱللّٰهِ *upon God* and عَلَا ٱللّٰهُ *God has ascended* are both in pause (see § 27) pronounced 'alallâh. The interposition of hamzah (see § 15) prevents this waçl *union*, thus عَلَاءُ ٱلدِّينِ 'alâ'u -l dini (*Aladdin*) *the sublimity of religion*. The 'alif maqçûrah, however written, is quiescent (see § 9 rem. *a*) as also are و of ـَوْ au and ي of ـَيْ ai. When attached to tanwin, radical final 'alif is quiescent, thus عَصًا *a stick* (see § 212 *b*); but it is also maqçûrah in ٱلْعَصَا *the stick*.

Rem. *c.* If a pronominal suffix be added to a word ending in ـَى as نَرَى *we see*, the ى is sometimes retained, but more often is changed into ا as نَرَاكَ for نَرَيكَ or نَرٰيكَ (all pronounced) narâka *we see thee.*

Rem. *d.* Some words ending in ـَاة âh may be written ـَوة or ـٰوة as حَيَوةٌ or حَيٰوةٌ *life*, صَلَوةٌ or صَلٰوةٌ *prayer*, زَكَوةٌ or زَكٰوةٌ *alms*: further we find ـَية or ـٰية for ـَاة in the loan word تَوْرَيةٌ or تَوْرٰيةٌ *Old Testament.*

8. Marks of the short vowels when doubled at the end of a word (see § 4) are pronounced thus ـً an, ـٍ in, ـٌ un, which is called تَنْوِينٌ tanwînun *adding of the letter nûn.*

Rem. *a.* Tanwîn of fatḥah takes ا after all consonants except ة, as بَابًا *gate*, but سِنَةً *drowsiness* (see § 308). When preceding ى it requires no ا as هُدًى *guidance.* Notwithstanding this 'alif, the vowel is short: thus bâbaⁿ (not âⁿ), but in pause (see § 27) bâbâ. We transliterate بَابًا bâbaⁿ and سِنَةً sinaḥan, but aⁿ and an are pronounced alike; except in pause, when an is not heard, whereas aⁿ sounds as â. In pause sinahan is read sinah (see end of § 2).

The following orthographic signs are also in use:

9. Sukûn *rest* ـْ is placed over the final consonant of all shut syllables (see § 25).

Rem. *a.* A consonant which has no following vowel is called حَرْفٌ سَاكِنٌ *a quiescent letter* (see § 4 rem. *b*).

Rem. *b.* Letters that are assimilated to a following letter, which receives in consequence tas͟hdîd (see § 11), are retained in writing but are not marked with sukûn; thus اَللُّغَةُ *the language,* أَرَدتُّ pronounced 'arattu (see § 14 *c*).

10. When part of a diphthong ي and و take sukûn, but this sign is very unusual over a 'alif maqçûrah (see § 7 rem. *b*) or other letter of prolongation.

11. Tashdîd *strengthening* ـّـ is marked over a double consonant and the letter's repetition saved; thus بَدَّلَ baddala *to substitute,* اَلْكُلُّ al kullu *the whole.*

Rem. *c.* Hamzah (see § 15) may be doubled and take tashdîd, thus سَآَّلٌ sa''âlun *a mendicant* from سَأَلَ sa'ala *to ask.*

14. The euphonic tashdîd follows a vowelless consonant, which, though expressed in writing, is passed over in pronunciation, in order to avoid a harshness of sound, and assimilated to a following consonant. It is used:—

(*a*) With the letters ت ث د ذ ر ز س ش ص ض ط ظ ل ن after اَلْ *the* (see § 345).

Rem. *a.* These letters are called اَلْحُرُوفُ الشَّمْسِيَّةُ *the solar letters* because شَمْسٌ *sun* begins with one of them, and for an analogous reason all other consonants are called اَلْحُرُوفُ الْقَمَرِيَّةُ *the lunar letters* from قَمَرٌ *moon.*

(*b*) With the letters ر ل م و ي after n with sukûn, as مِن رَّبِّهِ *from his Lord,* كِتَابٌ مُّبِينٌ *a perspicuous book,* which are read mirrabbihi, kitâbunmubînun. The n of the words مِنْ عَنْ أَنْ is often not written when they are combined with مَا, مَنْ or لَا.

REM. *b*. We may write أَنْ لَا or أَن لَّا or أَلَّا *that not*, and إِلَّا for إِن لَّا *if not*; but عَمَّا *from what* is better so written for عَنْ مَا, as is إِمَّا for إِنْ مَا *if* with مَا ٱلزَّائِدَةُ *redundant mâ* (see § 353*).

(*c*) With the letter ت after ث د ذ ض ط ظ in certain parts of the verb, as أَرَدتُّ *I wished*: this practice is, however, more than questionable.

REM. *b*. If the verb ends in ت it naturally unites with a second ت, as نَبَتُّ nabbattu *I sowed* or *planted* for نَبَتْتُ.

15. Hamzah *compression* (*of upper part of windpipe*) ـٔـ, to which a 'alif most commonly serves as عِمَادٌ 'imâd *support*, may almost be reckoned by Europeans as the alphabet's initial consonant. It is equivalent to the French h aspirée (which to English sense is not, except in Normandy, sounded), and it may be heard between the two words le onze and between la onzième. If our own definite article be pronounced before a vowel as before a consonant, we can only prevent liaison by employing hamzah; thus thö 'orange (ö as E in thE book). Arabs would transcribe a nice house anaishaus but an'aishaus for an ice house.

REM. *a*. When a connective 'alif (see § 18) requires vowelling, the vowel mark is better written without hamzah, thus اَلْ *the*, اِبْنٌ *son* (see § 19 rem. *d*).

REM. *c*. Hamzah is marked between ا and sukûn or the following vowel; but we find مَلَئِه *his chiefs*, خَاسِئِينَ *abject*, and even بَئْسٌ *grievous*.

Rem. *d.* Hamzaħ is most perceptible in the middle of a word as اَلْقُرَانُ for (see § 23) اَلْقُرْآنُ al qur'ânu (not qurânu) *the Corân.*

Rem *e.* Hamzaħ and 'alif are called أَلِفُ ٱلْقَطْعِ *the 'alif of severance.*

16. We have spoken in the preceding section of 'alif serving most commonly as 'imâd to hamzaħ; in certain circumstances this position may be taken by و or ى, the latter appearing without dots (see §§ 131 et seq., 238, 240, 316 *d* and 361 *a* rem.), thus مُنْشِئٌ *producer.*

17. Hamzaħ alone, instead of أ إ ؤ or ئ, is written,

(*a*) always at a word's end, after sukûn or a letter of prolongation, as جَاءَ *he came,* سُوءٌ *evil,* مَجِيءٌ *a coming,* ظِمْءٌ *thirst;* and in the middle of a word after 'alif of prolongation provided the hamzaħ bears fatḥaħ as acc. أَعْدَاءَكُمْ *your enemies,* but nom. أَعْدَآؤُكُمْ, dep. أَعْدَآئِكُمْ.

Note. For جَآءَ, أَعْدَآءَكُمْ see § 22, and for سُوٓءٌ, مَجِيٓءٌ see § 23 rem. *c.*

(*b*) frequently in the middle of words after و or ي of prolongation and after sukûn, as سُوءَى *a mischief* for سُوْأَى, مَشِيئَةٌ *wish* for مَشِيئَةٌ, يَسْئَلُ *he asks* for يَسْأَلُ; also after kasraħ and ḍammaħ before ي or و of prolongation; خَاطِـئِينَ khâṭi'îna *sinners* for خَاطِئِينَ, رُءُوسٌ ru'ûsun *heads* for رُؤُوسٌ. Sometimes it is improperly placed over the letter of prolongation, as خَطِيئَةٌ for خَطِيـئَةٌ or خَطِيئَةٌ khaṭî'aħun *sin.*

Rem. *b.* Hamzaħ may under certain circumstances be changed

into a weak letter, as مِيَةٌ for مِئَةٌ (see § 325 rem. *a*), نَبِيٌّ for نَبِيءٌ *prophet*, فَيٌّ for فَيْءٌ *shade*, رَاسٌ for رَأْسٌ *head*, بِيرٌ for بِئْرٌ *a cistern*, آلِهَةٌ for أَأْلِهَةٌ *gods*, آمَنَّا for أَأْمَنَّا *we believed.*

NOTE. For آلِهَةٌ, آمَنَّا see § 23, and for مَشِيئَةٌ, سُوءٌ rem. *c.*

REM. *c.* The name دَاوُودُ *David* is always pronounced dâ'ûd however it may be written.

18. Some Arabic words begin with connective 'alif over which is marked waçlah *sign of union* ٱ, hereinafter transliterated by hyphen, because the word and its predecessor are spoken as one; thus عَبْدُ ٱللّٰهِ 'abdu -llâhi *servant of God*, وَٱدْعُوهُ wa -d'ûhu *and call ye upon Him.*

19. Elision takes place to form the union

(*a*) with the vowel of أَلْ *the*, as يَوْمُ ٱلدِّينِ *the day of the judgment.*

NOTE. As regards ٱلَّذِي see § 347.

(*b*) in regular Imperatives of the first form, as قَالَ ٱصْبِرْ *he said, Be patient*; instead of اِصْبِرْ.

(*c*) in certain derivatives belonging to the seventh and following forms of the verbs (see § 35), as وَٱنْقَلَبُوا *and they were changed*; instead of اِنْقَلَبُوا.

(*d*) in اِبْنٌ *son*, اِثْنَانِ *two*, اِمْرَأَةٌ *a woman*, اِسْمٌ *name*, and a few other nouns.

REM. *c.* In most of these words the 'alif and vowel are prosthetic, i.e. prefixed to a vowelless initial consonant for the sake of euphony (see § 26).

Rem. *d.* It is obviously an error to begin a sentence with آ: in such case the connective 'alif is written without hamzah but with a vowel, as اَلْحَمْدُ لِلّٰهِ *Praise belongs to God.*

Rem. *f.* Waçlah and 'alif are called أَلِفُ ٱلْوَصْلِ *the 'alif of union.*

20. The connective 'alif may follow

(*a*) a short vowel, which then absorbs it (see § 18).

(*b*) a long vowel, which is then shortened in pronunciation to comply with § 25; as فِي ٱلْأَرْضِ fî -l 'arḍi to be read fil'arḍi *in the earth,* اِهْدِنَا ٱلصِّرَاطَ ihdinâ -l çirâṭa to be read ihdinaççirâṭa *guide us (on) the way*: but the suffixes of the 1st pers. sing. ـِي and نِي may assume before the article the older forms ـِيَ and نِيَ, as أَدْخِلْ بِيَ ٱلْبَيْتَ *cause me to enter the house,* سَأَصْرِفُ عَنْ آيَاتِيَ ٱلَّذِينَ (or آيَاتِي ٱلَّذِينَ) *I will divert from my signs those who.*

(*c*) a diphthong, which usually is resolved into two simple vowels; but أَوْ *or* and لَوْ *if* take kasra, thus ضَمِيرُ ٱلتَّوْكِيدِ أَوِ ٱلتَّأْكِيدِ *the pronoun of corroboration* (see § 530).

(*d*) sukûn over a consonant, which then most usually takes kasrah, as فِي ٱلِٱبْتِدَاءِ for فِي ٱلْ ٱبْتِدَاءِ *in the beginning,* مُحَمَّدٌ ٱلنَّبِيُّ (sometimes written مُحَمَّدُ نِ ٱلنَّبِيُّ) *Mahomet the prophet* pronounced muḥammaduninnabîyu, جُمْلَةٌ ٱسْمِيَّةٌ *a nominal sentence* (see § 513), وَلٰكِنِ ٱنْظُرْ *but look.* The pronouns أَنْتُمْ *you,* هُمْ *they*; the suffixes كُمْ *your, you,* هُمْ *their, them*; and the verbal termination تُمْ take ḍammah (in which they originally ended), as لَعَنَهُمُ ٱللّٰهُ *may God curse them* (see § 401 *f*): also

مُذْ *since* because contracted for مُنْذُ: whereas مِنْ *from* (see § 448) takes fatḥah before the article and elsewhere kasrah.

Rem. *a.* When هُمْ becomes هِمْ (see § 185 rem. *b*) the waçl may be made with ḍammah هِمُ or kasrah هِمِ.

21. The ٱ is altogether omitted

(*a*) from ٱسْمٌ in the formula بِسْمِ ٱللّٰهِ for بِٱسْمِ ٱللّٰهِ *in the name of God*, which by way of compensation is written بســمِ.

(*b*) from ٱبْنٌ in a genealogical series, with certain exceptions.

(*c*) from ٱلْ *the* preceded by لِ *to* (see § 356 *c*) as لِلْبَيَانِ *to the explanation* for لِٱلْبَيَانِ; or لَ *verily* (see § 361 *c*) as لَلرَّجُلُ *certainly the man* for لَٱلرَّجُلُ. When three lâms occur one is omitted, thus لِلّٰهِ *to God* for لِٱللّٰهِ.

(*d*) from words preceded by the interrogative particle أَ (see § 361 *a*).

22. Maddah *extension* ــٓ does not admit of transliteration, being either superfluous or an abbreviation or marking an abbreviation. Thus it is customary to omit 'alif which, with hamzah and a vowel or tanwîn, follows a 'alif of prolongation; then by way of compensation maddah is written over the remaining 'alif, as سَآئِلٌ *one who asks* for سَاإِلٌ, جَآءَ *he came* for جَاأَ, أَعْدَآءُكُمْ *your enemies* for أَعْدَاأُكُمْ.

23. Maddah and 'alif آ also represent a 'alif with hamzah and fatḥah followed by 'alif of prolongation أَا or by 'alif with hamzah and sukûn أَأْ, as آلَ *he returned* for أَالَ or أَأْلَ, آيَةٌ *a sign, verse* for أَايَةٌ for أَوَيَةٌ, آلِهَةٌ *gods* for أَأْلِهَةٌ, آمَنَّا *we believed* for أَأْمَنَّا, سَيِّآتٌ for سَيِّئَاتٌ plural of سَيِّئَةٌ *an evil* (see § 242 Note 2).

REM. *c.* Maddah is sometimes placed over و and ي of prolongation when followed by hamzah, as سُوٓءٌ, مَجِيٓءٌ, سُوٓءَى, مَشِيٓئَةٌ: it serves in manuscript to prevent hamzah appearing to be upon the letter of prolongation.

REM. *d.* The same mark ـٓ is written over abbreviations, as آلخ for إِلَى آخِرِهِ or إِلَى آخِرِهَا *to its end* i.e. *etcætera* (see § 451 *c*).

---

24. An open syllable ends with a long or short vowel.

25. A shut syllable ends with a consonant, and its vowel is most commonly short.

26. A syllable cannot begin with two consonants: foreign words commencing so are transcribed by Arabian grammarians with an additional vowel, thus *franks* becomes إِفْرَنْجٌ *Europeans* pronounced colloquially faranj or farang.

27. A syllable cannot end with two consonants, except بِٱلْوَقْفِ bi -l waqfi *in pause*, which ought to be made only when required by sense, but which is really more frequent; as لَهُ ٱلْمُلْكْ وَلَهُ ٱلْحَمْدْ (compare *Elementary Arabic: First reading book*, page ٢٧, top line) *to Him belong the dominion and the praise*, witness also the Moslem *credo* phonetically written as pronounced at Damascus لَا إِلٰهْ إِلَّا ٱللّٰهْ وَمُحَمَّدْ رَسُولْ ٱللّٰهْ lâ'ilâh: 'illallâh: wamuḥammadurrasûlullâh *There is no god but God and Muḥammad is His apostle.* In the Urdu translation of this book - will mark the shortest pause then , one of medium length and . as in English the longest.

NOTE. Professor de Goeje appends to vol ii § 95 *f* of Wright's Grammar an instructive footnote condemning pedantic speech, and he gives reference to a MS at Leyden. In fact case-endings are nearly always dropped in أَلدَّارِجُ al dârij *current speech*: throughout Arabia the proper name إِبْنُ رَشِيدٍ is pronounced ibrrashîd by Badawîn (Bedouins). The accusative is most often heard, as مَرْحَبًا marḥabañ (see § 435 *b*) *welcome* pronounced in pause marḥabâ (see § 8 rem. *a*).

28. The accent will not occasion difficulty to Englishmen who acquire pronunciation of Arabic consonants by reading the Corân aloud after a Moslem: it is designed to ensure grammatical accuracy; thus يُسَبِّحُ (see *Elementary Arabic: First reading book*, page ٢٦ bottom line) is pronounced yusabbíḥu for fear of saying yusábbiḥû. Colloquial accentuation differs with the locality; thus مُصْطَفَى ٱللّٰهِ muçṭafa-llâhi *chosen of God* is múçṭafa in Syria, and in Egypt muçṭáfa or even muçṭâfa.

---

32. Numbers were anciently expressed by letters whose numerical value may be learnt in the following order أَبْجَدْ هَوَّزْ حُطِّي كَلَمَنْ سَعْفَصْ قَرَشَتْ ثَخَذْ ضَظَغْ; six consonants, forming the last two words, being supplementary to the Hebrew and Aramaic alphabets. Between the analysis and text of *Elementary Arabic: First reading book* will be found a Table, which gives the Phœnician, modern Hebrew, and other alphabets. The Arabic figures now employed are

١	٢	٣	٤	٥	٦	٧	٨	٩	٠
1	2	3	4	5	6	7	8	9	0

and they are used in our order, thus ٥٠٦٣٨٩ 506389.

PART II.

ETYMOLOGY OR THE PARTS OF SPEECH.

33. Verbs are mostly triliteral (containing three radical letters) but some are quadriliteral.

34. From the first or ground-form are derived other forms expressing modifications of the idea conveyed by the first (see § 369 Table 3 et seq.).

35. The forms of the triliteral verb are fifteen, as follows:

اِفْعَوَّلَ	XIII	اِسْتَفْعَلَ	X	اِنْفَعَلَ	VII	أَفْعَلَ	IV	فَعَلَ	I
اِفْعَنْلَلَ	XIV	اِفْعَالَّ	XI	اِفْتَعَلَ	VIII	تَفَعَّلَ	V	فَعَّلَ	II
اِفْعَنْلَى	XV	اِفْعَوْعَلَ	XII	اِفْعَلَّ	IX	تَفَاعَلَ	VI	فَاعَلَ	III

Rem. *a.* The 3rd pers. sing. masc. Perf. active, being the simplest form of the verb, is used as paradigm, but for shortness' sake we translate it by the English infinitive; thus كَلَمَ *to wound* instead of *he has wounded.*

Rem. *b.* Arabian grammarians use the verb فَعَلَ as paradigm; hence the first radical of the triliteral verb is called اَلْفَآءُ al fâ', the second اَلْعَيْنُ al 'ain, and the third اَللَّامُ al lâm.

36. The *first* form is generally transitive or intransitive in signification, according to the vowel which accompanies its second radical.

37. The second radical's vowel is *a* in most transitive verbs, as ضَرَبَ *to beat*; and some intransitive, as رَشَدَ *to go the right way.*

38. Vowel *i* in similar position usually shows an intransitive signification, *u* invariably: the *i* indicating what is temporary or accidental, as سَلِمَ *to be safe*; whilst *u* (meaning rarely to become what one was not before, as شَرُفَ *to become noble*) indicates a permanent state or inherent quality, as حَسُنَ *to be beautiful.*

Rem. *a.* Many verbs of the form فَعِلَ are transitive according to our ideas.

Note. The following sections give a general view of some derived forms without taking into account whether the verbs govern an accusative, or by help of prepositions a dependent (see § 423).

40. The *second* form فَعَّلَ is in meaning intensive or extensive. Originally it implies an act done with force, during long, by a number, or repeatedly; as سَخِرَ *to mock* سَخَّرَ *to subject, treat as abject,* صَرَفَ *to turn, shift* صَرَّفَ the same but of several objects, صَلَبَ *to crucify* صَلَّبَ the same of many, فَصَلَ *to separate* فَصَّلَ *to divide into several pieces,* قَتَلَ *to kill* قَتَّلَ *to massacre,* قَطَعَ *to cut* قَطَّعَ *to mangle,* كَفَرَ *to cover up, ignore* كَفَّرَ *to efface,* مَدَّ *to extend* مَدَّدَ *to stretch much* or *often,* مَسَكَ *to hold* مَسَّكَ *to hold tight.*

41. Not less usual is the secondary signification, (*a*) verbs intransitive in the first form becoming transitive in the second; as أَدُبَ *to be well brought up* أَدَّبَ *to bestow a good education, punish,* تَبِرَ *to perish* تَبَّرَ *to destroy,* حَرُمَ *to be unlawful* حَرَّمَ *to*

forbid, دَمَرَ *to perish utterly* دَمَّرَ *to destroy entirely*, سَارَ *to go* سَيَّرَ *to make go*, قَوِيَ *to be strong* قَوَّى *to strengthen, encourage*, نَبَتَ *to spring forth* نَبَّتَ *to plant* or *sow*, and

(*b*) those transitive in the first, causative; as بَلَغَ *to reach, attain* بَلَّغَ *to bring*, ذَكَرَ *to remember* ذَكَّرَ *to remind*, عَدَا *to pass* عَدَّى *to make pass* and *to give* a verb *a transitive signification*, عَذَبَ *to abstain* عَذَّبَ *to restrain by punishment*, فَسَرَ *to discover* فَسَّرَ *to explain*, قَرُبَ *to be near* قَرَّبَ *to bring near*.

Rem. *b*. This form is often declarative or estimative, as صَدَقَ *to tell the truth* صَدَّقَ *to think that* one *tells the truth, believe* one, كَذَبَ *to lie* كَذَّبَ *to call* one *a liar*, فَضَلَ *to surpass* فَضَّلَ *to regard as superior, favour*.

Rem. *c*. This form is very frequently denominative, *i.e.* derived from a noun; as بَدَّلَ *to substitute* from بَدَلٌ *something given or received in exchange*, سَلَّمَ عَلَيْهِ *he said to him* سَلَامٌ عَلَيْكَ (*peace be upon thee*), صَوَّرَ *to fashion* from صُورَةٌ *an image*, ظَلَّلَ *to shade* from ظِلٌّ *shadow*, كَلَّمَ *to speak with* from كَلَامٌ *speech*, نَبَّأَ *to inform* from نَبَأٌ *news* (perhaps originally *something which has emerged* or *arisen*), نَوَّنَ *to write the letter nûn* from نُونٌ *n*.

Note. It is difficult to connect سَبَّحَ *to praise* with سَبَحَ *to swim*: accordingly the native grammarians call سَبَّحَ denominative of سُبْحَانٌ, see § 435 *a* Note. The verb عَزَّرَ (which generally means *he disciplined, chastized, constrained by punishment*) in the exceptional sense *he helped* may possibly be a denominative from the Hebrew ‘ezer *help* (see I Samuel vii. 12). The noun does not occur in Arabic with that signification.

43. The *third* form فَاعَلَ implies

(*a*) the effort or attempt to perform an act which the first form denotes as immediately affecting an object, the idea of reciprocity being sometimes added; as عَطَا *to receive* عَاطَى *to receive from each other, give mutually,* غَلَبَ *to overcome* غَالَبَ *to try to overcome,* قَرَأَ *to read* قَارَأَ *to read together, teach mutually,* لَأَمَ *to join together* لَاءَمَ *to reconcile,* مَدَّ *to extend* مَادَدَ and مَادَّ *to contend in pulling,* وَعَدَ *to promise* وَاعَدَ *to fix time and place for execution of a promise.*

(*b*) This form sometimes governs directly, not without the idea of reciprocity, when the first or fourth form governs its object by help of a preposition, as أَرْسَلَ إِلَى ٱلسُّلْطَانِ *he sent (a message) to the Sultan* رَاسَلَ ٱلسُّلْطَانَ *he interchanged messages, corresponded, with the Sultan,* قَالَ لَهُ *he said to him* something قَاوَلَهُ *he conversed with him.*

(*c*) When the first form denotes a quality or state (see § 75) فَاعَلَ indicates affecting a person by the quality or bringing him into the state, as حَسُنَ *to be good* or *kind* حَاسَنَهُ *he treated him kindly,* طَاعَ *to be submissive* طَاوَعَ *to comply with,* نَعِمَ *to lead a comfortable life* نَاعَمَهُ *he found him means of doing so.*

Rem. *a.* This form is sometimes denominative, as ضَاعَفَ *to double, multiply* from ضِعْفٌ *the like* or *equal.*

Rem. *c.* In *Elementary Arabic: First reading book* page ١٤ bottom line جَاوَزْنَا بِ may be rendered *We caused to pass* (see § 456 *b*).

Note. The form of the verb بَارَكَ *he blessed* may be due to Hebrew, from which it is most probably derived (see § 455 Note).

45. The *fourth* form أَفْعَلَ is factitive or causative, (*a*) verbs intransitive in the first form becoming transitive; as أَتَى *to come* آتَى، *to bring,* أَذِيَ *to experience damage* آذَى *to hurt,* أَسِفَ *to grieve* آسَفَ *to make grieve,* تَمَّ *to be finished* أَتَمَّ *to finish,* حَبَّ for حَبُبَ *to be an object of love* أَحَبَّ *to love* i.e. treat as an object of love, حَلَّ *to be lawful* أَحَلَّ *to make lawful,* حَيِيَ *to live* أَحْيَى *to bring to life,* خَرَجَ *to come forth* أَخْرَجَ *to produce,* [سَلِمَ *to be safe* أَسْلَمَ *to preserve*] سَنَدَ *to lean* أَسْنَدَ *to cause to lean, support,* شَمِتَ *to rejoice at another's trouble* أَشْمَتَ *to make so to rejoice,* صَلُحَ *to be good* أَصْلَحَ *to make good, do good, follow right action,* ضَلَّ *to err* أَضَلَّ *to lead into error,* ضَاعَ *to be lost* أَضَاعَ *to abandon,* طَاعَ *to be submissive* أَطَاعَ *to obey,* طَالَ *to be long* أَطَالَ *to prolong,* عَلَنَ *to be public* أَعْلَنَ *to publish,* غَرِقَ *to be drowned* أَغْرَقَ *to cause to drown,* فَرِغَ *to be empty* أَفْرَغَ *to empty by pouring out,* فَسَدَ *to be spoilt* أَفْسَدَ *to commit disorders,* مَاتَ *to die* أَمَاتَ *to cause to die,* نَذِرَ *to be on one's guard* أَنْذَرَ *to warn,* نَزَلَ *to descend* أَنْزَلَ *to send down,* نَعِمَ *to live agreeably* أَنْعَمَ *to bless,* نَفِقَ *to be expended* أَنْفَقَ *to expend,* نَكِرَ *to be strange* أَنْكَرَ *to regard as strange, disavow,* هَلَكَ *to perish* أَهْلَكَ *to destroy.*

(*b*) Verbs transitive in the first form become doubly transitive; as حَاطَ *to guard, observe* أَحَاطَ *to cause one's knowledge to encompass, comprehend,* دَخَلَ *to go into* أَدْخَلَ *to cause to enter,* رَأَى ٱلشَّيْءَ *he saw the thing* أَرَاهُ ٱلشَّيْءَ *he showed him the thing,* رَجَا *to hope for* أَرْجَى *to put off,* عَطَا *to receive* أَعْطَى *to give,*

غَشِيَ *to cover, conceal* أَغْشَى *to cause to cover,* قَرَأَ *to read* أَقْرَأَ *to teach reading* or *reciting,* لَقِيَ *to meet* أَلْقَى *to throw,* مَدَّ *to extend* أَمَدَّ *to cause increase,* وَرِثَ *to inherit* أَوْرَثَ *to cause to inherit,* وَقَى *to guard* أَوْقَى *to make to guard.*

REM. *a.* When both the second and fourth forms of a verb are causative they have in some cases different significations, in others the same; as أَذِنَ *to give ear to* أَذَّنَ and آذَنَ *to cause* people *to listen, announce, declare,* عَلِمَ *to know* عَلَّمَ *to teach* أَعْلَمَ *to inform,* نَجَا *to escape* نَجَّى and أَنْجَى *to deliver.*

REM. *b.* The fourth form, like the second, is sometimes declarative or estimative; as أَمُنَ *to be faithful* آمَنَ *to find trustworthy, believe,* حَمِدَ *to praise* أَحْمَدَ *to esteem praiseworthy.*

REM. *c.* This form is often denominative, as أَبْلَغَ *to speak eloquently* from بَلَاغَةٌ *eloquence,* أَثْمَرَ *to bear fruit* from ثَمَرٌ *fruit,* أَجْرَمَ *to be guilty* from جُرْمٌ *a crime,* أَحْسَنَ *to act well* from حَسَنٌ *good, beautiful,* أَخْطَأَ *to err* from خَطَأٌ *a blunder, fault,* أَرْسَلَ *to send* from رَسُولٌ *a message, apostle,* أَسَرَّ *to conceal* from سِرٌّ *a secret,* أَسْرَعَ *to make haste* from سُرْعَةٌ *promptitude,* أَسْلَمَ *to turn Moslem* from إِسْلَامٌ *Islâm**, أَسَآءَ *to do ill* from سُوٓءٌ *evil,* أَقْرَضَ *to lend* from قَرْضٌ *a loan,* أَقَامَ *to remain in a place* from مُقَامٌ *a place,* أَمْهَلَ *to grant a respite* or *delay* from مَهْلٌ *gentleness, leisurely acting.* There is another class of denominatives, as أَبَانَ *to become plain* from بَيِّنٌ *evident,* أَحْرَمَ *to enter the sacred*

* Islâm may mean in English the religion's geographical area, or the religion itself which is better called Islâmism as we say Judaism.

territory from حَرَمٌ *a holy place*, أَعْوَزَ *to become destitute* from عَوَزٌ *want*, أَفْلَسَ *to become penniless* from فَلْسٌ *a copper coin*, أَمْكَنَ *to find a place, become possible* from مَكَانٌ *a place*; and somewhat analogous is أَيْسَرَ *to arrive at ease* from يَسَرَ *to be easy*.

Note. Beside the above must be mentioned أَرَادَ *to wish* which cannot be immediately derived from رَادَ *to go to and fro*; أَشَارَ *to indicate, point out* from شَارَ *to exhibit*; أَصَابَ *to direct the course of* something *expressly at, hit the mark* whence the commoner meaning *to overtake, befall* from صَابَ *to rush down as water*; أَفْلَحَ *to be prosperous* from فَلَحَ *to plough*; أَفَاقَ *to recover from illness or a swoon* from فَاقَ *to be above*; أَقَلَّ *to treat as light, carry easily* from قَلَّ which means in Hebrew *to be light in weight*; أَلْأَكَ *to send* from the obsolete لَأَكَ; أَوْحَى from وَحَى both meaning *to inspire, suggest*; and أَيْقَنَ *to make sure* from يَقِنَ which means the same but is very unusual.

47. The *fifth* form تَفَعَّلَ is reflexive of the second, being (as are the next following forms) called مُطَاوِعٌ a verb *the grammatical agent of which complies with*, i.e. receives the effect of, *the action of the verb to which it is reflexive*; as أَذَّنَ *to announce* تَأَذَّنَ *to declare obligatory on oneself*, جَلَّى *to make manifest, show* تَجَلَّى *to make oneself manifest*, ذَكَّرَ *to remind* تَذَكَّرَ *to become reminded of*, رَأَّسَ *to appoint as chief* تَرَأَّسَ *to become chief*, طَيَّرَ *to make* a bird *fly* اِطَّيَّرَ (for تَطَيَّرَ) *to draw an omen concerning oneself* as from the flight of birds, قَوَّلَ *to cause to say, to make out that* a man *said* so and so تَقَوَّلَ *to make out falsely that* a man *said* so and so *with a view to one's own*

advantage, كَبَّرَ *to exalt* تَكَبَّرَ *to be proud,* كَلَّمَ *to address, accost* تَكَلَّمَ *to speak,* وَفَّى *to pay in full* تَوَفَّى *to receive payment in full,* and of God *to take to Himself,* وَكَّلَ *to make* someone else *to be one's wakíl,* i.e. a person left alone, an agent تَوَكَّلَ *to trust oneself to* an agent who is fully empowered to act on one's behalf, وَلَّاهُ ٱلْأَمْرَ *he put him* (*another*) *in charge of the matter* تَوَلَّى ٱلْأَمْرَ *he took charge of the matter himself.*

Rem. *b.* Some of Professor Wright's examples in § 47 are denominative, as تَنَبَّأَ *to call oneself a prophet* from نَبِيّ *a prophet.* In case of تَضَرَّعَ *to make humble supplication,* earnestness is denoted by the doubled middle radical and self-advantage by the prefixed ت in comparison with ضَرَعَ *to be humble.* Further we observe لَقِفَ *he caught up, swallowed* what was cast to him لَقَّفَ *to cast* a thing to another person *to be seized and swallowed* تَلَقَّفَ similar in sense to لَقِفَ but with the idea added of *taking for one's own advantage*: while تَمَدَّدَ *to stretch oneself* is reflexive of the first form مَدَّ *to extend.* We find also وَلِيَ *to be near* or *beside* وَلَّى *to turn one's side or back to another* تَوَلَّى *to turn aside.*

48. By way of secondary meaning we have the effective, i.e. expressing effect, as بَيَّنَ *to make distinct* تَبَيَّنَ *to appear clear,* عَدَّى *to give* a verb *a transitive signification* تَعَدَّى *to be transitive.*

50. The *sixth* form تَفَاعَلَ is connected with the third: it is reflexive, and frequently simulative especially when the ground form is intransitive, thus تَبَاءَسَ *to feign poverty* from بَئِسَ *to be poor.* Also we find تَخَاطَأَ *wrongly to attribute error to oneself*

which is reflexive and intensive of تَخَطَّأَ *to impute error* to another, from خَطِئَ *to do wrong.* More often it is reciprocal, as آمَرَ *to consult with* تَآمَرَ and تَوَامَرَ *to deliberate in common,* سَايَرَ *to accompany* تَسَايَرَ *to travel in company,* عَاوَنَ *to help* تَعَاوَنَ *to help one another,* قَاتَلَهُ *he fought with him* تَقَاتَلَا *the two fought with one another*; while مَادَدَ and مَادَّ *to contend in pulling* make تَمَادَدَ and تَمَادَّ of two persons *together to stretch* a cloth.

REM. *a.* When used of God تَبَارَكَ and تَعَالَى illustrate the reflexive force of this form: تَبَارَكَ ٱللّٰهُ *God has made Himself most blessed,* تَعَالَى ٱللّٰهُ *God has exalted Himself above all,* see § 401 rem.

REM. *c.* This form is appropriate to actions that take place bit by bit, as سَقَطَ *to fall* تَسَاقَطَ *to fall one by one* (as leaves).

NOTE. From غَبَنَ *to cheat* غَابَنَ (should mean if it existed) *of two persons that one cheated the other* and تَغَابَنَ means *of many that they cheated one another* whence تَغَابُنٌ *general deception,* see § 202.

52. The *seventh* form اِنْفَعَلَ is originally in certain ways reflexive of the first, and approaches to a passive, being sometimes effective, as بَجَسَ *to make flow* اِنْبَجَسَ *to gush,* جَلَا *to become clear, manifest* اِنْجَلَى of anxiety *to be cleared away,* سَبَأَ *to skin* اِنْسَبَأَ of the skin *to be stripped off,* سَاقَ *to drive* اِنْسَاقَ *to be driven,* قَطَعَ *to cut* اِنْقَطَعَ *to be cut off, to be ended, to end,* قَلَبَ *to change, invert* اِنْقَلَبَ *to be changed, translated* as by death.

53. This form may imply that a person allows of an act being done to himself, as جَرَّ *to drag* اِنْجَرَّ *to let oneself be dragged.*

NOTE. We employ اِنْجَأَثَّ *to split itself* as paradigm, though the word is little known.

55. The *eighth* form اِفْتَعَلَ is reflexive of the first; the reflex object being (*a*) the direct object, as سَتَرَ *to conceal* اِسْتَتَرَ *to conceal oneself*, فَرَقَ *to divide* اِفْتَرَقَ *to go asunder*, مَدَّ *to stretch* a thing اِمْتَدَّ of a thing *to stretch itself*, وَقَى *to guard* اِتَّقَى *to guard oneself, fear*, or

(*b*) the indirect object, implying for one's own advantage, as أَجَرَ *to reward* اِيتَجَرَ *to give alms seeking a reward*, خَارَ *to obtain good* اِخْتَارَ *to take to oneself that which seems good, choose* سَوِيَ *to be even with, equal to* اِسْتَوَى *to settle oneself, become firm*, صَفَا *to be pure and clear* اِصْطَفَى *to take to oneself that which is pure and clear*, عَدَا *to go beyond and leave behind* اِعْتَدَى *to do so for one's own evil ends, transgress consciously*, فَرَى *to cut out, manufacture* اِفْتَرَى *to do so for one's own evil purpose, forge lies*, نَقَمَ *to punish* اِنْتَقَمَ *to avenge oneself*, يَسَرَ *to play at hazard* اِتَّسَرَ *to divide by lot a slain beast.*

56. Occasionally, like the sixth form, it is reciprocal, as لَقِيَ *to meet* اِلْتَقَوْا and تَلَاقَوْا *they met one another.*

57. Sometimes we find it passive, especially in verbs wanting the seventh form (see § 113), as وَعَظَ *to admonish* اِتَّعَظَ *to be admonished*; also هَدَى *to direct* اِهْتَدَى *to be directed aright*, which however may mean *to find true direction.*

REM. *a.* In many verbs this form agrees nearly in meaning with the first, as بَدَأَ and اِبْتَدَأَ *to begin,* تَبِعَ and اِتَّبَعَ *to follow,* هَنَأَ and اهْتَنَأَ *to put right.*

NOTE. We find also بَئِسَ *to be poor* اِبْتَأَسَ *to abase oneself.*

59. The *ninth* form اِفْعَلَّ and the *eleventh* اِفْعَالَّ chiefly express colours or defects, being indistinguishable in sense; thus اِصْفَرَّ and اِصْفَارَّ *to be yellow.*

61. The *tenth* form اِسْتَفْعَلَ is often reflexive of the fourth, as أَحْيَا *to bring to life, preserve alive* اِسْتَحْيَا *to save alive for one's own advantage,* أَرْهَبَ *to cause fear* اِسْتَرْهَبَ *to call forth fear of oneself,* أَطَاعَ *to comply with a command* اِسْتَطَاعَ *to be able* (i.e. to obey oneself), أَغْنَى *to make rich* اِسْتَغْنَى *to make oneself independent,* أَقَرَّ *to cause to remain* اِسْتَقَرَّ *to stand firm,* أَقَامَ *to make stand upright* اِسْتَقَامَ *to hold oneself upright.*

62. This form may indicate a belief that some thing or person possesses the quality expressed by the first, as شُئِمَ (passive) *to be unlucky* اِسْتَشْأَمَ *to deem unlucky,* ضَعُفَ *to be weak* اِسْتَضْعَفَ *to find weak, despise,* طَابَ *to be sweet and pleasant* اِسْتَطَابَ *to find sweet and pleasant,* كَبُرَ *to be great* اِسْتَكْبَرَ *to be puffed up with pride.*

63. This form very frequently means asking or seeking what is indicated by the first, as أَذِنَ *to give permission* اِسْتَأْذَنَ *to ask permission,* سَقَى *to give drink* اِسْتَسْقَى *to ask for drink,* غَفَرَ *to pardon* اِسْتَغْفَرَ *to ask pardon,* فَهِمَ *to understand* اِسْتَفْهَمَ *to ask*

the meaning, قَرَأَ *to read* اِسْتَقْرَأَ *to ask* one *to read,* وَقَعَ *to befall* اِسْتَوْقَعَ *to look for* its *coming to pass.*

65. This form is sometimes denominative, as اِسْتَثْنَى *to except* from ثُنْيَا *a turning away from the course, an exception,* اِسْتَخْلَفَ *to appoint as successor, deputy* or *caliph* from خَلِيفَةٌ *successor.*

NOTE. In meaning اِسْتَيْسَرَ *to be easy* is identical with تَيَسَّرَ and nearly corresponds with يَسَرَ; while اِسْتَعَانَ *to ask help* may be derived from أَعَانَ *to help* or, better still, called a denominative of عَوْنٌ *help.*

66. The remaining forms of the triliteral verb need not be noticed here, as they do not occur in *Elementary Arabic: First reading book.*

---

67. Quadriliteral verbs are formed (*a*) by repeating a biliteral root, as غَرْغَرَ *to gargle*; (*b*) by adding a fourth letter, as جَلَطَ and جَلْمَطَ *to shave* the head; (*c*) as denominatives from nouns, often foreign, thus جَوْرَبَ *to put on* جَوْرَبٌ *stockings*; or (*d*) from certain common formulas, as بَسْمَلَ *to say* بِسْمِ ٱللّٰهِ.

68. There are three derived forms of the quadriliteral verb, which are conjugated in the paradigms (Table IV) of Wright's Grammar, viz.

IV اِفْعَلَلَّ III اِفْعَنْلَلَ II تَفَعْلَلَ I فَعْلَلَ

---

73. Nearly all verbal forms, primitive or derivative, have two voices, the *active* and the *passive*; but we must often translate the latter impersonally, as أُنْجُرَّ *a dragging took place*

يُشَارُ إِلَيْهِمْ *one points to them*, سُقِطَ فِي أَيْدِيهِمْ *a falling took place* (or, an onslaught was made) *upon their hands*, i.e. they bit their fingers for disappointment (see § 533).

75. We speak of neuter verbs, meaning those which express a state or condition and therefore have no passive voice, as حَكُمَ *to be wise*, but Arabian grammarians reckon them as active, distinguishing between ٱلْأَفْعَالُ ٱلْمُتَعَدِّيَةُ *transitive verbs* and ٱلْأَفْعَالُ غَيْرُ ٱلْمُتَعَدِّيَةِ *intransitive verbs* or ٱلْأَفْعَالُ ٱللَّازِمَةُ *verbs that are confined to the subject.*

77. An Arabic verb has two States, the *Perfect* indicating a finished act, and the *Imperfect* an act that is just commencing or in progress.

Rem. *a.* Acquaintance with grammar will teach how to employ these States in explaining the temporal relations (past, present, and future) which non-semitic languages express by tenses.

79. There are five moods: the Indicative which is common to the perfect and imperfect states; the Subjunctive, and Jussive (or Conditional) which are restricted to the imperfect; the Imperative which is expressed by a special form; and the Energetic which can be derived from the imperfect and from the imperative.

80. By way of Infinitives we have nomina actionis *nouns expressing the action or quality* (see § 195). In place of participles two verbal adjectives are used; nomen agentis denoting the agent, and nomen patientis the patient (see § 229).

81. There are three numbers, Singular, Dual, and Plural; likewise three persons. The genders are two, Masculine and Feminine; but distinction cannot in all cases be made, as أَقُولُ *I say*, where the speaker's sex is not disclosed.

---

83. Verbs are called *strong* when the three radical letters are retained throughout and undergo no change.

REM. To contain أ, و or ي causes a verb to be called *weak* (see § 126); but verbs in which the second and third radicals are identical (see § 120) we shall call strong.

NOTE. Students must spare no pains to learn the conjugations in § 369 Tables 1, 2 and 3; otherwise they will find the weak verbs difficult to impossibility.

84. The numbers, persons, and genders of the verbs are expressed by means of personal pronouns, annexed to the various moods and states. These may be connected, *i.e.* prefixed or suffixed, in which case they are to be learned from the conjugations; thus نَا *we* in كَلَمْنَا *we wounded,* تُمْ *ye* in كَلَمْتُمْ *ye wounded,* يَ *he* in يَكْلِمُ *he wounds* (see § 369 Table 1)*: or they may be separate.

89. The following table gives such separate personal pronouns as express the nominative:—

SINGULAR.

Feminine	Common	Masculine	
هِيَ *she*	. . . .	هُوَ *he*	3rd person
أَنْتِ *thou*	. . . .	أَنْتَ *thou*	2nd „
. . . .	أَنَا *I*	. . . .	1st „

---

* These pronouns are called مُسْتَتِرٌ *concealed* see § 513.

DUAL

Feminine	Common	Masculine	
. . . .	هُمَا *they two*	. . . .	3rd person
. . . .	أَنْتُمَا *ye two*	. . . .	2nd ,,

PLURAL

هُنَّ *they*	. . . .	هُمْ *they*	3rd ,,
أَنْتُنَّ *ye*	. . . .	أَنْتُمْ *ye*	2nd ,,
. . . .	نَحْنُ *we*	. . . .	1st ,,

REM. *c.* For the older forms هُمُ and أَنْتُمُ see § 20 *d.*

NOTE. In § 185 are given pronominal suffixes expressing the accusative, and those expressing the dependent in § 317.

90. Regarding first the active voice we observe that the 3rd pers. sing. masc. *perfect* of the ground form bears fatḥah always on the first and third radicals.

91. When the middle radical of the perfect has fatḥah a verb must take either ḍammah or kasrah in the imperfect; as بَطَلَ *to be worthless* يَبْطُلُ, ضَرَبَ *to strike* يَضْرِبُ which we write بَطَلَ ـُ and ضَرَبَ ـِ. Also أَثَرَ ـُ *to relate,* خَلَقَ ـُ *to create,* رَزَقَ ـُ *to provide,* سَكَنَ ـُ *to dwell,* شَكَرَ ـُ *to be thankful,* ظَلَمَ ـِ *to do wrong, injure,* عَرَشَ ـِ *to construct,* عَقَلَ ـِ *to understand,* فَسَقَ ـُ *to be impious,* نَتَقَ ـُ *to shake, wave,* نَزَعَ ـِ *to pull out,* نَصَرَ ـُ *to assist,* نَكَثَ ـُ *to break a promise.* Many verbs admit of both forms; as دَرَسَ *to study,* يَدْرُسُ and يَدْرِسُ which we shorten into دَرَسَ ـُـِ, also سَبَتَ ـُـِ *to keep Sabbath,* and عَكَفَ ـُـِ *to cling.*

REM. *a.* Verbs of which the second or third radical is a guttural (either أ, ح, خ, ع, غ, or ه) may be exceptional; as بَعَثَ ـَ *to send*, جَعَلَ ـَ *to make, place*, جَمَعَ ـَ *to collect*, خَسَأَ ـَ *to be driven away*, رَأَسَ ـَ *to be the head of*, سَبَحَ ـَ *to swim*, سَحَرَ ـَ *to fascinate, enchant*, شَفَعَ ـَ *to intercede*, صَعَقَ ـَ *to strike with lightning*, صَفَحَ ـَ *to pardon*, صَنَعَ ـَ *to make*, فَتَحَ ـَ *to open*, فَعَلَ ـَ *to do*, قَطَعَ ـَ *to cut*, قَهَرَ ـَ *to overcome*, نَسَخَ ـَ *to supersede, transcribe*, نَصَحَ ـَ *to counsel*, نَهَرَ ـَ of water *to flow*, نَهَى ـَ *to forbid*. Many however conform to the rule; as أَخَذَ ـُ *to take, seize*, بَلَغَ ـُ *to reach*, دَخَلَ ـُ *to enter*, رَجَعَ ـِ *to return*, زَعَمَ ـُ *to assert*. Some verbs have more than one form; as رَبَعَ ـَ ـِ *to take a fourth part*, صَلُحَ ـَ ـُ *to be good*, فَرَغَ ـَ ـُ *to be vacant*.

NOTE. As paradigm we use فَعُلَ ـُ ـِ.

92. When the second radical of the perfect has kasrah, the imperfect bears fathah; as أَثِمَ ـَ *to sin*, حَبِطَ ـَ *to be vain*, خَطِئَ ـَ *to do wrong, sin*, رَهِبَ ـَ *to fear*, سَفِهَ ـَ *to be lightwitted*, شَهِدَ ـَ *to testify*, صَحِبَ ـَ *to consort with*, صَعِقَ ـَ *to swoon*, صَغِرَ ـَ *to be small*, طَمِعَ ـَ *to desire*, عَجِبَ ـَ *to wonder*, عَجِلَ ـَ *to hasten*, عَمِلَ ـَ *to work, do*, عَهِدَ ـَ *to enjoin, covenant*.

REM. Exceptions are rare, as بَئِسَ ـَ ـِ *to be in distress or poverty*, حَضِرَ ـُ *to be present*, and مَاتَ *to die* for مَوِتَ (see § 157) which usually makes يَمُوتُ but sometimes يَمَاتُ or يَمِيتُ.

93. When the middle radical of the perfect has dammah the imperfect bears the same, as بَصُرَ ـُ *to see*, خَبُثَ ـُ *to be bad*,

رَحُبَ ـُـ *to be spacious,* سَفُهَ ـُـ *to be light-witted,* شَهُدَ ـُـ *to testify,* صَغُرَ ـُـ *to be small,* كَبُرَ ـُـ *to be great,* كَثُرَ ـُـ *to be numerous,* نَهُوَ ـُـ *to be intelligent.*

95. The *indicative* of the imperfect is distinguished by dammah on the third radical, as يَجْهَلُ *he is ignorant*; the *subjunctive* by fathah, as يَجْهَلَ; and the *jussive* by sukûn, as يَجْهَلْ.

96. A termination نَ of the indicative is only retained in the subjunctive and jussive when required as mark of gender; otherwise it and نِ are rejected.

97. The *energetics* are formed from the jussive by adding ـَنَّ or ـَنْ (subject to certain variations, which in case of Energetic I of the imperfect may be learnt from the paradigms in § 369) thus, يَبْعَثَنَّ, *he will certainly send* from يَبْعَثْ jussive of بَعَثَ. Energetic II of the imperfect and the two energetics of the imperative are omitted from § 369 as they do not occur in *Elementary Arabic: First reading book.*

98. The *imperative* is formed by substituting a prosthetic vowel for the prefix of the jussive's 2nd sing.: when the second radical bears fathah or kasrah this vowel is kasrah, and when dammah it is dammah; thus, اِجْعَلْ *make,* اِرْحَمْ *have mercy upon,* اِكْشِفْ *remove,* اِعْدِلْ *be just,* اُسْكُتْ *calm thyself,* اُطْلُبْ *seek*; and similarly with the feminine etc.

Rem *a.* Concerning prosthetic vowels see § 19, rem. *c.*

Rem. *b.* Fathah is never so employed.

100. From the active voice the *passive* is distinguished by altered vowels (see § 369, Table 2) on the first and second radicals.

Rem. It makes no difference what characteristic vowels are employed in the active voice.

101. Instead of a passive imperative the jussive is used.

---

102. The *derived forms* of strong verbs must be learned from § 369, Table 3; attention being at an early stage confined to the first seven and the tenth form, i.e. neglecting the ninth, eleventh and following.

107. The relation of passive to active will be found analogous to that in the ground form.

Rem. *a.* The imperfect passive of the first and fourth forms are identical in appearance.

111. When the verbal root begins with ت, ث, ج, د, ذ, ز, س, ش, ص, ض, ط or ظ the characteristic ت of the *fifth* and *sixth* forms may lose its vowel and form a double letter with the first radical, to which when necessary a prosthetic 'alif and kasrah must be added; as اِطَّيَّرَ يَطَّيَّرُ *to draw an omen concerning oneself* for تَطَيَّرَ يَتَطَيَّرُ, اِسَّاقَطَ يَسَّاقَطُ *to fall one by one* for تَسَاقَطَ يَتَسَاقَطُ.

112. The تَ of the fifth and sixth forms is sometimes omitted from those persons of the imperfect active to which تَ is prefixed; as تَلَقَّفُ *she swallows* for تَتَلَقَّفُ, تَذَكَّرُ *she becomes reminded of* for تَتَذَكَّرُ or تَذَّكَّرُ (see § 111).

115. If the first radical be ت or ث, characteristic ت of the *eighth* form unites with the initial ت into تّ and with initial ث into ثّ or ثّ; as اِتَّبَعَ *he followed* for اِتْتَبَعَ.

117. If the first radical be ص, ض, ط or ظ, characteristic ت is changed into ط; as اِصْطَفَيْتُ *I chose* from صَفَا ـُ (see § 55) and not اِصْتَفَيْتُ.

---

120. Verbs with the *middle radical doubled* are conjugated in § 369, Tables 5 *a*, *b* and *c*: they differ from other strong verbs in two ways.

(*a*) When both the initial and final radicals have vowels the middle rejects its vowel and becomes with the final a double letter bearing tashdîd; as جَنَّ ـُ *to cover*, حَطَّ ـُ of a burden *to put down*, حَقَّ ـِ *to be fitting*, خَرَّ ـِ *to fall down*, دَكَّ ـُ *to pound*, ذَلَّ ـِ *to be abased*, شَحَّ ـِ *to be avaricious*, شَدَّ ـِ *to be severe*, ظَنَّ ـُ *to think*, عَزَّ ـِ *to be potent*, غَلَّ ـُ *to insert*.

(*b*) If the initial radical is without a vowel and the final has one, then the middle radical throws its vowel to the initial and becomes with the final a double letter; as يَخِرُّ for يَخْرِرُ, يَدُكُّ for يَدْكُكُ, يَغُلُّ for يَغْلُلُ: but if the final radical be vowelless, no contraction is possible; as ظَنَنْتُ, يَذْلِلْ, يَحْطُطْ; and this must be specially noted in the perfect of verbs like حَبَّ for حَبُبَ *to become loved* which makes حَبُبْتُ and like مَسَّ for مَسِسَ *to touch* which makes مَسِسْتُ.

121. The jussive is sometimes identical with the subjunctive as يَمُدَّ for يَمْدُدْ.

124. In some derived forms will be found alternative vocalization: this is common when the doubled radical follows l. ... â, as مَادَّ for مَادَدَ, see § 25, rem.

---

126. Verbs are called *weak* when one of the three radical letters is subject to transformation or rejection.

128. Verbs with و or ي for a radical are unmistakeably weak, more so than those called hamzated.

129. Verbs may be doubly weak (§ 171): and even trebly, as أَوَى ـِ *to resort to* imperf. يَأْوِي impera. اِيوِ.

---

130. *Hamzated* verbs fall into three classes according as hamzaħ serves for first, second or third radical: they are conjugated in § 369, Tables 6 to 8, differing from strong verbs especially as regards the 'imâd (see § 15) in the following ways.

131. The 'alif with hamzaħ and sukûn أْ preceded by ḍammaħ becomes ؤْ, as دَنُؤْتَ *thou art mean* not دَنُأْتَ; preceded by kasraħ ئْ, as خَطِئْتُ *I have done wrong* not خَطِأْتُ.

132. It is said by some that و and ي represent sounds towards which hamzaħ is inclined by the preceding vowel.

Rem. *b.* Instances occur like أُوذِينَا *we were hurt* for أُؤْذِينَا, اِيذَنْ *give ear* for اِئْذَنْ, اِيتِ *come* for اِئْتِ (see § 175): but in imperatives following وَ or فَ the connective 'alif is rejected while hamzaħ with sukûn remains; thus فَأْتِ *so then come.*

133. Similarly أ becomes ؤ if preceded by fatḥaħ, as بَؤُسَ *to be brave* not بَأُسَ; إ becomes ئ if preceded by fatḥaħ, as بَئِسَ *to be in distress* not بَإِسَ; أ becomes ؤَ if preceded by ḍammaħ, as دَنُؤَ *to be ignoble* not دَنُأَ; أ becomes ئ if preceded by kasraħ, as

خَطِئ *to do wrong* not خَطَأ ; إ becomes ئ if preceded by ḍammah, as سُئِلَ (passive) *he was asked* not سُإِلَ.

REM. At the end of a word أ stands after fatḥah, thus يَقْرَأُ *he reads* but يَقْرَؤُهُ *he reads it.*

134. When preceded by a consonant with sukûn أ becomes ؤ, as يَبْؤُسُ imperfect of بَؤُسَ not يَبْأُسُ ; and إ becomes ئ as, not يَبْإِسُ but يَبْئِسُ which and يَبْأَسُ are imperfects of بَئِسَ.

135. If 'alif of prolongation follows radical أ at a word's beginning we write آ or آء or even أ (see § 23) as آمَرَ *to consult with* for أَامَرَ ; and so when radical أ follows أ, as آسَفَ *to make grieve* for أَأْسَفَ.

137. The verbs أَخَذَ ـُ *to take* أَمَرَ ـُ *to command* and أَكَلَ ـُ *to eat* make in the imperative خُذْ, مُرْ and كُلْ.

138. The imperative مُرْ may when following وَ or فَ recover its first radical, but not so خُذْ or كُلْ ; thus وَأْمُرْ or وَمُرْ but وَخُذْ, فَكُلْ.

139. In the eighth form of أَخَذَ the first radical becomes assimilated to ت, thus اِتَّخَذَ *to take for oneself*: this occurs with a few other verbs, but اِتَّجَرَ from أَجَرَ *to reward* is less common than اِيتَجَرَ which follows § 132, rem. *b.*

140. Loss of hamzah occasionally takes place and we have سَالَ يَسَالُ for سَأَلَ ـَ *to ask.* The vowel may even be transferred, as أَلَكَ *to send* for أَلْأَكَ whence مَلَكٌ for مَلْأَكٌ *an angel.*

141. *Weak verbs* specially so called likewise fall into three classes according as و or ي is the first, the second, or the third radical.

142. Verbs with و as *initial radical* (see § 369, Table 9) which have kasraħ for characteristic vowel of the imperfect and imperative, reject و in those forms. Thus وَلَدَ *to bear children* imperf. يَلِدُ, impera. لِدْ; وَعَدَ *to promise* imperf. يَعِدُ, impera. عِدْ; وَجَدَ *to find* imperf. يَجِدُ, impera. جِدْ; وَقَتَ *to fix a time or place* imperf. يَقِتُ, impera. قِتْ; وَكَلَ *to leave alone* imperf. يَكِلُ, impera. كِلْ; وَعَظَ *to warn* imperf. يَعِظُ, impera. عِظْ.

Rem. *a.* A few verbs, having (contrary to § 92) kasraħ in both perfect and imperfect, lose their initial radical, as وَثِقَ *to trust* يَثِقُ, وَرِثَ *to inherit* يَرِثُ, وَلِيَ *to be near* يَلِي.

143. But verbs with و as initial radical, which have fatḥaħ or ḍammaħ for characteristic vowel of the imperfect and imperative, retain و in those forms; as وَسِنَ *to doze* imperf. يَوْسَنُ, impera. اِيسَنْ for اِوْسَنْ; وَبُلَ *to be unwholesome* imperf. يَوْبُلُ, impera. اُوبُلْ; وَجِلَ *to fear* imperf. يَوْجَلُ, impera. اِيجَلْ for اِوْجَلْ.

144. In certain verbs initial و drops from the imperfect and imperative notwithstanding that fatḥaħ is the characteristic vowel of these forms; as وذر *to leave* يَذَرُ and ذَرْ, وَسِعَ *to be spacious* يَسَعُ and سَعْ, وَضَعَ *to put down* يَضَعُ and ضَعْ, وَقَعَ *to fall* يَقَعُ and قَعْ.

Rem. *b.* وذر is not used in the perfect.

145. If initial و be vowelless, a preceding kasraħ or ḍammaħ changes it into ي or و of prolongation as may be seen in § 143 with the imperatives of وَسِنَ وَبُلَ and وَجِلَ.

146. Verbs with ي as *initial radical* are inflected almost like strong verbs, thus يَسَرَ يَيْسِرُ (see § 369, Table 9).

147. But if initial ي be vowelless, a preceding kasraħ or ḍammaħ changes it into ي or و of prolongation; thus the imperative of يَسَرَ *to be easy* is اِيسِرْ for اِيْسِرْ and the fourth form is أَيْسَرَ يُوسِرُ *to arrive at ease.*

148. In the eighth form و and ي are assimilated to the characteristic ت, thus producing تّ, as اِتَّقَى *to fear* for اِوْتَقَى, of which the nomen agentis is مُتَّقٍ *devout.*

---

149. Verbs with و or ي as *middle radical* are conjugated in § 369, Tables 10 to 13: they differ from strong verbs only in the first, fourth, seventh, eighth and tenth forms.

150. In case the initial radical is without a vowel and the final has one, the vowel of the middle radical passes to the first and we employ a letter of prolongation homogeneous with the vowel which the first radical has now assumed; thus

with form	يَفْعُلُ	يَطْوُفُ	becomes	يَطُوفُ	I of	طَافَ ـُـ	*to circle*
„	يَفْعِلُ	يَدْيِنُ	„	يَدِينُ	I „	دَانَ ـِـ	*to obey*
„	يَفْعَلُ	يَخْوَفُ	„	يَخَافُ	I „	خَافَ ـَـ	*to fear*
„	do.	يَنْيَلُ	„	يَنَالُ	I „	نَالَ ـَـ	*to reach*
„	يُفْعَلُ	يُسْوَمُ	„	يُسَامُ	I „	سَامَ ـُـ	*to inflict*

with form أَفْعَلَ	أَفْوَزَ	becomes	أَفَازَ IV	of	فَازَ ـُ *to obtain*
„ do.	أَضْيَعَ	„	أَضَاعَ IV	„	ضَاعَ ـِ *to be lost*
„ يُفْعِلُ	يُذْوِقُ	„	يُذِيقُ IV	„	ذَاقَ ـُ *to taste*
„ اِسْتَفْعَلَ	اِسْتَقْوَمَ	„	اِسْتَقَامَ X	„	قَامَ ـُ *to stand*
„ يَسْتَفْعِلُ	يَسْتَطْيِبُ	„	يَسْتَطِيبُ X	„	طَابَ ـِ *to be good*

151. But if the final radical has sukûn, the long vowels ـَا â, ـِي î, ـُو û become short, according to § 25; thus

with form يَفْعُلْ	يَدُورْ	becomes	يَدُرْ I	of	دَارَ ـُ *to go round*
„ يَفْعِلْ	يَعِينْ	„	يَعِنْ I	„	عَانَ ـِ *to flow*
„ يَفْعَلْ	يَخَافْ	„	يَخَفْ I	„	خَافَ ـَ *to fear*
„ يَفْعِلْ	يَزِادْ	„	يَزِدْ I	„	زَادَ ـِ *to increase*
„ أَفْعَلْتَ	أَحَاطْتَ	„	أَحَطْتَ IV	„	حَاطَ ـُ *to guard*
„ يُفْعِلْ	يُقِيمْ	„	يُقِمْ IV	„	قَامَ ـُ *to stand*
„ أَفْعِلْ	أَضِيعْ	„	أَضِعْ IV	„	ضَاعَ ـِ *to be lost*

REM. يَكُنْ for يَكُونْ jussive of كَانَ *to be* is sometimes further abbreviated into يَكُ, see § 583 *c*.

NOTE. We have يَكُونَنَّ *he will certainly be* from يَكُنْ (see § 97) jussive of كَانَ ـُ *to be*: the letter of prolongation must reappear in obedience to § 150. So in the plural, thus لَا تَخَافُوا *fear ye not.*

152. It follows that the first form's imperative needs no prosthetic 'alif; thus

with form أُفْعُلْ أُكُونْ becomes كُنْ from كَانَ ـُ *to be*
„ اِفْعِلْ اِصِيرْ „ صِرْ „ صَارَ ـِ *to become*
„ اِفْعَلْ اِخَافْ „ خَفْ „ خَافَ ـَ *to fear*
„ اُفْعُلُوا اُتُوبُوا „ تُوبُوا „ تَابَ ـُ *to repent*

153. If three open syllables follow in immediate succession, the first of which has fatḥah, then 'alif of prolongation takes the middle radical's place; thus

with form فَعَلَ نَوَرَ becomes نَارَ I of نَارَ ـُ *to shine*
„ do. غَيَبَ „ غَابَ I „ غَابَ ـِ *to be absent*
„ فَعِلَ كَوِدَ „ كَادَ I „ كَادَ ـَ *to be on the point of*
„ فَعُلَ طَوُلَ „ طَالَ I „ طَالَ ـُ *to be long*
„ اِنْفَعَلَ اِنْسَوَقَ „ اِنْسَاقَ VII „ سَاقَ ـُ *to drive*
„ يَفْتَعِلُ يَخْتَيِرُ „ يَخْتَارُ VIII „ خَارَ ـِ *to be good*

154. But if the first syllable's vowel be ḍammah, and و or ي bear kasrah, we discard ḍammah, taking kasrah into its place, and adopt ي of prolongation instead of the middle radical; as

with form فُعِلَ قُوِلَ becomes قِيلَ passive of قَالَ ـُ *to say.*

155. If the first radical has fatḥah and the third sukûn, three cases arise.

(*a*) The middle radical is و or ي with fatḥah; when we discard it and its vowel, placing, if it was و, ḍammah on the first radical, and kasrah if it was ي: thus

with form فَعَلْتَ قَوَمْتَ becomes قُمْتَ from قَامَ يـ to stand

„ do. سَيَرْتَ „ سِرْتَ „ سَارَ يـ to go

(*b*) The middle radical is و with ḍammah or ي with kasrah; when we discard it and its vowel, but we place a vowel homogeneous with it upon the first radical: as

with form فَعُلْتَ طَوُلْتَ becomes طُلْتَ from طَالَ يـ to be long

„ فَعِلْتَ نَيِلْتَ „ نِلْتَ „ نَالَ يـ to reach

(*c*) The middle radical is و with kasrah; when we discard it and its vowel, placing kasrah on the first radical: as

with form فَعِلْتَ خَوِفْتَ becomes خِفْتَ from خَافَ يـ to fear

„ do. مَوِتْتَ „ مِتَّ „ مَاتَ يـ to die

156. In certain passive forms the ي of prolongation is shortened into kasrah, when the third radical bears sukûn; thus دِينْتَ (for دُيِنْتَ) becomes دِنْتَ *thou wast obeyed*, which is identical in form with دِنْتَ *thou hast obeyed*.

157. Most verbs with و as middle radical take ḍammah in the imperfect, and most with ي take kasrah; but some of the form فَعِلَ take fatḥah. Thus

كَادَ for كَوِدَ *to be on the point of* makes يَكَادُ for يَكْوَدُ

خَافَ „ خَوِفَ *to fear* „ يَخَافُ „ يَخْوَفُ

شَاءَ „ شَيِئَ *to wish* „ يَشَاءُ „ يَشْيَأُ

نَامَ for نَوِمَ *to sleep* makes يَنَامُ for يَنْوَمُ

نَالَ „ نَيِلَ *to reach* „ يَنَالُ „ يَنْيَلُ.

We have mentioned (§ 92, rem.) مَاتَ for مَوِتَ *to die.*

---

164. Verbs with و or ي as *final radical* are conjugated in § 369, Tables 14 to 18: they are of five kinds:—

(i) Final و	of form فَعَلَ	as دَنَا	*to be near*	for دَنَوَ
(ii) „ ي		„ بَغَى	*to seek*	„ بَغَيَ
(iii) „ و	„ فَعِلَ	„ رَضِيَ	*to be pleased*	„ رَضِوَ
(iv) „ ي		„ فَنِيَ	*to perish*	
(v) „ و	„ فَعُلَ	„ نَهُوَ	*to be intelligent, prudent*	

165. One of three things must happen: the final radical retains its consonantal power, or resolves itself into a vowel, or is elided.

166. At the beginning of a syllable two things are possible.

(*a*) The third radical maintains its power as a consonant,

in ـَـوَا awâ as عَتَوَا *they two* (masc.) *were disobedient*

„ ـَـيَا ayâ „ جَزَيَا *they two* (masc.) *rewarded*

„ ـُـوَ uwa „ يَبْلُوَ *he may try*

„ ـُـوَا uwâ „ يَعْفُوَانِ *they two* (masc.) *condone*

„ ـِـيَ iya „ عَمِيَ *he was blind*

„ ـِـيَا iyâ „ غَنِيَا *they two* (masc.) *were rich*;

also when following sukûn, as عَدْوٌ *a transgressing*, رِضْوَانٌ *grace*, *favour* (see § 212 *a*). The letter و in ـِوَ iwa and in ـِوَا iwâ always becomes ي, as بُلِيَ *he was tried* for بُلِوَ. The letter ي is never found in ـُيَ uya or in ـُيَا uyâ, though we have تُبُيِّنَ and the like in verbs with و or ي as middle radical.

(*b*) The third radical is elided between a short vowel and î or û: this involves contraction

(i) either into a long vowel; namely

ـُوُو uwû into ـُو û as يَدْعُونَ *they* (masc.) *call* for يَدْعُوُونَ
ـِيُو iyû „ ـُو û „ يَجْرُونَ *they* (masc.) *flow* „ يَجْرِيُونَ
ـُوِي uwî „ ـِي î „ تَرْجِينَ *thou* (fem.) *hopest* „ تَرْجُوِينَ
ـِيِي iyî „ ـِي î „ تَسْقِينَ *thou* (fem.) *givest drink*, „ تَسْقِيِينَ

(ii) or into a diphthong; namely

ـَوُو awû into ـَوْ au as صَفَوْا *they* (masc.) *were clear* for صَفَوُوا
ـَيُو ayû „ ـَوْ au „ نَهَوْا *they* (masc.) *forbade* „ نَهَيُوا
ـَيِي ayî „ ـَيْ ai „ تَنْسَيْنَ *thou* (fem.) *forgettest* „ تَنْسَيِينَ

167. At the end of a syllable the third radical is either (*a*) vocalized or (*b*) elided, whether (i) it stands there naturally as in خُفِيتُ *I was hidden*, or (ii) after losing a short vowel as in يَخْفَى *he is hidden* for يَخْفَيُ. The following cases arise.

a. (i) It is vocalized when naturally so placed, as follows:

(a) if the preceding vowel be homogeneous

ـُوْ uw becomes ـُو û as نَهُوتُ *I was prudent*
ـِيْ iy „ ـِي î „ غَشِيتُ *I covered*

(b) if the preceding vowel be heteregeneous

ـَـوْ aw becomes ـَـوْ au as نَجَوْتُ *I escaped*

ـَـيْ ay „ ـَـيْ ai „ هَدَيْتُ *I directed*

(ii) It is vocalized if so placed by loss of a short vowel, thus

ـَـوْ aw becomes ـَـا â as عَلَا *to be high* for عَلَوَ

ـَـيْ ay „ ـَـى a „ جَزَى *to reward* „ جَزَيَ

ـُـوْ uw „ ـُـو û „ يَعْدُو *he transgresses* „ يَعْدُوُ

ـِـيْ iy „ ـِـي î „ يَفْرِي *he cuts out* „ يَفْرِيُ

b. (i) It is elided when naturally so placed in the imperative and jussive, thus

اُدْعُ *call thou* (masc.) for اُدْعُو and يَدْعُ for يَدْعُو

اِبْغِ *seek thou* (masc.) „ اِبْغِي „ يَبْغِ „ يَبْغِي

اِرْضَ *be thou content* (masc.) „ اِرْضَى „ يَرْضَ „ يَرْضَى

(ii) It is elided when so placed in the nomina agentis (see § 80) before tanwîn of ḍammaħ and kasraħ, which vowels disappear, while the tanwîn passes back to kasraħ of the second radical; thus

with forms فَاعِلٌ and فَاعِلٍ عَاصِوٌ become عَاصٍ *a striker*

„ مُفَعِّلٌ „ مُفَعِّلٍ مُجَلِّيٌ „ مُجَلٍّ *one who reveals*

„ مُفَاعِلٌ „ مُفَاعِلٍ مُعَادِيٌ „ مُعَادٍ *one at enmity*

„ مُفْعِلٌ „ مُفْعِلٍ مُلْقِيٌ „ مُلْقٍ *a thrower*

„ مُفْتَعِلٌ „ مُفْتَعِلٍ مُعْتَدِيٌ „ مُعْتَدٍ *transgressor*

So with all the first eight forms and tenth (see §§ 236, 311).

NOTE. The distinction in *a* (ii) between the final syllables of علا for علو and جزى for جزي is mechanical and not phonetic (see § 7, rem. *b*).

169. Final و becomes ى in all derived forms of the verb, thus II عَدَّى, III عَادَى, IV أَنْجى, V تَعَدَّى, VI تَنَاجَى, VII اِنْجَلَى, VIII اِعْتَدَى, etc.

170. To form the nomen patientis مَفْعُولٌ of these verbs, radical و coalesces with و of prolongation, as مَعْضُوٌّ *struck with a stick* for مَعْضُووٌ, مَبْلُوٌّ *tried* for مَبْلُووٌ; but radical ي converts و of prolongation into ي and the two coalesce, with kasrah preceding instead of dammah, as مَهْدِيٌّ *one led aright* for مَهْدُويٌ. Verbs like رَضِيَ for رَضِوَ admit of either form.

---

171. *Doubly weak* verbs are of two classes: *first* those with both hamzah and و or ي among their radicals; and *second* those in which و or ي occurs twice or which contain و and ي.

172. Of the first class there are three sorts, each admitting two varieties according to the position of hamzah.

(i) Hamzated verbs with initial و or ي
(ii) " middle و or ي
(iii) " final و or ي

173. In sort (i) hamzah serves as middle or final radical, and such verbs are inflected like both classes to which they belong.

174. In sort (ii) hamzah serves (*a*) for initial radical, as آدَ or ءَادَ for أَوَدَ *to fatigue*, آلَ or ءَالَ for أَوَلَ *to return*; and (*b*) for final radical, as سَآءَ for سَوَءَ *to be evil*, جَآءَ for جَيَأَ *to come*,

شَآءَ for شَيِءَ *to wish.* The following table shows such verbs inflected like both classes to which they belong.

	a		*b*	
Perf. sing. 3rd masc.	آدَ	سَآءَ	جَآءَ	شَآءَ
„ „ 2nd „	أُدْتَ	سُؤْتَ	جِئْتَ	شِئْتَ
Imperf. indic.	يَؤُودُ	يَسُوءُ	يَجِيءُ	يَشَآءُ
Imperative	أُدْ	سُؤْ	جِئْ	شَأْ
Passive perfect	إِيدَ	سِيءَ	جِيءَ	شِيءَ

NOTE. We can write أُدتَّ for أُدْتَ in accordance with § 14 *c.*

175. In sort (iii) hamzah serves (*a*) for initial radical, as أَتَى *to come,* أَذِيَ *to be hurt*; and (*b*) for middle radical, as نَأَى *to be far*: such verbs are inflected like both classes to which they belong, thus

	a		*b*
Perf. sing. 3rd masc.	أَتَى	أَذِيَ	نَأَى
„ „ „ fem.	أَتَتْ	أَذِيَتْ	نَأَتْ
„ „ 2nd masc.	أَتَيْتَ	أَذِيتَ	نَأَيْتَ
Imperf. indic.	يَأْتِي	يَأْذَى	يَنْأَى
Imperative	اِيتِ	اِيذَ	اِنْأَ
Nomen agentis	آتٍ	آذٍ	نَآءٍ

REM. *a.* In the imperative أَتَى has also تِ for اِيتِ and اِئْتِ, see § 132, rem. *b.*

176. From certain parts of رَأَى hamzated 'alif may be elided: as (indic. and subj.) تَرَى *thou* (masc.) *seest*, نَرَى *we see*; (subj. and juss.) يَرَوْا *they* (masc.) *see*; but (perf.) رَأَيْتُ *I saw*, رَأَوْا *they* (masc.) *saw*.

REM. *c*. Radical hamzated 'alif is elided from the fourth form when meaning *to show*, as أَرِ *show thou* (masc.), أُرِي *I show*.

177. Of the second class (see § 171) there are two sorts.

178. In sort (i) و or ي is the initial and final radical, as وَقَى *to guard*, وَفَى *to be faithful to one's engagement*, وَلِيَ *to be near* (see § 142, rem. *a*); and such verbs are inflected like both classes to which they belong, thus

Perf. sing. 3rd masc.	وَقَى	وَلِيَ
" " " fem.	وَقَتْ	وَلِيَتْ
" " 2nd masc.	وَقَيْتَ	وَلِيتَ
Imperf. indic.	يَقِي	يَلِي
Imperative	قِ	لِ

179. In sort (ii) و or ي is the middle and final radical, as غَوَى *to go astray*, قَوِيَ *to be strong*, سَوِيَ *to be even with, equal to*; حَيِيَ *to live*; and in such verbs the second radical undergoes no change: thus

Perf. sing. 3rd masc.	غَوَى	قَوِيَ	حَيِيَ
" " " fem.	غَوَتْ	قَوِيَتْ	حَيِيَتْ
" " 2nd masc.	غَوَيْتَ	قَوِيتَ	حَيِيتَ
Imperf. indic.	يَغْوِي	يَقْوَى	يَحْيَا
Imperative	اِغْوِ	اِقْوَ	اِحْيَ

Rem. *a.* We write يَحْيَا, as above, to distinguish the word from يَحْيَى *John the Baptist* and to prevent the union of two ي; as also in اَلدُّنْيَا (not اَلدُّنْيَى) fem. of اَلْأَدْنَى *the nearest* (see § 295 *b*).

Rem. *b.* حَيِيَ may be contracted to حَيَّ, see § 120.

---

182. The verb لَيْسَ *he is not* has no imperfect or imperative; its perfect is inflected like verbs with ي for middle radical; thus

1st	2nd f.	2nd m.	3rd f.	3rd m.	
لَسْتُ	لَسْتِ	لَسْتَ	لَيْسَتْ	لَيْسَ	Sing.
	لَسْتُمَا	لَسْتُمَا	لَيْسَتَا	لَيْسَا	Dual
لَسْنَا	لَسْتُنَّ	لَسْتُمْ	لَسْنَ	لَيْسُوا	Plur.

We may perhaps call لَيْسَ a substantive verb, because it implies non-existence without connotation of time or change; it is mentioned in §§ 442, 559, 560 and 587 *d*.

Rem. *a.* لَيْسَ is compounded of لَا *not* and the obsolete يسَ or أَيْسَ *existence, being*; as may be learned in studying Hebrew, Aramaic, and Assyrian.

183. The verbs of praise and blame are نِعْمَ *to be good* and بِئْسَ *to be bad*: they are exclamatory, and when a nominative follows, it must be defined, as بِئْسَ ٱلْمَصِيرُ *a bad issue is that!*

Rem. *a.* The verb may be joined to following conjunctive مَا, as بِئْسَمَا خَلَفْتُمُونِي *evil have ye wrought in mine absence.*

---

185. We give here a table of the *pronominal suffixes* which follow verbs in order to express the accusative, the nominative pronouns having been mentioned in § 89.

SINGULAR.

Feminine	Common	Masculine	
هَا *her*	. . .	هُ *him*	3rd person
كِ *thee*	. . .	كَ *thee*	2nd "
. . .	نِي *me*	. . .	1st "

DUAL.

Feminine	Common	Masculine	
. . .	هُمَا *them both*	. . .	3rd "
. . .	كُمَا *you both*	. . .	2nd "

PLURAL.

Feminine	Common	Masculine	
هُنَّ *them*	. . .	هُمْ *them*	3rd "
كُنَّ *you*	. . .	كُمْ *you*	2nd "
. . .	نَا *us*	. . .	1st "

REM. *a.* For the dependent case, see § 317.

REM. *b.* The ḍammah of هُ, هُمَا, هُمْ, and هُنَّ is changed after ـِ, ـِي, and ـَيْ into kasrah; as أَرْجِهِ *do thou* (masc.) *put him off,* يَهْدِيهِمْ *he directs them,* اِغْشَيْهِ *do thou* (fem.) *cover it.*

REM. *d.* For the older forms ـِي, نِي, هُمُ, and كُمُ see § 20.

186. An accusative suffix causes change to its verb when

(*a*) the word ends with a superfluous 'alif (see § 7, rem. *a*) which is elided, thus اِحْذَرُوا *do ye* (masc.) *beware,* but اِحْذَرُوهُمْ *beware of them.*

(*b*) To avoid cacophony we retain in the Perf. pl. 2nd masc. ـُو û which the language employed at an earlier stage, thus مَكَرْتُمْ *ye* (masc.) *have contrived,* but مَكَرْتُمُوهُ *ye have contrived it.*

(*e*) As mentioned in § 7 rem. *c* ـَى a becomes ـَا â.

188. Sometimes the pronominal object is expressed by a suffix attached to the word إِيَّا ʾīyâ, which cannot stand alone; thus إِيَّاكَ *thee*, but the 1st sing. is إِيَّايَ *me*.

189. A pronominal suffix with إِيَّا is used,

(*a*) if one desires to avoid attaching two suffixes to the same verb, as أَعْطَانِي إِيَّاهُ or أَعْطَانِيهِ *he gave it to me*: also to avoid repetition of the governing verb when a pronoun is coupled by وَ *and* (see § 578) with a substantive or with a pronominal suffix, as أَهْلَكْتَهُمْ وَإِيَّايَ or أَهْلَكْتَهُمْ وَأَهْلَكْتَنِي *thou hast destroyed them and me*:

(*b*) when a pronoun is, for the sake of emphasis, placed before the verb; as إِيَّاكَ نَعْبُدُ وَإِيَّاكَ نَسْتَعِينُ *Thee only do we worship and to Thee alone we cry for help* (see § 431 rem.).

Arabian grammarians divide parts of speech into three; (*a*) اَلْإِسْمُ *the noun* in large sense, (*b*) اَلْفِعْلُ *the action, verb*, and (*c*) اَلْحَرْفُ *the particle.*

---

190. The *noun* (اَلْإِسْمُ nomen) is of six kinds.

(i) The *nomen substantivum* more especially called اَلْإِسْمُ as well as اَلْمَوْصُوفُ or اَلْمَنْعُوتُ *qualificabile*: to it adjectives can be attached. This when deverbal we shall call nomen verbi and treat in § 195 et seq.

(ii) The adjective, or descriptive epithet.

(iii) The numeral, or noun of number.

(iv) The demonstrative pronoun, or noun of indication.

(v) The conjunctive pronoun.

(vi) The personal pronoun, or substitute for a thing or person not mentioned.

Rem. *a.* Nouns substantive and adjective must be treated together, they being in form almost identical. We give (iii) numerals in §§ 318 to 328; (iv and v) demonstrative, conjunctive, and interrogative pronouns in §§ 340 to 353*: the (vi) personal pronouns, which have been treated in §§ 84, 89 and 185 to 189, will be mentioned again at § 317.

191. In respect of their origin nouns are divisible into (*a*) primitive and (*b*) derivative.

(*a*) Primitive nouns are substantives; as أَرْضٌ *earth*, أُمٌّ *mother*, إِنْسَانٌ *man*, آيَةٌ *sign, miracle, message, verse*, بِئْرٌ *a well*, بَدَلٌ *a substitute*, بَلَدٌ *country, land*, بَابٌ *gate*, ثُعْبَانٌ *serpent*, جَبَلٌ *mountain*, جَسَدٌ *a body, red gold*, حَجَرٌ *a stone*, حُوتٌ *fish*, رَأْسٌ *head*, رِجْزٌ *plague*, رَجُلٌ *a man*, رِجْلٌ *foot*, زَوْجٌ *spouse*, سِبْطٌ *grandchild, tribe*, سَبِيلٌ *road*, سَنَةٌ *a year*, سُورٌ *a wall*, اَلشَّمْسُ *the sun*, صَنَمٌ *idol*, صُورَةٌ *image*, ضِفْدِعٌ *frog*, طُوفَانٌ *deluge*, عِجْلٌ *calf*, عَصًا *a stick*, عَيْنٌ *eye, spring of water*, فَرَسٌ *mare, horse*, فُلْكٌ *ark, ship*, قِرْدٌ *a monkey*, قَسَمٌ *an oath*, قَلْبٌ *a heart*, قَمَرٌ *a moon*, كَلَامٌ *speech*, لَوْحٌ *table, tablet*, لَيْلٌ *night*, مَالٌ *property*, مَآءٌ *water* (whence مَاهَ ـُـ *to be full of water*), نَفْسٌ *soul, self*, نَهْرٌ *runnel, rill*, نَهَارٌ *day*, وَجْهٌ *face*, يَمٌّ *sea*, يَوْمٌ *day*.

(*b*) Derivative nouns may be substantive or adjective; and are either deverbal, as تَفْضِيلٌ *pre-eminence* from فَضَّلَ *to regard as superior*, أَدِيبٌ *lettered, polite* from أَدُبَ . ـُـ *to be well brought up*; or they are denominative, as سُورَةٌ *a line of bricks, a chapter* from سُورٌ *a wall,* مَسِيحِيٌّ *Christian* from اَلْمَسِيحُ *the anointed, Christ.*

Rem. *a.* Arabic dictionaries catalogue words under their radical letters; those compiled by Orientals are mostly arranged in order of the final, and by Europeans of the initial radical. All place first the verb, even though it be derivative and a noun its etymon (*i.e.* an original, primitive, or root word). To distinguish may be difficult; but any noun which is used as maçdar (see § 195) will best be considered deverbal: thus إِفْكٌ *a falsehood* beside being a substantive is infinitive of أَفَكَ ـِ *to beguile, cause to put on a false appearance* which has also the infinitive أَفْكٌ. Lane* gives بَحْرٌ *sea, great river,* because it is cleft or trenched in the earth, as derivative of بَحَرَ ـَ *to split*; whereas some may wish to regard *sea* as a primitive noun. It is well to treat substantives of foreign origin as etymons; thus, صِرَاطٌ *way* from via strata, جِنْسٌ *sort, kind* from γένος *genus,* شَيْطَانٌ שטן *Satan,* سَبْتٌ שבת *sabbath,* اَلتَّوْرَاةُ תורה *the Old Testament,* اَلْإِنْجِيلُ *the Gospel* from εὐαγγέλιον, كُرْسِيٌّ *seat* etc. etc. Also we have اَلْعَالَمِينَ (plural, oblique case) *the mundane rational creatures* (see § 302 *e*). Words which Arabians admit to be borrowed are called by them مُعَرَّبٌ *arabicized.*

Rem. *b.* Arabian grammarians unmethodically divide the nouns into categories which overlap.

Note. The following defective substantives are primitive

---

* An Arabic-English Lexicon by E. W. Lane. London: Williams & Norgate, 1863 to 1893.

nouns; اِبْنٌ *son*, أَخٌ *brother*, اِسْمٌ *name*, دَمٌ *blood*, سَنَةٌ *year*, لُغَةٌ *language*, يَدٌ *hand*. Many nouns may be called either deverbal or primitive; thus, قَرْيَةٌ *a village*, رِيحٌ *wind*, نَجْمٌ *a star*, وَلَدٌ *a child*, and مَنٌّ according to origin *manna* or *grace, favour*.

192. Deverbal nouns are divisible into two principal classes:

(i) nomina verbi which are by nature substantives, but also serve as adjectives;

(ii) nomina agentis and nomina patientis which by nature are adjectives, but also serve as substantives (see § 230).

193. The following four sorts of deverbal nouns are connected with the nomina verbi:

(i) nomina vicis, that express the doing of an action once;

(ii) nomina specici, nouns of kind and manner;

(iii) nomina loci et temporis, nouns of time and place (see § 221);

(iv) nomina instrumenti, denoting the instrument (see § 228).

194. Denominative nouns are divisible into six classes:

(i) nomen unitatis, denoting the individual (see § 246);

(ii) nomen abundantiæ, denoting a place of abundance;

(iii) nomen vasis, denoting a vessel (وِعَاءٌ);

(iv) nomen relativum, which we shall call the relative adjective (see § 249);

(v) nomen abstractum qualitatis, the abstract noun of quality;

(vi) nomen deminutivum, the diminutive.

195. Nomina verbi are *deverbal nouns*, abstract and concrete. The former (known as مَصَادِرُ maçâdir, plural of مَصْدَرٌ maçdar *source*, and as أَسْمَآءُ ٱلْفِعْلِ *nomina actionis*) are infinitives; the latter are substantives pure and simple. When a noun is maçdar it cannot be used in the plural, and according to some grammarians (see § 292 *d*) is of either gender: in such case it nearly corresponds with the English infinitive and can govern an accusative, which obviously may not be when it appears as a simple substantive. The following verse employs كِتَابٌ in both ways.

كَتَبْتُ وَقَدْ أَيْقَنْتُ عِنْدَ كِتَابِهَا

بِأَنَّ يَدِي تَفْنَى وَيَبْقَى كِتَابُهَا

I wrote (it) and I felt sure at the time of writing it
That my hand would perish and its (the hand's) writing endure.

NOTE. Professor Wright uses the term nomina verbi as synonymous with maçâdir, infinitives and nomina actionis; whereas I require a category wide enough to include all words in the succeeding sections. Without this change the Grammatical Analysis of my First reading book could not have been compiled.

196. Nomina verbi from the groundform of triliteral verbs are very numerous. The following specimens will serve our present purpose.

1 فَعْلٌ as خَلْقٌ *creation*, شَيْءٌ *a thing*.

2 فَعَلٌ „ عَرَضٌ *frail goods*, حَالٌ *state* (see § 207 *a*).

4 فِعْلٌ „ حِفْظٌ *guarding*, دِينٌ *religion*, *judgment*.

6 فُعْلٌ as عُرْفٌ *top-knot, an elevated place,* شُحٌّ *covetousness.*

7 فُعَلٌ „ هُدًى *guidance* (see § 212 *b*).

8 فَعْلَةٌ „ رَحْمَةٌ *mercy,* رَجْفَةٌ *convulsion.*

9 فَعَلَةٌ „ حَسَنَةٌ *a boon,* حَيَاةٌ *life.*

10 فَعِلَةٌ „ كَلِمَةٌ *a word,* نَكِرَةٌ *ignorance.*

11 فِعْلَةٌ „ قِيمَةٌ *value,* فِتْنَةٌ *trial,* قِلَّةٌ *paucity.*

12 فُعْلَةٌ „ نُسْخَةٌ *text,* ظُلَّةٌ *canopy.*

22 فِعْلَانٌ „ إِتْيَانٌ *coming.*

23 فُعْلَانٌ „ فُرْقَانٌ *criterion,* قُرْآنٌ *reading.*

25 فَعَالٌ „ بَلَاغٌ *delivery,* وَبَالٌ *mischief,* ضَلَالٌ *error.*

26 فِعَالٌ „ عِقَابٌ *chastisement,* لِقَاءٌ *meeting,* عِمَادٌ *support.*

27 فُعَالٌ „ خُوَارٌ *lowing.*

28 فَعَالَةٌ „ شَهَادَةٌ *testimony.*

29 فِعَالَةٌ „ خِلَافَةٌ *caliphate,* قِيٰمَةٌ *resurrection.*

32 فَعُولٌ „ رَسُولٌ *message, apostle.*

37 فَعِيلٌ „ نَبِيٌّ *prophet* (see § 17 *b*, rem. *b*).

38 فَعِيلَةٌ „ بَيِّنَةٌ *evidence,* سَيِّئَةٌ *evil,* مَدِينَةٌ *a city.*

39 مَفْعَلٌ „ مَرْحَبٌ *roominess* (see Ps. cxviii. 5 מרחב).

40 مَفْعِلٌ „ مَصِيرٌ *returning, issue,* مَجِيءٌ *coming.*

42 مَفْعَلَةٌ „ مَحَبَّةٌ *love* (see § 204).

43 مَفْعِلَةٌ „ مَوْعِظَةٌ *admonition,* مَعْذِرَةٌ *excuse.*

Rem. The forms numbered 39 to 43 commence with مَ ma: and if infinitive are called مَصْدَرٌ مِيمِيٌّ.

Note. Beside being feminine of رَابِطٌ *connector*, nomen agentis of its verb, اَلرَّابِطَةُ *the copulative* is nomen verbi. Similarly عَاقِبَةٌ *end* is nomen verbi of unusual form.

197. Most verbs have only one infinitive (nomen actionis) to their first form, and very few more than two or three apiece; exact information must be obtained from dictionaries.

198. When infinitives are few, deverbal nouns (nomina verbi) are very numerous.

No. 1. When infinitives these are from transitive verbs of form فَعَلَ and فَعِلَ. We have nomina verbi أَجْرٌ *reward*, أَمْرٌ *command*, جَمْعٌ *assembly*, حَمْدٌ *praise*, خَلْفٌ *posterity*, سَهْلٌ *a plain*, صَبْرٌ *patience*, صَدْرٌ *breast*, عَرْشٌ *throne*, عَطْفٌ *connection*, عَهْدٌ *covenant*, فَصْلٌ *separation*, قَرْضٌ *loan*, مَكْرٌ *plot*, مَهْلٌ *gentleness*, نَقْصٌ *diminution*.

No. 2. When infinitives these are from intransitive verbs of form فَعِلَ, except عَمَلٌ *work*, *rection* which is from a transitive verb. For nomina verbi we have أَبَدٌ *perpetuity*, أَجَلٌ *fixed term*, خَبَرٌ *announcement*, *enunciation*, طَمَعٌ *desire*, عَدَدٌ *a number*, غَضَبٌ *anger*.

No. 4 has إِذْنٌ *permission*, إِصْرٌ *burden*, ذِكْرٌ *admonition*, سِحْرٌ *sorcery*, ضِعْفٌ *a like*, عِلْمٌ *science*.

No. 6 has رُشْدٌ *true direction*, سُوءٌ *evil*, مُلْكٌ *dominion*.

No. 8 has رَغْبَةٌ *desire*, كَثْرَةٌ *abundance*, قِطْعَةٌ *a piece*, لَفْظَةٌ *an expression, a word,* and جَنَّةٌ *a garden* by which the ground is covered, from جَنَّ ـُ *to cover.*

No. 11 has حِطَّةٌ *unloading,* ذِلَّةٌ *ignominy,* قِلَّةٌ *paucity.*

No. 12 has أُمَّةٌ *a course of acting, one course which people follow in religion, people of a particular religion* and so *a nation, a people,* جُمْلَةٌ *an aggregate, a sentence, clause.*

No. 25 has بَيَانٌ *perspicacity,* بَيَاضٌ *whiteness.*

No. 26 has كِتَابٌ *writing, a book,* حِجَابٌ *obstacle, veil, partition,* خِلَافٌ *a contrary,* and إِلٰهٌ *a god* which however may be etymon of أَلَهَ ـَ *to adore.*

No. 27 expresses sounds, as in the instance given above, viz. خُوَارٌ *lowing.*

No. 29 expresses office etc., as خِلَافَةٌ *the office of* خَلِيفَةٌ *caliph, successor,* وِلَايَةٌ *governorship, province,* حِكَايَةٌ *imitation, narration,* رِسَالَةٌ *a message, letter.*

No. 37 has by form بَشِيرٌ *herald,* وَلِيٌّ *protector,* رَشِيدٌ *one who directs,* كَلِيمٌ *interlocutor,* وَكِيلٌ *an authorized agent,* and سَفِيهٌ *a fool* which are akin to nomina agentis and may be taken as adjectives of the form فَعِيلٌ.

No. 38 has خَطِيئَةٌ *sin,* also written خَطِيَّةٌ, see § **17**, rem. *b.*

199. If a verb has two or three meanings, to be distinguished by characteristic vowels, there may be one or more nouns for each; thus, مَعْرِفَةٌ *knowledge* and عِرْفَانٌ *spiritual insight* from عَرَفَ ـِ *to know*; also عِرَافَةٌ *to become* عَرِيف *over a people* from

عَرَفَ ـُـ *to be chief*, عَرِيفٌ meaning *soothsayer* or *chief*; further we find عَرْفٌ *sweet smell* from عَرِفَ ـَـ *to scent perfume.*

200. If a verb has more meanings than forms there may be several nomina actionis in correspondence; thus شَفْعٌ *a pair* and شَفَاعَةٌ *intercession* from شَفَعَ ـَـ *to double* and *to intercede.*

201. Infinitives are used both in an active and a passive sense, there being no separate form to distinguish; thus أَخْذُهُ from أَخَذَ *to take* means *his taking* another or *his being taken*, سَمْعٌ *sense of hearing* and *oral tradition* from سَمِعَ ـَـ *to hear.*

202. The following nomina verbi from derived forms of the strong triliteral verb are also nomina actionis.

II تَفْعِيلٌ as تَبْعِيضٌ *dividing into portions*, تَرْكِيبٌ *combining*, تَعْرِيفٌ *definition*, تَعْلِيلٌ *assigning a cause*, تَفْصِيلٌ *exposition*, تَمْيِيزٌ *specification*, تَوْكِيدٌ *corroboration.*

III فِعَالٌ „ خِطَابٌ *a discourse.*

مُفَاعَلَةٌ „ مُبَالَغَةٌ *exaggeration, intensiveness*, مُغَالَبَةٌ *effort to overcome*, مُقَارَبَةٌ *appropinquation.*

IV إِفْعَالٌ „ إِسْنَادٌ *an act of supporting*, إِصْلَاحٌ *good ordering.*

V تَفَعُّلٌ „ تَضَرُّعٌ *abasement.*

VI تَفَاعُلٌ „ تَغَابُنٌ *over-reaching.*

VII اِنْفِعَالٌ „ اِنْقِلَابٌ *transition.*

VIII اِفْتِعَالٌ „ اِبْتِدَآءٌ *beginning*, اِشْتِمَالٌ *comprehension*, اِنْتِقَامٌ *vengeance.*

X اِسْتِفْعَالٌ as اِسْتِثْنَآءٌ *exception,* اِسْتِغْفَارٌ *an act of asking pardon,* اِسْتِفْهَامٌ *interrogation,* اِسْتِكْبَارٌ *arrogant pride.*

REM. In form مُفَاعَلَةٌ is identical with the feminine passive participle.

NOTE. As will be seen from its meaning, the word عَذَابٌ *punishment* is connected with the second form, viz. عَذَّبَ *to punish* (see § 41), to which it serves as اَلْمَفْعُولُ ٱلْمُطْلَقُ see § 426.

---

204. Nouns derived from verbs with the *middle radical doubled* observe the rules in § 120; thus غُلٌّ *fetter* for غُلْلٌ, حَقٌّ *truth* for حَقْقٌ, دَكٌّ *crumbled soil* for دَكْكٌ, رَبٌّ *lord* for رَبْبٌ, مَحَبَّةٌ *love* for مَحْبَبَةٌ, حِطَّةٌ *unloading,* حِسٌّ *a sense,* عِلَّةٌ *a malady, weakness.*

205. Nouns from *hamzated* verbs observe the rules in §§ 131 to 135.

206. Verbs treated in §§ 142 and 144 with و as *first radical* may drop it from the noun and then they add ـَةٌ by way of compensation: thus, from وَضَعَ يَضَعُ *to put down* we have وَضْعٌ *position* and ضَعَةٌ *humiliation,* from وَصَفَ يَصِفُ *to describe* is صِفَةٌ *a qualificative*; while from وَعَدَ يَعِدُ *to promise* we have both وَعْدٌ and عِدَةٌ which mean *a promising,* and from وَصَلَ يَصِلُ *to reach, attain* are وَصْلَةٌ *a means of connection* and صِلَةٌ *a conjunctive.*

NOTE. We find the substantive سِنَةٌ *drowsiness* as well as the infinitive وَسَنٌ *a sleeping* from وَسِنَ *to sleep* which makes يَوْسَنُ in the imperfect (see § 143).

207. Nouns from verbs with و or ي as *middle radical* observe the rules in §§ 150 etc.

(*a*) Those of the form فَعْلٌ remain unchanged, as خَوْفٌ *fear*, غَيْبٌ *secret*, فَوْزٌ *prize*, قَوْلٌ *a saying*, نَوْمٌ *slumber.* Those like فَعَلٌ follow § 153, as حَالٌ *state, condition* for حَوَلٌ. Those like مَفْعِلٌ most commonly follow § 150, as مَصِيرٌ *returning, issue* for مَصْيِرٌ.

(*b*) If و be preceded by kasraĥ it mostly becomes ي; as قِيَمَةٌ *resurrection* for قِيَامَةٌ (see § 6, rem. *a*) for قِوَامَةٌ, قِيمَةٌ *price* for قِوْمَةٌ, both from قَامَ ـُ *to stand.*

(*c*) In the fourth and tenth forms the second radical is elided, its vowel passing back to the first, and ـَةٌ being added to the word's end; thus إِرَادَةٌ *wish* for إِرْوَادٌ, إِضَافَةٌ *annexation* for إِضْيَافٌ, اِسْتِعَانَةٌ *appeal for help* instead of اِسْتِعْوَانٌ.

210. From these verbs we have nouns of the form فَعْلُولَةٌ as دَيْمُومَةٌ *duration* from دَامَ ـُ *to last.*

212. Nouns from verbs with و or ي as *final radical* experience assimilation into يّ in the form فَعْلٌ if و be the second and ي the third radical, thus غَيٌّ *error* for غَوْيٌ; but we find وّ in قُوَّةٌ *force* for قُوْيَةٌ of form فُعْلَةٌ. When the middle radical is strong the following rules hold.

(*a*) The third radical is retained if the second bears sukûn, as حَلْيٌ *an ornament*, دَعْوَةٌ *an invocation*, خُفْيَةٌ *concealment* (see § 166 *a*).

(*b*) Nouns of the forms فَعَلٌ, فِعَلٌ, and فُعَلٌ are usually written with final ى, which is quiescent, while tanwîn falls upon the second radical's fatḥaħ; thus هُدًى *guidance* for هُدَيٌ, حَيٌّ *a tribe* from حَوَى يَحْوِي *to gather*. Sometimes radical و is written ا, as also in primitive nouns, thus عَصًا *a stick* for عَصَوٌ.

(*c*) Nouns of the form فَعَلَةٌ with و as final radical may end in ـَاةٌ, as صَلَاةٌ for صَلَوَةٌ (see § 7, rem. *d*, and compare § 294, rem. *a*).

(*d*) Nouns of the forms فَعَالٌ, فِعَالٌ and فُعَالٌ change the final radical into hamzaħ, as بَلَآءٌ *trial* for بَلَاوٌ, سَمَآءٌ *heaven* for سَمَاوٌ, لِقَآءٌ *meeting* for لِقَايٌ, وِعَآءٌ *receptacle* for وِعَايٌ. This occurs in nomina verbi of the fourth, seventh etc. forms as إِنْتِهَآءٌ *end, limit* from نَهَى ـَـ *to forbid.*

---

221. Nouns of *time and place* are formed from the imperfect active of a verb's ground form by substituting مَ for its prefix: the second radical bears fatḥaħ, if fatḥaħ or ḍammaħ be characteristic of the imperfect, but kasraħ if kasraħ. Thus, شَرِبَ *to drink*, makes يَشْرَبُ whence مَشْرَبٌ *drinking-place*, كَتَبَ *to write* يَكْتُبُ whence مَكْتَبٌ *place of writing, school*, نَزَلَ *to descend* يَنْزِلُ whence مَنْزِلٌ *halting place*, صَدَرَ *to proceed* يَصْدُرُ whence مَصْدَرٌ *the place whence anything proceeds* (see § 195).

REM. *a.* A noun of time and place is called اِسْمُ ٱلظَّرْفِ *the noun of vessel.*

REM. *b.* A few nouns take kasraħ irregularly, as مَسْجِدٌ *place of prostration, a mosque*, مَشْرِقٌ *time* or *place of rising, the east*, مَغْرِبٌ *place of setting, the west*, مَسْقِطٌ *place where anything falls.*

222. Nouns of time and place from verbs with و or ي as *initial radical* have kasraħ to the second syllable and always

retain the first radical; thus مَوْعِدٌ *time* or *place of appointment* from وَعَدَ *to promise* (see § 142), مَوْضِعٌ *a place where anything is put down, a place* from وَضَعَ *to put* (see § 144).

223. Those from verbs with و or ي as *middle radical* experience change in accordance with § 150, thus مَكَانٌ *place of existence* for مَكْوَنٌ from كَانَ *to be, exist.*

REM. Verbs with ي as middle radical commonly retain it, thus مَصِيرٌ *place of returning,* مَجِيءٌ *place of arrival.*

224. Those from verbs with و or ي as *final radical* always have fatḥah (notwithstanding § 221) to the second syllable and they suffer the contraction explained in § 212 *b*; thus, مَنْجًى *place of refuge* for مَنْجَيٌ for مَنْجَوٌ from نَجَا ـُ *to escape.*

226. Some nouns of time and place from verbs with و or ي as *initial radical* take the form مِفْعَالٌ (see § 228); as مِيقَاتٌ *appointed time* or *place* from وَقَتَ ـِ *to fix a time,* مِيلَادٌ *time of birth* from وَلَدَ ـِ *to bear a child.* In both these examples ي replaces و according to § 145

227. Those from derived forms are identical in form with the nomina patientis, as مُبْتَدَأٌ *place of beginning, inchoative.*

228. Nouns of *instrument* denote the intransitive agent and take the form مِفْعَلٌ, مِفْعَالٌ or مِفْعَلَةٌ; as مِفْتَحٌ and مِفْتَاحٌ *a key* from فَتَحَ ـَ *to open.* Initial و becomes ي as in § 226, thus مِيثَاقٌ *a covenant* from وَثِقَ ـِ *to trust.*

229. We have already mentioned in § 80 the nomen agentis and nomen patientis; they are *deverbal adjectives* often used as substantives.

230. In the ground form nomina agentis are like فَاعِلٌ and nomina patientis like مَفْعُولٌ: thus كَاتِبٌ *a writer, clerk* مَكْتُوبٌ *written, script* from كَتَبَ ـُ *to write*; مَالِكٌ *possessor* مَمْلُوكٌ *owned* from مَلَكَ ـِ *to possess*; عَارِفٌ *a discerner* مَعْرُوفٌ *recognized, approved* from عَرَفَ ـِ *to know*; تَابِعٌ *follower* مَتْبُوعٌ *followed*, حَاذِفٌ *clipper* مَحْذُوفٌ *eliminated*, حَامِدٌ *one who praises* مَحْمُودٌ *praiseworthy*, رَابِطٌ *that which binds* مَرْبُوطٌ *bound*, جَامِعٌ *that which collects, great mosque* مَجْمُوعٌ *assembled*, جَاهِلٌ *ignorant*, كَارِهٌ *hating*, حَافِظٌ *preserver*, نَاقِصٌ *deficient*, بَاطِلٌ *vain, worthless*, بَالِغٌ *one who attains*, خَالِدٌ *one who stays long, abides*, شَارِعٌ *manifest*, صَالِحٌ *pious, that which is right*, عَالِمٌ *one who knows, a scholar*, كَافِرٌ *one who ignores God's benefits, an unbeliever*, لَازِمٌ *intransitive*, وَاقِعٌ *falling*.

NOTE. As regards nomina patientis, we have mentioned in § 73 the impersonal manner in which passive verbs must often be translated, and shall treat اَلْمَغْضُوبُ عَلَيْهِمْ *the objects of anger* in § 533.

232. From the ground form there are other deverbal adjectives of which the following are specimens.

1. فَعْلٌ as سَهْلٌ *easy*, خَيْرٌ *good, excellent* (see § 242, Note 1).
2. فَعَلٌ „ حَسَنٌ *good, beautiful*.
3. فَعِلٌ „ أَسِفٌ *afflicted*, نَكِدٌ *churlish*, صَعِقٌ *thunderstruck, swooning*.

11. فَعِيلٌ as أَلِيمٌ *painful,* بَصِيرٌ *seeing,* حَكِيمٌ *wise,* حَلِيمٌ *clement,* خَبِيرٌ *well acquainted,* سَرِيعٌ *prompt,* عَزِيزٌ *powerful,* قَدِيرٌ *able,* أَمِينٌ *trustworthy,* كَبِيرٌ *great.*

12. فَعُولٌ „ شَكُورٌ *grateful,* غَفُورٌ of God *forgiving,* أَكُولٌ *voracious.*

13. فَعْلَانُ „ غَضْبَانُ *angry.*

14. فَعْلَانٌ „ رَحْمَانٌ *merciful* (a borrowed word).

16. أَفْعَلُ „ أَبْيَضُ *white,* أَجْمَعُ *all* (see § 537), أَصْفَرُ *yellow,* of a horse *grey.*

NOTE 1. We use No 16 to express colours and defects.

REM. *c.* When derived from transitive verbs فَعِيلٌ may have a passive sense; as حَثِيثٌ *urged on, swift,* حَقِيقٌ *fitting,* حَمِيدٌ *praiseworthy,* شَدِيدٌ *severe,* قَتِيلٌ *slain,* كَحِيلٌ *treated with kuḥl.*

NOTE 2. Much of the Corân is almost in the nature of rhymed prose, wherein ـُون may rhyme with ـِين, ـُور with ـِير etc., but the rules are more lax than in classical rhymed prose*; for instance رَحِيم *merciful,* عَظِيم *mighty,* عَلِيم *skilful,* etc. are used to rhyme with مُبِين *manifest,* رَاحِمِين *merciful,* سَاجِدِين *prostrating themselves,* مُسْلِمِين *Moslems,* شَاكِرِين *thankful,* صَادِقِين *truthful,* صَاغِرِين *contemptible,* ظَالِمِين *wrongdoers,* غَافِرِين *those who pardon,* غَافِلِين *neglectors,* غَالِبِين *victors,*

* Specimens of rhymed prose are to be found at pp. 168 to 181 of "Wright's Reading book" which I hope to reproduce as *Elementary Arabic: Third reading book.*

فَاسِقِين *impious,* قَاهِرُون *subduers,* نَاظِرِين *beholders,* and the like.

233. Adjectives of form فَعَّالٌ are intensive, as from سَآئِلٌ *asking* we have سَئَّالٌ *importunate, a beggar.*

Rem. *a.* We use this form to indicate occupations, as صَرَّافٌ *a money-changer,* قَوَّاسٌ *a bow-maker, cavass.*

Rem. *b.* There are other intensive adjectives, as قَيُّومٌ *everlasting.*

234. The elative, اِسْمُ ٱلتَّفْضِيلِ *the noun of pre-eminence,* is of form أَفْعَلُ as أَحْسَنُ *more* or *most beautiful.*

Rem. *a.* When superlative these adjectives must have the article as اَلْأَرْحَمُ *the most merciful,* or be in construct state (see § 475) as أَكْثَرُهُمْ *most of them,* and if feminine (see § 295 *b*) are of form فُعْلَى as اَلْكَلِمَةُ ٱلْحُسْنَى *the most gracious word.*

235. No elative should be derived from adjectives which have already the form أَفْعَلُ, thus the comparative of أَبْيَضُ *white* is أَشَدُّ بَيَاضًا *stronger as to whiteness*: but elatives are sometimes formed, though contrary to strict rule, from the derived forms of verbs.

236. Next as to the derived forms in which we have (*a*) nomina agentis:

II مُعَذِّبٌ *chastizer,* مُفَسِّرٌ *explanatory, commentator.*

III مُطَاوِعٌ *compliant,* مُقَارِنٌ *contemporaneous.*

IV مُهْلِكٌ *destroyer,* مُمْكِنٌ *possible,* مُجْرِمٌ *guilty,* مُحْسِنٌ *well-doer,* مُصْلِحٌ *one who puts to rights,* مُفْسِدٌ *transgressor,* مُفْلِحٌ *prosperous.*

5—2

V مُتَحَرِّكٌ *in motion.*

VI مُتَشَابِهٌ *uniform,* i.e. part resembling part, مُتَقَابِلٌ *facing each other.*

VII مُنْقَلِبٌ *one who reverts.*

VIII مُنْتَقِمٌ *avenger,* مُسْتَتِرٌ *hiding oneself.*

X مُسْتَكْبِرٌ *haughty.*

and (*b*) nomina patientis:

II مُتَبَّرٌ *destroyed,* مُسَخَّرٌ *held in subjection,* مُفَصَّلٌ *separated,* مُقَرَّبٌ *brought near,* مُحَرَّمٌ *forbidden, inviolable,* مُقَدَّرٌ *ordained, predestined.*

III مُفَاعَلٌ.

IV مُنْكَرٌ *disapproved,* مُسْنَدٌ *that which is supported, attribute,* مُطْلَقٌ *set free.*

V مُتَفَعَّلٌ.

VIII مُبْتَدَأٌ *inchoative* etc.

237. Adjectives derived from verbs with the *middle radical doubled* observe the rules in § 120; thus ضَالٌّ *erring* for ضَالِلٌ, أَشَدُّ *stronger* or *most strong* for أَشْدَدُ, مُتِمٌّ *one who perfects* for مُتْمِمٌ, مُضِلٌّ *causing error,* تَامٌّ *entire, perfect,* كَافٌّ *repulsing.*

238. Adjectives from *hamzated* verbs observe the rules in §§ 131 to 135; thus سَائِلٌ *one who asks* not سَاإِلٌ, بَئِسٌ *grievous* not بَإِسٌ, مُؤْمِنٌ *believer* not مُأْمِنٌ, مُؤَنَّثٌ *feminine.*

239. Adjectives from verbs with و or ي as *initial radical* observe §§ 147 and 148, thus مُتَّصِلٌ *joined.*

Rem. *a*. Preceded by kasraħ أ becomes ئ as قَارِئٌ *reader* not قَارِأٌ.

240. Nomina agentis from verbs of the first form with و or ي as *middle radical* substitute for that letter ئ (i.e. hamzaħ and ‘imâd, see § 16); thus طَآئِرٌ *flying, a bird, evil omen* from طَارَ ـِ *to fly* and not طَايِرٌ, عَائِدٌ *one who returns,* نَائِمٌ *sleeping.*

241. Nomina patientis from verbs of the first form with و or ي as middle radical, in case of و elide it and throw back its vowel to the first radical; thus مَخُوفٌ *to be feared* for مَخْوُوفٌ: but in case of ي its elision must be marked by substituting kasraħ for ḍammaħ, and then و of prolongation becomes ي; thus مَدِينٌ *one who receives recompense* for مَدْيُونٌ.

Rem. Sometimes we find an uncontracted form, as مَدْيُونٌ *a debtor.*

242. Adjectives of form فَعِيلٌ from verbs with و or ي as middle radical become فَيِّلٌ and sometimes فَيْلٌ: thus, for طَيِيبٌ from طَابَ ـِ we have طَيِّبٌ *good, sound, agreeable*; for بَيِينٌ from بَانَ ـِ is بَيِّنٌ *evident*; for سَوِيءٌ from سَآءَ ـُ is سَيِّءٌ *wicked*; for مَوِيتٌ from مَاتَ ـُ is مَيِّتٌ *dead,* and for its opposite حَيِيٌ from حَيَّ ـَ we have حَيٌّ *living*; also for خَيِيرٌ from خَارَ ـِ is خَيِّرٌ *excellent,* هَيِّنٌ *easy* for هَوِينٌ, سَيِّدٌ *chief, lord.*

Note 1. In § 232 is to be found خَيْرٌ under form فَعْلٌ: it is from خَارَ ـِ *to choose* and means *to be chosen* whence the elative خَيْرٌ مِنْ *choosable rather than, better than*: its opposite شَرٌّ *bad, worse* is also used as elative.

NOTE 2. We may consider بَيِّنَةٌ and سَيِّئَةٌ (see § 196, No. 38) as substantives derived from the adjectives بَيِّنٌ and سَيِّءٌ.

243. Adjectives from the derived forms of verbs with و or ي as middle radical follow in respect of it the rules of their Imperfects, thus مُبِينٌ *manifest* like يُبِينُ IV of بَانَ ـِ *to be distinct*, مُصِيبٌ *that which strikes home* like يُصِيبُ IV of صَابَ ـُ (see § 45, Note), مُضَافٌ *annexed* like يُضَافُ IV passive of ضَافَ ـِ *to incline*, مُسْتَقِيمٌ *straight* like يَسْتَقِيمُ X of قَامَ ـُ *to stand*.

NOTE 1. For ضَرْبَةٌ مُصِيبَةٌ *a blow that hits* we find مُصِيبَةٌ which we may render *a mischance*.

NOTE 2. Be it observed that the nomina agentis and patientis of Form VII are identical, and so with Form VIII.

244. We have treated in § 167 *b* (ii) the nomina agentis of verbs with و or ى as *final radical*, and the nomina patientis in § 170, which last section gives rules applicable to adjectives of forms فَعُولٌ and فَعِيلٌ; thus عَدُوٌّ *hostile, an enemy* for عَدُووٌ, عَلِيٌّ *high, sublime* for عَلِيوٌ, غَنِيٌّ *rich, self-sufficing* for غَنِييٌ.

NOTE. In the Corân عَدُوٌّ is sometimes a collective noun.

245. Adjectives, whose second radical bears fatḥah, from verbs with ي or و (which we now write ى) as final radical, reject their final vowel.

(*a*) If triptote (see § 308) tanwîn is transferred to the second radical (compare § 212 *b*); thus مُعْطًى *given* nomen patientis IV of عَطَا ـُ for مُعْطَوٌ, مُثَنًّى *dual*, مُسْتَثْنًى *an exception*.

(*b*) If diptote there is only the vowel to reject; thus أَرْضَى *better* or *best pleased* for أَرْضَوُ.

---

246. Nomina unitatis *nouns of individuality*, which specify one from a genus or one part of a whole, are formed by adding ـَة to the collective noun (see §§ 292 *a*, 306 rem.). Thus, بَقَرَةٌ *one head of cattle* (*ox* or *cow*, ثَوْرٌ being usual for *a bull*) from بَقَرٌ *cattle*, ثَمَرَةٌ *a fruit* from ثَمَرٌ *fruit*, جَرَادَةٌ *a grasshopper*, *locust* from جَرَادٌ, سَحَابَةٌ *a cloud* from سَحَابٌ (for سُورَةٌ see § 191 *b*), ضَلَالَةٌ *an error* (by some considered nomen verbi, see § 196, No. 28) from ضَلَالٌ, غَمَامَةٌ *a cloud* from غَمَامٌ, قَمْلَةٌ *a louse* from قَمْلٌ *lice*, لَيْلَةٌ *a night* from لَيْلٌ *night*, شَجَرَةٌ *a tree* from شَجَرٌ.

NOTE. We find also سَلْوَاةٌ *a quail* from سَلْوَى *quail*.

249. The *relative adjective* اَلنِّسْبَةُ is formed by adding ـِيٌّ to the word from which it is derived, and denotes some thing or person connected therewith. Thus, شَمْسِيٌّ *solar* from اَلشَّمْسُ *the sun*, قَمَرِيٌّ *lunar* from قَمَرٌ *moon*, عَرَبِيٌّ *Arabian* from اَلْعَرَبُ *the Arabs*, اِنْكِلِيزِيٌّ *English* from اَلْاِنْكِلِيزُ *the English collectively*, قَلْبِيٌّ *mental* from قَلْبٌ *a heart*, شَرْقِيٌّ *saracen* شَرْقِيَّةٌ *sirocco* from اَلشَّرْقُ *the east*, اِسْمِيٌّ *nominal* from اِسْمٌ, ظَرْفِيٌّ *local* from ظَرْفٌ, حَالِيٌّ *circumstantial* from حَالٌ, فِعْلِيٌّ *verbal* from فِعْلٌ.

250. But the derivatives cannot always be formed so simply: certain terminations are rejected, and other changes arise. Thus مَكَّةُ *Mecca* مَكِّيٌّ, أُمَّةٌ (see § 198, No. 12) أُمِّيٌّ *illiterate*, اَلْمَدِينَةُ

Medina مَدَنِيٌّ, اَلْمُسْلِمُونَ *the Moslems* مُسْلِمِيٌّ, لَفْظَةٌ *a word* لَفْظِيٌّ, مَعْنًى *signification* مَعْنَوِيٌّ, حَقِيقَةٌ *reality* حَقِيقِيٌّ, and the Prophet's tribe قُرَيْشٌ makes قُرَشِيٌّ.

---

269. The diminutive is of form فُعَيْلٌ thus حُسَيْنٌ from حَسَنٌ *beautiful.*

---

289. Nouns substantive must in *gender* be masculine, feminine, or common, for Arabic has no neuter.

290. Nouns are said to be *feminine* (*a*) by signification, or (*b*) by form; as,

(*a*) أُمٌّ *a mother,* عَجُوزٌ *an old woman,* مَرْيَمُ *Mary,* عَيْنٌ *an eye,* يَدٌ *a hand.*

Rem. Masculine are رَأْسٌ *a head,* and وَجْهٌ *a face.*

(*b*) بَقَرَةٌ *an ox* or *cow,* سُورَةٌ *a chapter,* جَنَّةٌ *a garden,* بُشْرَى *good news.*

Rem. A few nouns ending in ـَةٌ are masculine because only used of males, as خَلِيفَةٌ *caliph.*

291. Certain nouns are feminine only by usage; as أَرْضٌ *earth,* دَارٌ *a mansion,* رِيحٌ *wind,* اَلشَّمْسُ *the sun,* عَصًا *a stick,* نَفْسٌ *a soul, self,* نَارٌ *fire.*

292. Many are said to be masculine by form and feminine by signification: together with others, these are of *common* gender; thus,

(*a*) Collective nouns which form nomina unitatis (see § 246) chiefly denoting animals and plants: but سَلْوَى *quail* is usually masculine.

(*b*) Collective nouns denoting rational beings and not forming nomina unitatis, as خَلْفٌ *posterity*, مَلَأٌ *chieftains*, قَوْمٌ *one's people* or *tribe*. But أَهْلٌ and آلٌ *one's household, people* are masculine only.

(*d*) Deverbal nouns when infinitives (maçâdir, see § 195).

(*e*) Words regarded as such. But كَانَ *to be* is feminine, as كَانَ ٱلتَّامَّةُ *the complete kâna* (see § 441): so also usually are particles, as أَنْ ٱلْمَصْدَرِيَّةُ *the 'an which with its verb is equivalent to a maçdar* (see § 488), أَنِ ٱلْمُفَسِّرَةُ *the explicative 'an* (see § 367 *e*), إِنِ ٱلشَّرْطِيَّةُ *the conditional 'in* (see § 367 *f*), إِنِ ٱلنَّافِيَةُ *the negative 'in* (see § 362 *k*).

(*f*) Certain nouns among which are the following; بَشَرٌ *a human being, humankind*, حَالٌ *state*, سَبِيلٌ *road*, سَمَآءٌ *heaven*, صِرَاطٌ *a way*, فُلْكٌ *a ship*, لَيْلٌ *night*, مُلْكٌ *dominion*, هُدًى *guidance*.

293. From most adjectives and some substantives of the masculine gender, feminines are formed ending in ـَةٌ, ـَى, or ـَآءُ.

Rem. Of these ـَةٌ is appended without further change, but feminines in ـَى and ـَآءُ are distinct in form from the masculine.

294. The most usual termination is ـَةٌ; thus, آخِرٌ (for أَاخِرٌ) *latter, last* آخِرَةٌ, حَاضِرٌ *present* حَاضِرَةٌ, قِرْدٌ *monkey* قِرْدَةٌ *she-monkey*, مَكِّيٌّ *Meccan* مَكِّيَّةٌ.

REM. *a*. A dropped radical may be replaced, as سَمَاوَةٌ from سَمَآءٌ *heaven* (see § 212 *d*): but مُصْطَفَاةٌ (for مُصْطَفَيَةٌ) from مُصْطَفًى *chosen*.

REM. *b*. ـَـةٌ (see end of § 2 and § 8, rem. *a*) is a compromise in orthography between the old pausal form ـَـهْ, and ـَـت which we find in رَحْمَتْ *mercy*, كَلِمَتْ *word* for the more modern رَحْمَةٌ and كَلِمَةٌ. We write أُخْتٌ *sister* for أَخَوَةٌ.

295. Feminines ending in ـَـى are derived,

(*a*) from adjectives of form فَعْلَانُ which make فَعْلَى, as غَضْبَانُ *angry* غَضْبَى;

(*b*) from adjectives of form أَفْعَلُ when superlative (being defined by the article or following noun, see § 234, rem. *a*) in which case the feminine is فُعْلَى; as, اَلْأَحْسَنُ *the most beautiful* اَلْحُسْنَى, اَلْأَدْنَى *the nearest* اَلدُّنْيَا (see § 179, rem. *a*), اَلْأَكْبَرُ *the greatest* كُبْرَى ٱلْمَدَآئِنِ *the greatest of the cities*.

REM. *b*. The feminine of اَلْأَوَّلُ (for اَلْأَوْءَلُ or اَلْأَاْوَلُ) *the first* (see § 328) is اَلْأُولَى, and that of آخَرُ (for أَأْخَرُ) *other*, *another* is أُخْرَى.

296. Feminines ending in ـَـآءُ are derived from adjectives of form أَفْعَلُ which are not elatives, as أَبْيَضُ *white* بَيْضَآءُ, أَجْمَعُ *all* جَمْعَآءُ. There are feminines which have no masculine, as عَرْبَآءُ *most Arab* which should come (irregularly, being elative) from أَعْرَبُ.

297. All adjectives do not invariably employ their feminine forms, and some few have none. Only let the meaning be clear and there may be a laxity as regards form: thus,

(*a*) فَعُولٌ is of both genders when active in signification and attached to a singular substantive, as رَجُلٌ شَكُورٌ *a grateful man* and اِمْرَأَةٌ شَكُورٌ *a grateful woman*; also when active in meaning and predicate to a substantive or pronoun in the singular, as هِيَ شَكُورٌ *she is grateful*, ظَنَنْتُهَا صَبُورًا *I thought her patient.* If however no substantive or pronoun be expressed we must, in order to make our meaning clear, employ the feminine form فَعُولَةٌ, as رَأَيْتُ شَكُورَةً *I saw a grateful woman*, مَا لَهُ حَمُولَةٌ *he has not a she-camel to carry loads*: also, this is required when the adjective is passive by signification, as مَا لَهُ نَاقَةٌ حَلُوبَةٌ *he has not a she-camel to milk* i.e. to be milked.

NOTE. Being only used of God غَفُورٌ *forgiving* has no feminine.

REM. *a*. Exceptions are to be found, as عَدُوٌّ *hostile, an enemy* fem. عَدُوَّةٌ.

(*b*) فَعِيلٌ is of both genders when passive in signification and attached to a singular substantive, as اِمْرَأَةٌ قَتِيلٌ *a slain woman*; also when passive in meaning and predicate to a substantive or pronoun in the singular, as هِيَ حَثِيثٌ *she is swift*, اَلْعَيْنُ كَحِيلٌ *the eye is treated with kuhl.* But if no substantive or pronoun be expressed we must, in order to make our meaning clear, employ فَعِيلَةٌ, as رَأَيْتُ قَتِيلَةً *I saw a slain woman*: also, this is required when the adjective is active by signification; whether transitive, as اِمْرَأَةٌ عَلِيمَةٌ *a skilful woman*, عَجُوزٌ خَبِيرَةٌ *an experienced old woman*; or intransitive, as رِيحٌ عَزِيزَةٌ *a powerful wind.*

REM. Exceptions are to be found in either case; as

هٰذِهِ ٱلْفِعْلَةُ حَمِيدَةٌ *this way of acting is praiseworthy*, and on the other hand رَحْمَةُ ٱللّٰهِ قَرِيبٌ *the mercy of God is near.*

(*c*) Similar peculiarities are to be remarked in certain others.

NOTE. Adjectives of form أَفْعَلُ when comparative are of common gender.

REM. *b*. Adjectives applicable to females only do not usually form a feminine, as أَنْتِ طَالِقٌ *thou* (fem.) *art divorced* because a wife cannot say أَنْتَ طَالِقٌ.

---

298. Nouns have (like verbs, see § 81) three *numbers*, the singular, dual, and plural.

299. A *dual* is formed by adding ـَانِ to the singular after elision of the final vowel or tanwin; as بَحْرٌ *sea* بَحْرَانِ, أُمَّةٌ *a nation* أُمَّتَانِ.

REM. *b*. If the singular ends in quiescent ى, or ا which was و, the original letter may be restored; as عَصًا *a staff* عَصَوَانِ.

REM. *e*. If the third radical has been elided before ة in the singular, it is not restored; thus, لُغَةٌ *a language* for لُغَوَةٌ makes لُغَتَانِ.

---

300. There are two kinds of *plurals*.

(*a*) That which, having only a single form, is called pluralis sanus, the *sound* or perfect plural.

(*b*) That which, having various forms, is called pluralis fractus, the *broken* plural; being more or less altered from the singular.

301. The sound plural of masculine nouns is formed by adding ـُونَ to the singular (see § 308), as قَاهِرٌ *a conqueror* قَاهِرُونَ, عَابِدٌ *a worshipper* عَابِدُونَ. The sound plural of feminine nouns is formed by writing ـَاتٌ for ـَةٌ when they have that termination in the singular, or when without it by adding ـَاتٌ; as حَسَنَةٌ *a boon* حَسَنَاتٌ, ثَمَرَةٌ *a fruit* ثَمَرَاتٌ, طَيِّبَةٌ *good* طَيِّبَاتٌ, رَمَضَانُ *the month of ramaḍân* رَمَضَانَاتٌ.

Rem. *a.* If the singular ends in 'alif maqçûrah̄ (see § 7, rem. *b*) with or without tanwîn (see § 245), as مُصْطَفًى *chosen* for مُصْطَفَيٌ, أَعْلَى *higher, highest* for أَعْلَيُ; or in kasrah̄ with tanwîn (see § 167, *b* ii), as عَمٍ *blind* for عَمِيٌ, مُفْتَرٍ *one who invents lies* for مُفْتَرِيٌ, مُتَّقٍ *devout* (see § 148) for مُتَّقِيٌ; or in quiescent ي preceded by kasrah̄ (see § 314, rem. *b*), as اَلْعَمِي *the blind (man)* for اَلْعَمِيُ: then § 166 *b* must be obeyed in the forming of the plurals. Thus,

Nominative	مُصْطَفَوْنَ	أَعْلَوْنَ	عَمُونَ	مُفْتَرُونَ
for	مُصْطَفَيُونَ	أَعْلَيُونَ	عَمِيُونَ	مُفْتَرِيُونَ
Oblique	مُصْطَفَيْنَ	أَعْلَيْنَ	عَمِينَ	مُفْتَرِينَ
for	مُصْطَفَيِينَ	أَعْلَيِينَ	عَمِيِينَ	مُفْتَرِيِينَ

The singular of اَلْعَمِي illustrates § 167 *a* (ii) in changing from ـِيُ iy to ـِي î, and the plural differs nothing from that of عَمٍ see § 314, rem. *a*. Of feminines we may note غَضْبَى *angry* غَضْبَيَاتٌ, اَلْكُبْرَى *the greatest* اَلْكُبْرَيَاتُ (see § 303 *b*).

Rem. *b.* Feminine substantives with sukûn to the middle

radical may undergo change; as أَرْضٌ *earth* أَرَضَاتٌ, قَرْيَةٌ *a village* قَرَيَاتٌ.

Rem. *c.* A final radical dropped as in § 212 *c* must reappear; thus صَلَاةٌ *prayer* صَلَوَاتٌ, مُصْطَفَاةٌ (feminine of مُصْطَفًى) *chosen* مُصْطَفَيَاتٌ (see § 294, rem. *a*).

Rem. *d.* A final radical dropped before ـَةٌ sometimes reappears, as سَنَةٌ *a year* سَنَوَاتٌ and سَنَهَاتٌ; but مِئَةٌ *a hundred* for مِئْيَةٌ makes مِئَاتٌ (see § 325, rem. *a*).

Rem. *e.* We have mentioned in § 294, rem. *a* سَمٰوَةٌ *heaven* which makes سَمَاوَاتٌ and سَمٰوَاتٌ (see § 6, rem. *a*).

302. The sound plural masculine is formed from :—

(*a*) Certain diminutives and proper names.

(*b*) Deverbal adjectives which form their feminines by adding ـَةٌ, as ضَالٌّ *erring* ضَالُّونَ.

(*c*) Adjectives of form أَفْعَلُ which are elatives, as أَكْثَرُ *more* or *most numerous* أَكْثَرُونَ: also the corroboratives of كُلٌّ viz. أَجْمَعُ *all* etc. making أَجْمَعُونَ etc. (see § 539, rem. *a*).

(*d*) The relative adjectives (see § 249) as بَدَوِيٌّ (irregularly from بَدْوٌ *a desert*) *a badawī* بَدَوِيُّونَ *badawīn* (*bedouins*). This termination is often shortened to ـُونَ.

(*e*) A few words, among which are اِبْنٌ *a son* (for بَنْيٌ) بَنُونَ, أَرْضٌ *earth* أَرَضُونَ, عَالَمٌ *one of the four classes of created beings* عَالَمُونَ (see § 191, rem. *a*), ذُو *owner* (see § 340, rem. *c*), etc.

Rem. *a.* It must be SPECIALLY NOTED that adjectives have the sound plural masculine only when joined to substantives, expressed or understood, denoting rational creatures.

REM. *b.* From substantives and adjectives that have the sound plural masculine there may be formed a broken plural, especially from adjectives used substantively.

REM. *c.* Certain numerals given in § 323 have the form of sound plural masculine.

REM. *d.* Some feminine nouns in ـَةٌ, especially those from which the final radical (ه, و, or ي) has been elided, form a sound plural masculine, the termination ـَةٌ disappearing; as سَنَةٌ *a year* سِنُونَ, oblique case سِنِينَ.

303. The sound plural feminine is formed from :—

(*a*) All nouns ending in ـَةٌ, as رِسَالَةٌ *message* رِسَالَاتٌ, آيَةٌ *a sign* آيَاتٌ.

REM. Some grammarians express this rule less comprehensively.

(*b*) Feminine adjectives, the masculine gender of which has a sound plural, as مُؤْمِنَاتٌ *believing* (*women*) from مُؤْمِنٌ.

(*c*) Names of the letters and months, as well as certain other nouns.

304. The following are forms of broken plural, from triliteral roots, numbered as in the Grammar of Professor Wright.

فَعِيلٌ 25.	فُعْلَانٌ 19.	أَفْعُلٌ 13.	فُعَّلٌ 7.	فُعَلٌ 1.
فُعُولَةٌ 26.	فُعَلَاءُ 20.	أَفْعَالٌ 14.	فُعَّالٌ 8.	فُعْلٌ 2.
فِعَالَةٌ 27.	أَفْعِلَاءُ 21.	أَفْعِلَةٌ 15.	فَعَلَةٌ 9.	فُعُلٌ 3.
فَعَلٌ 28.	فَعْلَى 22.	فَوَاعِلُ 16.	فُعَلَةٌ 10.	فِعَلٌ 4.
فَعْلٌ 29.	فَعَالٍ 23.	فَعَائِلُ 17.	فِعَلَةٌ 11.	فِعَالٌ 5.
	فَعَالِي 24.	فِعْلَانٌ 18.	فِعْلَةٌ 12.	فُعُولٌ 6.

In the next table an example of, at least, one noun (substantive or adjective) appears to each plural, but space forbids us to attempt illustrating each singular form.

1. فُعَلٌ plural of فُعْلَةٌ فُعْلَى فَعْلَةٌ فِعْلَةٌ as

جُمَلٌ *a sentence* جُمْلَةٌ, صُوَرٌ *a form* صُورَةٌ, أُمَمٌ *a nation* أُمَّةٌ.

2. فُعْلٌ plural of أَفْعَلُ فَعْلَآءُ فَعَالٌ فِعَالٌ فُعَالٌ فَاعِلٌ as

بِيضٌ (for بُيْضٌ) *white* أَبْيَضُ.

3. فُعُلٌ plural of فَعَالٌ فِعَالٌ فُعَالٌ فَعِيلٌ فَعِيلَةٌ فَعُولٌ فَعْلٌ فَعَلٌ فَعَلَةٌ فِعَلٌ فُعُلٌ فَاعِلٌ as

رُسُلٌ *a message, messenger, apostle* رَسُولٌ, كُتُبٌ *a book* كِتَابٌ.

REM. In nearly all cases the form فُعْلٌ is admissible, as بُشْرٌ *a herald* بَشِيرٌ.

4. فِعَلٌ plural of فِعْلَةٌ فَعْلَةٌ فَعَلَةٌ as

حِكَمٌ *a maxim* حِكْمَةٌ.

5. فِعَالٌ plural of فَعْلٌ فِعْلٌ فُعْلٌ فَعْلَةٌ فِعْلَةٌ فُعْلَةٌ فَعَلٌ فَعَلَةٌ فُعُلٌ فُعَلٌ فُعْلَى فَعْلَانُ فُعْلَانٌ فَعْلَانٌ فَعِيلٌ فَاعِلٌ as

ثِمَارٌ *a fruit* ثَمَرَةٌ, جِبَالٌ *a mountain* جَبَلٌ, رِيَاحٌ *a wind* رِيحٌ, ثِقَالٌ *heavy* ثَقِيلٌ, رِجَالٌ *a man* رَجُلٌ.

REM. نِسَآءٌ is plural of اِمْرَأَةٌ *a woman* (see § 305, rem. *e*).

6. فُعُولٌ plural of فَعْلٌ فِعْلٌ فُعْلٌ فَعَلٌ فَعِلٌ فَعْلَةٌ فِعْلَةٌ فُعْلَةٌ فَعَلَةٌ فَاعِلٌ as

حُلِيٌّ *an ornament* حَلْيٌ, رُؤُوسٌ *head* رَأْسٌ, صُدُورٌ *breast* صَدْرٌ

(for حُلُويٌ), نَجْمٌ *star* نُجُومٌ, فَلْسٌ *a copper coin* فُلُوسٌ, شَكْلٌ *form, figure* شُكُولٌ, حَرْفٌ *letter* (of the alphabet), *particle* حُرُوفٌ, نَفْسٌ *soul, self* نُفُوسٌ, ذَكَرٌ *a male* ذُكُورٌ, سَاجِدٌ *prostrate* سُجُودٌ.

7. فُعَّلٌ plural of فَاعِلٌ فَاعِلَةٌ as

سَاجِدٌ *prostrate* سُجَّدٌ, شَارِعٌ *manifest* شُرَّعٌ.

8. فُعَّالٌ plural of فَاعِلٌ as

طَالِبٌ *seeker* طُلَّابٌ.

9. فَعَلَةٌ plural of فَاعِلٌ فَعِيلٌ as

سَاحِرٌ *magician* سَحَرَةٌ.

10. فُعَلَةٌ plural of فَاعِلٌ as

قَاضٍ (for قَاضِيٌ) *a judge* قُضَاةٌ (for قُضَيَةٌ).

11. فِعَلَةٌ plural of فُعْلٌ فَعْلٌ فِعْلٌ as

قِرْدٌ *an ape* قِرَدَةٌ.

12. فِعْلَةٌ plural of فَعْلٌ فَعَلٌ فَعَالٌ فُعَالٌ فَعِيلٌ as

أَخٌ (for أَخَوٌ) *a brother* إِخْوَةٌ.

13. أَفْعُلٌ plural of فَعْلٌ فَعَلٌ فِعْلٌ فُعْلٌ فَعَلَةٌ and some other feminine quadriliterals, as

نَفْسٌ *soul, self* أَنْفُسٌ, فَلْسٌ *a copper coin* أَفْلُسٌ, يَدٌ (for يَدْيٌ) *hand* أَيْدٍ (for أَيْدُيٌ), رِجْلٌ *leg, foot* أَرْجُلٌ.

14. أَفْعَالٌ plural of فَعِيلٌ فَاعِلٌ and triliterals of all forms, as عُرْفٌ *uppermost part, forelock, cock's comb* أَعْرَافٌ, نَهْرٌ *river* أَنْهَارٌ, أَلْفٌ *thousand* آلَافٌ, صَنَمٌ *idol* أَصْنَامٌ, اِبْنٌ (for بَنَيٌ) *son* أَبْنَآءٌ, اِسْمٌ (for سِمْوٌ) *name* أَسْمَآءٌ, عَمَلٌ *work* أَعْمَالٌ, سِبْطٌ *tribe* أَسْبَاطٌ, غُلٌّ *fetter* أَغْلَالٌ, شَكْلٌ *form, figure* أَشْكَالٌ, وَلَدٌ *a child* أَوْلَادٌ, زَوْجٌ *spouse* أَزْوَاجٌ, مَالٌ *riches* أَمْوَالٌ, لَوْحٌ *table* أَلْوَاحٌ, يَوْمٌ *day* أَيَّامٌ (for أَيْوَامٌ), صَاحِبٌ *a companion* أَصْحَابٌ.

REM. There are a few other singulars which take this plural, as عَدُوٌّ *hostile* أَعْدَآءٌ; but أَشْيَآءُ (not أَشْيَآءٌ) is the plural of شَيْءٌ *thing*.

15. أَفْعِلَةٌ plural of فَعَالٌ فِعَالٌ and other quadriliterals, also فَعْلٌ فِعْلٌ فُعْلٌ فَعَلٌ فُعَلٌ as إِلٰهٌ *a god* آلِهَةٌ (for أَأْلِهَةٌ), وِعَآءٌ *receptacle* أَوْعِيَةٌ, جَوَابٌ *answer, complement* أَجْوِبَةٌ.

16. فَوَاعِلُ plural of فَاعَلٌ فَاعِلٌ فَاعِلَةٌ فَاعِلَآءُ as تَابِعٌ *follower, appositive* تَوَابِعُ, سَاكِنَةٌ *female dweller* سَوَاكِنُ.

17. فَعَآئِلُ plural of some feminine quadriliterals, with or without ة in addition, as مَدِينَةٌ *a city* مَدَآئِنُ, خَبِيثَةٌ *foul* خَبَآئِثُ, كَرِيمَةٌ *noble* كَرَآئِمُ.

18. فِعْلَانٌ plural of فِعْلٌ فَعْلٌ فِعَالٌ فَعَالٌ فُعَلٌ فَعَلٌ فُعْلٌ فَاعِلٌ فَعَلَانٌ فُعَيْلَةٌ فُعَيْلٌ فَعُولٌ فَعِيلٌ as

حُوتٌ *a fish* حِيتَانٌ, أَخٌ (for أَخَوٌ) *a brother* إِخْوَانٌ.

19. فُعْلَانٌ plural of فَاعِلٌ فَعِيلٌ فِعَالٌ فُعَالٌ فَعَلٌ فِعْلٌ فَعْلٌ أَفْعَلُ as

ذَكَرٌ *a male* ذُكْرَانٌ, أَبْيَضُ *white* بِيضَانٌ (for بُيْضَانٌ) *whites* opposed to سُودَانٌ (plural of أَسْوَدُ) *blacks.*

20. فُعَلَآءُ plural of فَاعِلٌ فَعِيلٌ as

سَفِيهٌ *fool* سُفَهَآءُ, عَالِمٌ *scholar* عُلَمَآءُ.

21. أَفْعِلَآءُ plural of فَعِيلٌ as

نَبِيٌّ for نَبِيٓءٌ (see § 17 *b*, rem. *b*) *a prophet* أَنْبِيَآءُ.

22. فَعْلَى plural of فَعْلَانُ أَفْعَلُ فَاعِلٌ فَعِلٌ فَعِيلٌ as

مَيِّتٌ (for مَوِيتٌ) *dead* مَوْتَى.

23. فَعَالٍ plural of فَعْلَوَةٌ فِعْلِيَةٌ فِعْلَاةٌ فِعْلَى فَعْلَى فَعْلَآءُ as

فَتْوَى *a legal opinion* فَتَاوٍ.

Rem. For declension see §§ 312 and 314, rem. *b*.

24. فَعَالَى plural of فَعِيلٌ فَعْلَانُ فِعْلِيَةٌ فُعْلَى فِعْلَى فَعْلَى فَعْلَآءُ فَاعِلَةٌ فُعَالَةٌ فِعَالَةٌ فَعَالَةٌ فَعِيلَةٌ نَعْلٌ فَعِلٌ as

فَتْوَى *a legal opinion* فَتَاوَى, زَاوِيَةٌ *a corner, a class in school* زَوَايَا (for زَوَايِى as in § 179, rem. *a*).

25. فَعِيلٌ plural of فَاعِلٌ فِعَالٌ فَعَلٌ فَعْلٌ as

حِمَارٌ *an ass* حَمِيرٌ.

26. فُعُولَةٌ plural of فَعْلٌ فَعَلٌ as

بَعْلٌ *a husband* بُعُولَةٌ.

27. فِعَالَةٌ plural of فَعْلٌ فَعَلٌ فَاعِلٌ as

صَاحِبٌ *a companion* صِحَابَةٌ (also صَحَابَةٌ).

28. فَعَلٌ plural of فَعْلَةٌ فَعَلَةٌ فَاعِلٌ as

آيَةٌ (for أَوْيَةٌ) *sign, miracle, message, verse* آيٌ (for أَوْيٌ).

29. فَعْلٌ plural of فَاعِلٌ as

صَاحِبٌ *a companion* صَحْبٌ.

REM. *a.* These rules are not without exception nor are they by any means exhaustive.

REM. *c.* Beside عِبَادٌ br. pl. 5, عَبْدٌ *slave* has fourteen other broken plurals. When a singular has more than one meaning and several plurals, there may be a correspondence: thus خَلِيفَةٌ *a caliph* usually follows No. 20 خُلَفَآءُ *caliphs*, but خَلِيفَةٌ *successor, deputy* makes No. 17 خَلَآئِفُ which by rule is restricted to feminines. There are four meanings to عَيْنٌ beside its being the letter's name, and there are four plurals (three broken and a pl. of pl. أَعْيُنَاتٌ) of which No. 13 أَعْيُنٌ signifies *eyes* and *fountains*. A word which takes the sound plural may have also one or more broken plurals.

305. The following are forms of broken plural from singular nouns with four or more consonants.

1. فَعَالِلُ plural of quadriliterals, with or without ة in addition, (*a*) whose four consonants are radical, and (*b*) formed from triliteral roots by prefixing أ ت or م ; as

ضِفْدِعٌ *a frog* ضَفَادِعُ, مَشْرِقٌ *the east* مَشَارِقُ, مَغْرِبٌ *the west* مَغَارِبُ, مَنَارَةٌ *candlestick, minaret* مَنَاوِرُ and مَنَآئِرُ (compare § 240) vulg. مَنَايِر, مَصْدَرٌ *source* مَصَادِرُ, مَكْتَبٌ *school* مَكَاتِبُ.

2. فَعَالِيلُ plural of quinqueliterals, with or without ة in addition, of which the penult is a letter of prolongation; as مَكْتُوبٌ *written* مَكَاتِيبُ, مَلْعُونٌ *accursed* مَلَاعِينُ, كُرْسِيٌّ *a chair* كَرَاسِيُّ, مِيقَاتٌ (see § 226) مَوَاقِيتُ.

3. فَعَالِلَةٌ plural of many relative adjectives (see § 249) and other nouns with four or more letters; as مَغْرِبِيٌّ *a Moor* مَغَارِبَةٌ, فِرْعَوْنُ *Pharaoh* فَرَاعِنَةٌ, (مَلَكٌ) مَلْأَكٌ *angel* مَلَآئِكَةٌ.

Rem. *e.* A few nouns have anomalous plurals, as اِمْرَأَةٌ *a woman* (see § 304, No. 5 rem.) نِسَآءٌ, إِنْسَانٌ *a human being* أُنَاسٌ; this we may abbreviate to نَاسٌ especially with the article, thus اَلنَّاسُ, much as اَلْإِلٰهُ has become اَللّٰهُ.

306. We have noted the restriction (§ 302, rem. *a*) that masculine sound plurals can only be used of rational beings: they are said by grammarians to mean several individuals; whereas the broken plural is by nature a collective and feminine in gender, being generally represented by the feminine singular pronoun; thus كَتَبْنَا فِي ٱلْأَلْوَاحِ فَخُذْهَا *we have written upon the tablets, so take them.*

Rem. Beside broken plurals there are the two sorts of collectives which have been mentioned in § 292 *a* and *b*:

(*a*) generic nouns (أَسْمَآءُ ٱلْجِنْسِ) which form nomina unitatis (see § 246); and

(*b*) nouns to which attaches the idea of collectiveness (أَسْمَآءُ ٱلْجَمْعِ or أَشْبَاهُ ٱلْجَمْعِ *likenesses of the plural*) and which do not form nomina unitatis; as أُمَّةٌ *a section of a nation*, قَوْمٌ *a people*, etc, thus مِنَ ٱلْقَوْمِ أُمَّةٌ يَهْدُونَ *of the people there is a section who direct* (not *which directs*) *others.*

NOTE. As nomen verbi أُمَّةٌ appears in § 198, No. 12, and as singular of أُمَمٌ in § 304, No. 1. Beside being nomen verbi (§ 198, No. 25), نَبَاتٌ with the signification of *plants* is a collective, of sort (*a*) though without nomen unitatis, and makes a plural نَبَاتَاتٌ.

307. In case of nouns which have only one plural there can be no difficulty of selection; but, while the rest are called plurals of abundance, those broken plurals in § 304 numbered 12, 13, 14 and 15 as well as the sound plurals, are called plurals of paucity, being used when the objects denoted are ten or less. Thus سِتَّةُ أَيَّامٍ *six days* br. pl. 14 (for أَيْوَامٍ) of يَوْمٌ *a day.*

---

308. In Arabic there are three cases, Nominative, Dependent and Accusative, each with its case-ending or sign: we shall however speak of the Oblique case when one and the same sign indicates both Dependent and Accusative. The following tables show how to decline *undefined* nouns which are not in construct state (see § 313) by means of فَلْسٌ *a copper coin*, لَيْلَةٌ *a night*, نُجُومٌ *stars* (br. pl. 6 of نَجْمٌ), مُلْكَانِ *two dominions*, حَسَنَتَانِ *two boons*, خَالِدُونَ *dwellers*, طَيِّبَاتٌ *good things*, أَحْسَنُ *better*,

بَيْضَآءُ (fem.) *white*, تَوَابِعُ *followers* (br. pl. 16 of تَابِعٌ). Nouns ending with ةٌ, whether broken plural or singular, mark the accusative differently (see § 8, rem. *a*) from other triptotes, i.e. nouns with three case-endings.

Triptote or First Declension.

	Masc. sing.	Fem. sing.	Broken pl.
Nominative	فَلْسٌ	لَيْلَةٌ	نُجُومٌ
Dependent	فَلْسٍ	لَيْلَةٍ	نُجُومٍ
Accusative	فَلْسًا	لَيْلَةً	نُجُومًا

Dual.

	Masculine	Feminine
Nominative	مُلْكَانِ	حَسَنَتَانِ
Oblique	مُلْكَيْنِ	حَسَنَتَيْنِ

Sound Plural.

	Masculine	Feminine
Nominative	خَالِدُونَ	طَيِّبَاتٌ
Oblique	خَالِدِينَ	طَيِّبَاتٍ

Except in the sound plural (see § 302) it makes no difference whether the noun be adjective or otherwise; and so with diptotes, i.e. nouns with not more than two case-endings.

Diptote or Second Declension.

	Masc. sing.	Fem. sing.	Broken pl.
Nominative	أَحْسَنُ	بَيْضَآءُ	تَوَابِعُ
Oblique	أَحْسَنَ	بَيْضَآءَ	تَوَابِعَ

In the dual diptotes and triptotes are alike, thus Nom. أَحْسَنَانِ, Obl. أَحْسَنَيْنِ and so in the sound plural.

NOTE. For declension of جَوَارٍ see § 312.

REM. *b*. No colloquial dialect of Arabic employs case-endings regularly; duals are rare, and in sound plurals only the oblique case is used.

309. We call nouns diptote when ending in ـُ, ـَى, or ـَـِ: such are the following.

(*a*) Broken plurals in § 304 numbered 16, 17, 20, 21, 22, 23 and 24; also those in § 305 numbered 1 and 2; beside a few others.

(*b*) Various nouns, more especially adjectives such as are found in § 232, Nos. 13 and 16, also in §§ 234, 295 and 296; beside others.

(*c*) Many proper names, as مَكَّةُ *Mecca*; especially if foreign to Arabic, as إِسْرَائِيلُ *Israel*, دَاوُدُ *David*, فِرْعَوْنُ *Pharaoh*, هٰرُونُ *Aaron*, يُوسُفُ *Joseph*, آدَمُ *Adam*, إِبْلِيسُ *Eblis*, مِصْرُ *Egypt*. Exceptional are such as consist of three letters, the second of which has sukûn or is a letter of prolongation, thus نُوحٌ *Noah*.

REM. *e*. There are said to be nine reasons why a noun is debarred from taking tanwin.

310. Nouns ending in ـًا or ـًى (for ـَوْ or ـَيْ see §§ 212 *b* and 245) have the same form in all three cases; thus

for عَصَوٌ, عَصَوٍ or عَصَوًا we write عَصًا *a stick*

„ هُدَيٌ, هُدَيٍ „ هُدَيًا „ هُدًى *guidance*

Similarly we leave unchanged nouns ending in ـَى (see § 309) such as غَضْبَى (fem.) *angry*, أَدْنَى *nearer*, مُوسَى *Moses*.

311. With nouns ending in ـٍ (for ـٍوْ, ـٍيْ or ـًيْ see § 167 *b* (ii) and § 369, Table 18) it is somewhat different, for we write

دَاعِيًا *a preacher* as the Accusative of دَاعٍ i.e. دَاعِوٌ

نَافِيًا *negative* „ نَافٍ „ نَافِيٌ

مُعْتَدِيًا *transgressor* „ مُعْتَدٍ „ مُعْتَدِيٌ

أَيْدِيًا *hands* „ أَيْدٍ „ أَيْدِيٌ (br. pl. 13)

following in this the analogy of § 166 *a*.

312. There are however certain broken plurals ending with ـٍ which is held to represent ـِيُ. They do not follow either of the last two rules; thus جَارِيَةٌ *a girl* has br. pl. 16 جَوَارٍ in the Nominative and Dependent, but جَوَارِيَ in the Accusative; so also صَحْرَآءُ *a desert* has br. pl. 23 Nom. and Dep. صَحَارٍ, but Accusative صَحَارِيَ.

---

313. Undefined nouns become *defined*: 1. by prefixing the article أَلْ *the*; 2. (*a*) by adding a defined noun in the dependent case, or (*b*) by adding a pronominal suffix. While remaining undefined a noun may be put in construct state (see § 475) by the addition of an undefined noun in dependent case.

Rem. Proper names are in themselves defined, as are the pronouns هُوَ *he* etc. and words like ذَا *this, that* (see §§ 340 et seq.).

Note. A noun cannot have two determinatives; thus ٱلْأَعْرَافُ *the uppermost parts* and أَعْرَافُ ٱلْحِجَابِ *the uppermost parts of the partition.*

314. When a noun is defined by the article, the following cases arise.

(*a*) If it be triptote it loses the tanwin; thus

Nominative . . اَلْفَلْسُ . . اَللَّيْلَةُ . . اَلنُّجُومُ

Dependent . . اَلْفَلْسِ . . اَللَّيْلَةِ . . اَلنُّجُومِ

Accusative . . اَلْفَلْسَ . . اَللَّيْلَةَ . . اَلنُّجُومَ

REM. From the accusative final ا has disappeared along with tanwin: so also from words like اَلْأَيْدِيَ defined acc. of أَيْدٍ.

(*b*) If diptote it becomes triptote; thus

Nominative . اَلْأَحْسَنُ . . اَلْبَيْضَآءُ . . اَلتَّوَابِعُ

Dependent . اَلْأَحْسَنِ . . اَلْبَيْضَآءِ . . اَلتَّوَابِعِ

Accusative . اَلْأَحْسَنَ . . اَلْبَيْضَآءَ . . اَلتَّوَابِعَ

(*c*) If sound plural feminine it loses tanwin; thus

Nominative . اَلطَّيِّبَاتُ   Oblique . اَلطَّيِّبَاتِ

REM. *a*. Prefixing the article causes no change in the dual or sound plural masculine.

REM. *b*. From the termination ـٍ tanwin is lost and ي reappears, as اَلْمُلْقِي *the thrower* from مُلْقٍ, اَلْعَمِي *the blind* (*man*) from عَمٍ, اَلْأَيْدِي *the hands* from أَيْدٍ.

NOTE. Nouns ending in ـًا or ـًى (for ـَوٌ or ـَيٌ see § 310) merely lose the tanwin, as اَلْعَصَا, اَلْهُدَى.

315. The following cases arise when a noun is in construct state, i.e. when it is مُضَافٌ *annexed* to a noun in the dependent case.

(*a*) We decline singulars and broken plurals as if defined by the article; thus

Nom.	طُلَّابُ ٱلْعِلْمِ	*the seekers of knowledge.*	مَشَارِقُ ٱلْأَرْضِ	*the eastern parts of the earth.*
Dep.	طُلَّابِ ٱلْعِلْمِ		مَشَارِقِ ٱلْأَرْضِ	
Acc.	طُلَّابَ ٱلْعِلْمِ		مَشَارِقَ ٱلْأَرْضِ	

NOTE. As to كُلٌّ *all* see § 482.

REM. *a*. Certain defective substantives (see § 191, Note) lengthen their final vowel after rejecting tanwīn; thus

Nom. أَخُو *brother* for أَخٌ, Dep. أَخِي for أَخٍ, Acc. أَخَا for أَخًا.

(*b*) The dual loses نِ from its termination, as

وَلَدَا ٱلْمَلِكِ *the two children of the king* for وَلَدَانِ, بَيْنَ يَدَيْ رَحْمَتِهِ *between the two hands of* (*i.e. before*) *his mercy* for يَدَيْنِ.

(*c*) The sound plural masculine loses نَ from its termination, as

أَرْسِلْ بَنِي إِسْرَآئِيلَ *send the sons of Israel* for بَنِينَ.

316. When the noun is defined by a pronominal suffix the following cases arise.

(*a*) Triptotes and feminine sound plurals lose tanwīn, duals and masculine sound plurals the termination نِ or نَ; thus يَدُهَا *her hand* from يَدٌ, عَصَاهُ *his stick* from عَصًا, كَلِمَاتُنَا *our words* from كَلِمَاتٌ, يَدَيَّ *my two hands* يَدَيْكَ *thy two hands* from يَدَيْنِ, بَالِغُوهُ *the attainers of it* from بَالِغُونَ.

NOTE. In the Nominative and Dependent we have أَيْدِينَا *our hands* and in the Accusative أَيْدِيَنَا from أَيْدٍ Acc. أَيْدِيًا.

(*b*) The singulars, broken plurals, and feminine sound plurals lose their final vowel before ـِي *of me, my* (see § 317); thus رَبِّي *my Lord* from رَبٌّ, أَعْمَالِي *my works* from أَعْمَالٌ, جَنَّاتِي *my gardens* from جَنَّاتٌ. Having lost its case-endings the noun becomes, so to speak, indeclinable.

(*c*) When a noun ends in ة we use the original form, viz. ت; thus آلِهَتُكَ *thy gods* from آلِهَةٌ.

(*d*) When a noun ends in hamzah, the ʽimâd (عِمَادٌ) *support* (see § 16) is subject to change; thus from نِسَآءٌ we have Nom. نِسَآؤُنَا *our women*, Dep. نِسَآئِنَا, Acc. نِسَآءَنَا, and from مَجِيءٌ we have مَجِيؤُكَ *thy coming*, Dep. مَجِيئِكَ, Acc. مَجِيئَكَ (see § 17 *b*).

REM. As regards words referred to in § 315, rem. *a* we must note, Nom. أَخُوهُ *his brother*, Dep. أَخِيهِ, Acc. أَخَاهُ; but أَخِي *my brother* in all three cases.

---

317. The pronominal suffixes which express the dependent are similar to those given in § 185 except that ـِي *of me, my* takes the place of ـنِي; thus حِفْظُهُمَا *the guarding of them both.*

REM. *a.* Beside مَعِي *along with me* we have by reverting to the older form مَعِيَ (see § 20 *b*). When attached to a word ending with ـَا, ـَى, ـِي, ـَيْ, ـُو or ـَوْ the suffix ـِي becomes يَ, as عَصَايَ *my stick*; and in most cases, together with the final letter, it becomes يَّ, as عَلَيَّ *upon me* (see § 358, rem. *a*). On أَخٌ etc. see § 316, rem.

REM. *b*. Like نِي, we find ـِي especially in the vocative, shortened to ـِ; thus يَا قَوْمِ *O my people* for قَوْمِي, رَبِّ *(O) my Lord* for رَبِّي (see § 438 *a*, rem. *b*).

REM. *c*. Changes occur similar to those in § 185, rem. *b*; thus بِإِذْنِهِ *by the permission of him*, لِنَاظِرِيهِمْ *to the beholders of them*, عَلَيْهِمْ *upon them*, بَيْنَ يَدَيْهِ *between his two hands*.

---

318. The *cardinal numbers* from one to ten are:

Fem.	Masc.		Fem.	Masc.	
خَمْسَةٌ	خَمْسٌ	5	إِحْدَى	أَحَدٌ	1
سِتَّةٌ	سِتٌّ	6	وَاحِدَةٌ	وَاحِدٌ	1
سَبْعَةٌ	سَبْعٌ	7	اِثْنَتَانِ or ثِنْتَانِ	اِثْنَانِ	2
ثَمَانِيَةٌ	ثَمَانٍ	8	ثَلَاثَةٌ	ثَلَاثٌ	3
تِسْعَةٌ	تِسْعٌ	9	أَرْبَعَةٌ	أَرْبَعٌ	4
عَشَرَةٌ	عَشْرٌ	10			

REM. *a*. For ثَلٰثٌ and words like it see § 6, rem. *a*. The radical letters of سِتٌّ are سدس (see § 328, rem. *c*).

319. The cardinal numbers from 3 to 10 take the feminine form, when the objects numbered are of the masculine gender; and conversely, the masculine form, when the objects numbered are feminine: as سِتَّةُ أَيَّامٍ *six days*, سَبْعُ آيَاتٍ *seven verses*.

320. Excepting the duals اِثْنَانِ, and اِثْنَتَانِ or ثِنْتَانِ, the cardinal numbers from 1 to 10 are triptote; ثَمَانٍ standing for ثَمَانِيٌ (see § 311) Accusative ثَمَانِيًا.

321. Cardinal numbers from 3 to 10 are substantives : either (*a*) they follow the objects numbered and stand in apposition, as رِجَالٍ ثَلَاثَةٍ *of three men* i.e. of men, a triad ; or (*b*) they are followed by a plural noun in the dependent case, as سِتَّةُ أَيَّامٍ *six days.* For the multiples of 100 see § 325 and § 496, rem. *a.*

REM. When these numerals take the article they lose tanwîn, as also when in construct state or defined by a pronominal suffix; while ثَمَانٍ has Nom. and Dep. ثَمَانِي Acc. ثَمَانِيَ.

322. The cardinal numbers from eleven to nineteen are :

	Masc.	Fem.
11	أَحَدَ عَشَرَ	إِحْدَى عَشْرَةَ
12	اِثْنَا عَشَرَ	اِثْنَتَا عَشْرَةَ ثِنْتَا عَشْرَةَ
13	ثَلَاثَةَ عَشَرَ	ثَلَاثَ عَشْرَةَ
14	أَرْبَعَةَ عَشَرَ	أَرْبَعَ عَشْرَةَ
15	خَمْسَةَ عَشَرَ	خَمْسَ عَشْرَةَ
16	سِتَّةَ عَشَرَ	سِتَّ عَشْرَةَ
17	سَبْعَةَ عَشَرَ	سَبْعَ عَشْرَةَ
18	ثَمَانِيَةَ عَشَرَ	ثَمَانِيَ عَشْرَةَ
19	تِسْعَةَ عَشَرَ	تِسْعَ عَشْرَةَ

REM. *a.* We find ثَمَانِ عَشْرَةَ and other forms, for ثَمَانِيَ عَشْرَةَ.

REM. *b.* These cardinal numbers are followed by the objects numbered in the accusative singular (see § 444 *e*, rem. *b*).

REM. *c.* These numerals may be called indeclinable, except اِثْنَا عَشَرَ and اِثْنَتَا (ثِنْتَا) عَشْرَةَ which have an oblique case اِثْنَيْ عَشَرَ and اِثْنَتَيْ (ثِنْتَيْ) عَشْرَةَ.

REM. *d.* Since long ago these compound numerals suffered contraction into one word, and are further corrupted in colloquial dialects.

323. The cardinal numbers from twenty to ninety are:

20 عِشْرُونَ	40 أَرْبَعُونَ	60 سِتُّونَ	80 ثَمَانُونَ
30 ثَلَاثُونَ	50 خَمْسُونَ	70 سَبْعُونَ	90 تِسْعُونَ

REM. *a.* For ثَلٰثُونَ and ثَمٰنُونَ see § 6, rem. *a.*

REM. *b.* While of common gender these numerals are declined as masculine sound plurals, taking an oblique case in ـِينَ; thus عِشْرِينَ, ثَلَاثِينَ, أَرْبَعِينَ, etc. They are substantives and usually take after them the objects numbered in the accusative singular (see § 499).

324. Numerals compounded of units and tens require وَ *and* between the unit and the ten; thus Nom. تِسْعٌ وَخَمْسُونَ *nine and fifty, fifty nine*, Dep. تِسْعٍ وَخَمْسِينَ, Acc. تِسْعًا وَخَمْسِينَ.

325. The multiples of مِائَةٌ *one hundred* are as follows:

200 مِائَتَانِ, 300 ثَلَاثُ مِائَةٍ, 400 أَرْبَعُ مِائَةٍ, etc.

REM. *a.* For مِائَةٌ we may write مِئَةٌ and (see § 17 *b*, rem. *b*) مِيَةٌ, which last represents the usual pronunciation. There are other plurals beside the one mentioned in § 301, rem. *d.*

326. The multiples of أَلْفٌ *one thousand* are as follows:

2000 أَلْفَانِ, 3000 ثَلَاثَةُ آلَافٍ, 4000 أَرْبَعَةُ آلَافٍ, etc.

REM. There are other plurals of أَلْفٌ beside آلَافٌ.

328. The *ordinal* numbers are adjectives; thus, masc. اَلْأَوَّلُ fem. اَلْأُولَى *the first*, masc. ثَانٍ fem. ثَانِيَةٌ *second*, masc. ثَالِثٌ fem. ثَالِثَةٌ *third*, masc. رَابِعٌ fem. رَابِعَةٌ *fourth*, etc.

REM. *a*. The radical letters of الأَوَّلُ (see § 295, rem. *b*) and الأُولَى (for الأُؤْلَى or أَلْوُولَى) are أول or وأل. These words have plurals, and will be further treated in § 486, rem. *a*, and § 493.

REM. *c*. From masc. سَادِسٌ fem. سَادِسَةٌ *sixth* we can obtain the radical letters of سِتٌّ given in § 318, rem. *a*, as also from the fraction سُدْسٌ *a sixth part.*

---

340. The simple *demonstrative pronoun* is ذَا *this, that,* which in course of declension takes many forms, the commonest plural being, masc. أُلَى fem. أُلَآءِ *these, those.*

REM. *c*. Closely connected by origin with ذَا is ذُو *possessor*, which is also declined, making in the singular feminine Nom. ذَاتُ Dep. ذَاتِ Acc. ذَاتَ, none of which is found except in construct state (see § 475).

REM. *d*. By prefixing كَ *like* to ذَا we get كَذَا *thus, so and so,* see § 362 *bb*.

341. From the simple demonstrative pronoun compounds, which admit of declension, are formed (*a*) by appending كَ كِ كُمْ كُمَا or كُنَّ either (i) alone, or (ii) with لِ interposed; also (*b*) by prefixing هَا.

a (i) ذَاكَ *that* is used whatever the sex or number of persons addressed; but we may say to a woman ذَاكِ, to two persons ذَاكُمَا, etc. The plurals أُلَاكَ and أُلَآئِكَ and أُولَآئِكَ, with short first syllable, *those* are of common gender.

(ii) Similarly ذَالِكَ or ذٰلِكَ *that* is used in conjunction with pronominal suffixes of the second person; thus فِي ذٰلِكُمْ *therein O you.*

Rem. By prefixing كَ *like* to ذٰلِكَ we get كَذٰلِكَ *in like manner, so,* see § 463.

b. The particle هَا (which is also an interjection, see § 368) we may prefix to ذَا and write هٰذَا *this*; which word has a singular feminine هٰذِهِ, and as one of its plurals هَاؤُلَآءِ or هٰؤُلَآءِ *these* of common gender.

345. We find in Arabic only one *article,* viz. أَلْ, which is called the instrument of definition and always written in conjunction with the following word; thus قُرْآنٌ *a reading* اَلْقُرْآنُ *the reading, the Corân.*

Rem. *a.* The article is also called لَامُ ٱلتَّعْرِيفِ ('alif being merely prosthetic, see § 19, rem. *c*) *the lâm of definition,* and it has two uses:

(i) لَامُ ٱلْعَهْدِ *the article of familiarity* when its presence implies that the word, to which it is attached, expresses a thing or person known to the hearer; thus يَرِثُونَ ٱلْأَرْضَ *they shall inherit the earth,* i.e. the earth which we know:

(ii) لَامُ ٱلْجِنْسِ *the generic article,* not implying that the word, to which it is prefixed, expresses an individual person or thing; in this case it shows the genus by indicating one member of a class; thus فَلِأُمِّهِ ٱلسُّدُسُ *his mother shall have a sixth,* إِذَا جَآءَتْهُمُ ٱلْحَسَنَةُ *whenever a boon comes to them.*

Note. Arabic and some other languages are more regular than English in respect of the generic article, for one says "Man is mortal" but "The horse is a quadruped," whereas in these cases we must write اَلْإِنْسَانُ *l'homme* and اَلْفَرَسُ *le cheval* (see § 527).

346. Among the *conjunctive pronouns* are masc. اَلَّذِي fem. اَلَّتِي *who, which, that*; مَنْ *he who, she who, whoever*; مَا *that which, whatever.* They are also called relative pronouns and, with exception of اَلَّذِي, may be interrogative (see § 351).

347. As may be found in § 20 *b*, initial ال of اَلَّذِي represents the article, to which is joined لَ (see § 341 *a* ii) and ذَا or ذُو (see § 340). Of the many forms taken in declension we must, beside اَلَّتِي the feminine singular, mention the masculine plural اَلَّذِينَ. When used adjectivally these words refer to a definite substantive with which they agree in gender, number, and case; thus اَللّٰهُ ٱلَّذِي خَلَقَهُ *God who created it,* اَلْأَرْضِ ٱلَّتِي بَارَكْنَا فِيهَا *the land which We blessed*: when used substantively however they have the meaning of مَنْ or مَا, thus أَغْرَقْنَا ٱلَّذِينَ *We drowned those who.*

Rem. The nominatives must originally have been اَللَّذُو and اَللَّذُونَ but in place of these words the oblique case is always used (see § 308, rem. *b*) and a shortened form.

348. The conjunctive pronouns مَنْ and مَا are indeclinable: the former refers to beings endowed with reason, as مُوسَى وَمَنْ مَعَهُ *Moses and those who (are) with him*; while the latter is used of all other objects, as بِمَا فَعَلَ *by reason of that which he has done.* Unlike اَلَّذِي these words can never be used adjectivally.

351. All conjunctive pronouns may be *interrogative* except اَلَّذِي, thus مَنْ أَنْتَ *who art thou?* مَا فَعَلَ *what has he done?* see § 570.

Rem. The interrogative مَا is usually shortened to مَ when joined with a preposition, thus لِمَ *why?* i.e. because of what? So also كَمَا *the like of what?* becomes كَمْ *how much?*

353*. The pronouns مَنْ and مَا are sometimes indefinite. Of this sort is مَا ٱلْمَصْدَرِيَّة *the mâ which introduces a clause equivalent to a maçdar* (see §§ 488 and 514); thus مِنْ بَعْدِ مَا جِئْتَ *after that thou camest* which is equivalent to مِنْ بَعْدِ مَجِيئِكَ *after thy coming.* We find the indefinite مَا in conditional clauses (مَا ٱلشَّرْطِيَّة § 406), also in reference to time (مَا ٱلدَّيْمُومَة §§ 367 *p* and 407); when added to certain adverbs it gives them a conditional and general signification, thus حَيْثُ *where* حَيْثُمَا *wherever*, أَيْنَ *where?* أَيْنَمَا *wherever.* If appended to إِنَّ, أَنَّ, etc., it hinders their regimen (مَا ٱلْكَافَّة § 436, rem. *d*); attached to a conjunction or preposition (مَا ٱلزَّائِدَة § 470, rem. *f*) it usually does not; and there are other uses for which it serves.

Note. Similar to the adverbs mentioned above is مَهْمَا (for مَامَا) *whatever* from مَا *what.*

---

354. The *particles* are of four sorts; viz. prepositions, adverbs, conjunctions, and interjections.

355. The *prepositions* are divided into separable, i.e. those written as separate words, and inseparable, i.e. those which are united in writing with the following word.

356. The inseparable prepositions consist of one consonant with its vowel. They are:—

(a) بِ *by, by means of, by reason of, for the reason, in, on, with, to, of, in exchange for*, see § 456.

(c) لِ *belonging to, for the use of, to, due to, in, for, of*, see § 453.

(d) وَ *by* in swearing, see § 462.

Rem. *a.* Changes occur after بِ similar to those in § 185, rem. *b*, as بِهِمْ, بِهِ; see also § 20, rem. *a*.

Rem. *b.* Before a pronominal suffix the preposition لِ becomes لَ, as لَهُ, لَكُمْ etc.; except with ـِي *me* when we have لِي.

Rem. *c.* Sometimes كَ *like* is reckoned among prepositions: it will be treated in § 463.

357. The separable prepositions are of two sorts: firstly, those which have different terminations and are biliteral or triliteral; secondly, those which are substantives in the accusative singular and end in ـَ, having lost tanwin on account of the following noun (see § 478 *b*).

358. The separable prepositions of the first sort are:—

(a) إِلَى *to, towards, until*, see § 451.

(b) حَتَّى *till, up to*, see § 452.

(c) عَلَى *over, upon, against, to, for, on account of, concerning, by means of, incumbent upon*, see § 459.

(d) عَنْ *from, away from, of*, see § 449.

(e) فِي *in, into, over, among, upon, on, concerning, treating of*, see § 455.

(f) لَدُنْ or لَدَى *with, beside, near.*

(g) مَعَ or مَعْ *with, along with,* see § 457.

(h) مِنْ *of, to, from, on, out of,* see § 20 *d* and § 448.

(i) مُنْذُ or مُذْ *from* a certain time, *since.*

REM. *a.* Before suffixes the final syllables of إِلَى, عَلَى, and لَدَى are diphthongs; thus إِلَيْكَ *to thee,* عَلَيْنَا *over us.* Changes occur similar to those in § 185, rem. *b*; إِلَيْهِنَّ *to them* (fem.), عَلَيْهِمَا *over them both.* With ـِي *me* we have إِلَيَّ *to me* etc., and فِيَّ in case of فِي as كِتَابٌ فِيَّ *a letter relating to me* (see § 317, rem. *a*).

REM. *b.* In connection with ـِي we double the ن of عَنْ, مِنْ, and لَدُنْ, thus مِنِّي *from me.* The ن of عَنْ and مِنْ is assimilated in connection with مَنْ or مَا, thus عَتَوْا عَمَّا *they turned disdainfully from that which* for عَنْ مَا (see § 14 *b*, rem. *b*).

359. Separable prepositions of the second sort have been described in § 357 and will be noticed in § 444 *b.* Among them are بَعْدَ *after,* بَيْنَ *between,* تَحْتَ *under,* خَلْفَ *behind,* دُونَ *below,* عِنْدَ *beside, in the mind of,* فَوْقَ *above, over,* قَبْلَ *before* of time (see §§ 464 to 470).

---

360. The *adverbs* are of three sorts; firstly, particles some inseparable and some separable; secondly, indeclinable substantives ending in ـُ; thirdly, nouns in the accusative.

361. The inseparable adverbial particles are :—

(a) أَ, interrogative, see § 566.

REM. When this أ is followed by إ we use ى instead of ا

as 'imâd (see § 16) to hamzah and write the two thus أئِ, as أَئِنَّ لَنَا لَأَجْرًا *shall there indeed be to us a reward?*

(*b*) سَ (abbreviation of سَوْفَ see § 364 *e*) prefixed to a verb in the imperfect to express more emphatically its future sense.

(*c*) لَ *verily, surely, certainly* (see § 590). As لَئِنْ كَشَفْتَ عَنَّا ٱلرِّجْزَ لَنُؤْمِنَنَّ لَكَ وَلَنُرْسِلَنَّ *Verily if thou removest from us the plague, surely we will believe with thee, and we will certainly send.* This la is always affirmative, and of it there are said to be five sorts.

362. Among the separable adverbial particles are:

(*b*) إِذْ and إِذَا *behold! lo!* Of these إِذَا is followed only by a nominal proposition (see § 513) and refers to the same time as the preceding statement.

(*e*) أَلَا *truly*, see § 568.

(*k*) إِنْ *not*, called إِنِ ٱلنَّافِيَةُ *the negative 'in*, see § 558.

(*m*) إِنَّ *verily* precedes a noun in the accusative or one of the pronominal suffixes given in § 185; but the 1st singular can be إِنَّنِي or إِنِّي and the 1st plural إِنَّنَا or إِنَّا. In such case the suffix هُ may be ضَمِيرُ ٱلشَّأْنِ *the pronoun of the fact*, not being needed to express the sentence's meaning, thus إِنَّهُ أَنَا ٱللّٰهُ *verily I am God* (see § 367 *g*). By means of إِنَّ the subject may be introduced, upon which often follows a predicate with لَ (see § 361 *c*) as انَّ هٰذَا لَسَاحِرٌ عَلِيمٌ *verily this (man) is a skilled magician.* For government by إِنَّ see § 436.

(*n*) إِنَّمَا *only*, see § 436, rem. *d*, and § 585.

(*q*) إِي *yes, yea*; used with an oath, as إِي وَٱللّٰهِ *yes by God*, whence the vulgar أَيْوَا and in Nubia أَيْوَلْ for which at Damascus اي نعم is said.

(*s*) أَيْنَ *where?* أَيْنَمَا *wherever*, see § 353*.

(*u*) بَلَى *yes, yea* sometimes to be translated *on the contrary*, for to a negative statement it gives contradiction. Compare *si* in French.

(*z*) قَدْ is usually employed with the perfect (see §§ 402, 403 *b*) to express more emphatically its past sense: when used with the imperfect we render قَدْ *sometimes.*

(*bb*) كَذَا *thus* (§ 340, rem. *d*) and كَذٰلِكَ *in like manner* (see § 341 *a*, rem.).

(*dd*) لَا *not* is used:—

(i) as negative of the future and of the indefinite present, see §§ 408 *e*, rem. *a*, 439, 555, and 584 *a*;

(ii) as representative of the other negatives after وَ *and*, see §§ 482 *d* rem., 560, and 580;

(iii) as negative of the jussive, see §§ 417 *b* and 420.

(*ee*) لٰكِنَّ, لٰكِنْ, often with وَ prefixed *but, yet* (see § 584 *b*). We place لٰكِنَّ only before nouns and pronominal suffixes in the accusative case (see § 436). With the 1st person we may write لٰكِنِّي, لٰكِنَّا as well as لٰكِنَّنِي, لٰكِنَّنَا.

(*ff*) لَمْ *not* is used solely with the jussive which is then perfect in sense, see §§ 412 and 418.

(*gg*) لَمَّا *not yet*, joined to the jussive.

(*hh*) لَنْ *not* a contraction of لَا أَنْ (i.e. لَا يَكُونُ أَنْ *it will not be that*) is followed by the subjunctive, see §§ 411, 415 *a* i, and 556.

(*kk*) مَا *not* negative of the definite or absolute present, see §§ 408 *e*, rem. *a*, and 531; also of the past see § 557.

(*mm*) نَعَمْ *yes, yea* (for نَعِمَ *it is agreeable*) affirms the preceding statement.

(*oo*) هَلْ interrogative, see § 567.

(*qq*) هُنَا demonstrative *here*; whence (see § 341 for an analogy) هُنَالِكَ *there.*

363. We have treated in §§ 357 and 359 certain accusative substantives which serve as prepositions; the same nouns may be used as adverbs, but they must invariably end in ـُ. Thus بَعْدُ, مِنْ بَعْدُ *afterwards*; حَيْثُ *where*, مِنْ حَيْثُ *whence*, إِلَى حَيْثُ *whither*, حَيْثُمَا *wherever* (see §§ 353* and 406); قَبْلُ, مِنْ قَبْلُ *beforehand.*

364. The Arabic language would however be poor in adverbs but for the adverbial accusative, which is extensively used as will be learned from § 440 et sqq. Here we may mention أَبَدًا *ever*, جَمِيعًا *all together.* Also, of the same class are the adverbs :—

(*e*) سَوْفَ *in the end* prefixed to the imperfect to express real futurity, see §§ 361 *b*, 408 *c*, and 587 *d*.

(*g*) كَيْفَ *how?*

Rem. *b*. For لَعَلَّ see §§ 436, rem. *f*, and 442, rem. *g* (2).

365. The *conjunctions*, like prepositions and adverbs, are some inseparable and some separable.

366. The inseparable conjunctions are :—

(*a*) وَ *and*, see §§ 576 to 583.

(*b*) فَ *so, and so, so that, and thereupon, then*, see §§ 406 *c*, 415 *d*, 540, 576, and 587.

Rem. These conjunctions وَ and فَ may be preceded by the interrogative أ (see § 566).

(*c*) لِ. This may be (i) the li of command (see 417 *a*) which is usually prefixed to the 3rd sing. of the jussive, to give it an imperative sense; and when following وَ or فَ is written without kasrah thus لْ: or (ii) the li which governs the subjunctive and means *that, so that, in order that* (see §§ 411 and 415 *b*).

367. Among the separable conjunctions are these :—

(*a*) إِذْ *when* is prefixed to a verbal or nominal proposition and refers to the past; thus وَإِذْ أَنْجَيْنَاكُمْ *and (remember the time) when We delivered you.*

(*b*) إِذَا *whenever*, see § 405.

(*d*) أَمَّا, followed by فَ, *as for, as regards*, see § 576.

(*e*) أَنْ *that, so that, in order that* governs the subjunctive (see §§ 411 and 415 *a* i); also the perfect and indicative (see § 415 *a* ii): it is used after certain prepositions (see §§ 470, rem. *f*, and 488). Notice must here be taken of أَنِ ٱلْمُفَسِّرَةُ *the explicative 'an*, which introduces a quotation, as أَوْحَيْنَا إِلَى مُوسَى أَنْ أَلْقِ عَصَاكَ *We revealed to Moses (saying) Throw down thy rod.*

(*f*) إِنْ *if* called إِنِ ٱلشَّرْطِيَّةُ *the conditional 'in*, see §§ 406 *b*, 413, 417 *c* i, and 588. The compounds are:—

وَإِنْ *although* (in which sense it is not usually followed by an apodosis*), *and if*;

لَئِنْ *verily if*, see § 361 *c*;

إِلَّا (for إِنْ لَا see § 14 *b*, rem. *b*) *if not*, but commonly meaning *except* and with a preceding negative *only*, see § 586 *a*;

إِمَّا (for إِنْ مَا see § 14 *b*, rem. *b*, and § 353*) *if* and when repeated إِمَّا . . . . . وَإِمَّا *either* . . . . . *or*, as إِمَّا أَنْ تُلْقِيَ وَإِمَّا أَنْ نَكُونَ نَحْنُ ٱلْمُلْقِينَ (*choose*) *either that thou dost throw or that we be the throwers.*

(*g*) أَنَّ *that.* Like إِنَّ it precedes a noun in the accusative or one of the pronominal suffixes given in § 185; the 1st singular being أَنَّنِي or أَنِّي and the 1st plural أَنَّنَا or أَنَّا. In such case the suffix هُ may be pronoun of the fact (see § 362 *m*) as بِأَنَّهُ كَانَتْ تَأْتِيهِمْ رُسُلٌ *because apostles used to come to them.* Beside بِأَنَّ we have لِأَنَّ which also means *because*, and كَأَنَّ *as though*, see §§ 436 and 470, rem. *f*.

---

* The apodosis of a sentence is the consequent clause, which expresses a result; as distinguished from the precedent clause, called protasis, which is conditional.

(*h*) أَوْ *or* as حَاشِرٌ أَوْ خَاسِرٌ *a gatherer or a loser.*

(*i*) ثُمَّ *then, and then,* implying succession at an interval.

(*k*) حَتَّى *till,* see §§ 405, rem. *c*, 415 *c*, and 452, rem. *c*. Beside being a conjunction حَتَّى is a preposition, see § 358 *b*.

(*n*) لَمَّا *after, when,* is used with the perfect.

(*o*) لَوْ *if,* see §§ 404 and 588.

وَلَوْ *even though.*

(*p*) مَا *as long as, as far as*; used with the perfect (see § 407) and jussive (see § 418): it is called the mâ of duration (see § 353*).

---

368. The *interjections* are numerous: among them we find يَا *O*! which is used before nouns (see § 438 *a*) without the article, as يَا قَوْمُ *O people*; أَيُّهَا or يَا أَيُّهَا *O*! used before nouns (see § 438 *b*) with the article, as يَا أَيُّهَا ٱلنَّاسُ *O men*; هَا *lo*! as هَا أَنْتُمْ أُولَاءِ *lo ye are those.*

---

369. The following pages supply paradigms of the verbs. First of all it is essential that Tables 1 and 2 be thoroughly well learnt; thus with كَلَمَ ـِ *to wound* (see § 35, rem. *a*).

kalama kalamat kalamta kalamti kalamtu
kalamâ kalamatâ kalamtumâ
kalamû kalamna kalamtum kalamtunna kalamnâ

yaklimu taklimu taklimu taklimîna 'aklimu
yaklimâni taklimâni taklimâni
yaklimûna yaklimna taklimûna taklimna naklimu

Also to be found in Table 1 are قَتَلَ ـُ *to kill*; جَمَعَ ـَ *to collect*; خَسِرَ ـَ *to lose*; and سَرُعَ ـُ *to be quick*.

Table 3 gives كَلَّمَ *to wound much* and *to address, accost*; قَاتَلَ *to fight with*; أَسْلَمَ *to turn Moslem*; تَكَلَّمَ *to speak*; تَقَاتَلَ *to fight with one another*; اِنْبَجَسَ *to gush*; اِفْتَرَقَ *to go asunder*; اِسْتَغْفَرَ *to ask pardon*; اِصْفَرَّ and اِصْفَارَّ *to be yellow*.

Table 5 *a b* and *c* give مَدَّ ـُ *to stretch*; حَبَّ ـِ *to be an object of love*; مَسَّ ـُ *to touch*; مَدَّدَ *to stretch much* or *often*; مَادَدَ and مَادَّ *to contend in pulling*; أَمَدَّ *to increase*; تَمَدَّدَ *to stretch oneself*; تَمَادَدَ and تَمَادَّ of two persons *together to stretch* a cloth; اِنْجَرَّ *to let oneself be dragged*; اِمْتَدَّ *to stretch oneself, to become extended*; اِسْتَمَدَّ *to ask succour*.

Table 6 gives أَدَبَ ـِ *to invite*; أَدُبَ ـُ *to be well brought up*; أَثَرَ ـُ *to relate*; أَلَهَ ـَ *to adore*; أَلِمَ ـَ *to suffer*; أَدَّبَ *to bestow a good education, punish*; آمَرَ *to consult with*; آسَفَ *to afflict*; تَأَذَّنَ *to proclaim*; تَآمَرَ and تَوَامَرَ *to deliberate in common*; اِيتَجَرَ and اِتَّجَرَ *to give alms, receive wages*; اِسْتَأْذَنَ *to ask permission*.

Table 7 gives بَؤُسَ ـُ *to be brave*; بَئِسَ ـَ *to be in distress*; سَأَلَ ـَ *to interrogate*; رَأَّسَ *to appoint as chief*; لَاءَمَ *to reconcile*; أَلْأَكَ *to send*; تَرَأَّسَ *to become chief*; تَبَاءَسَ *to feign poverty*; اِنْجَأَثَ *to split itself*; اِبْتَأَسَ *to abase oneself*; اِسْتَشْأَمَ *to deem unlucky*.

Table 8 gives هَنَأَ ـِ *to be pleasant*; دَنُؤَ ـُ *to be mean*; قَرَأَ ـَ *to read*; خَطِئَ ـَ *to do wrong*; نَبَّأَ *to inform*; قَارَأَ *to read together with, teach mutually*; أَقْرَأَ *to teach* one *to read* or *recite*; تَنَبَّأَ *to call oneself a prophet*; تَخَاطَأَ *wrongly to attribute error to oneself*; اِنْسَبَأَ of skin *to be stripped off*; اِهْتَنَأَ *to administer well*; اِسْتَقْرَأَ *to desire* one *to read*.

Table 9 gives وَعَدَ ـِ *to promise*; وَرِثَ ـِ *to inherit*; وَجِلَ ـَ *to fear*; يَسَرَ ـِ *to play at hazard* and *to be easy*; أَوْرَثَ *to cause to inherit*; أَيْقَنَ *to feel sure*; اِتَّعَظَ *to be admonished*; اِتَّسَرَ *to divide by lot a slain beast*; اِسْتَوْقَعَ *to expect*; اِسْتَيْسَرَ *to be easy*.

Tables 10 to 13 give قَالَ ـُ *to say*; سَارَ ـِ *to go*; خَافَ ـَ (for خَوِفَ) *to fear*; صَوَّرَ *to fashion*; سَيَّرَ *to make go*; طَاوَعَ *to comply with*; سَايَرَ *to accompany*; أَحَاطَ *to encompass, comprehend*; تَقَوَّلَ (see § 47) *to counterfeit, forge*; تَبَيَّنَ *to appear clear*; تَعَاوَنَ *to help one another*; تَسَايَرَ *to travel in company*; اِنْسَاقَ *to be driven*; اِخْتَارَ *to choose*; اِسْتَقَامَ *to hold oneself upright*.

Tables 14 to 18 give رَجَا ـُ *to hope for*; هَدَى ـِ *to direct*; نَسِيَ ـَ *to forget*; رَضِيَ ـَ *to be pleased*; عَدَّى *to make pass* and *to give* a verb *a transitive signification*; عَاطَى *to give mutually*; أَرْجَى *to put off*; تَجَلَّى *to make oneself manifest*; تَعَالَى *to exalt oneself*; اِنْجَلَى *to be cleared away*; اِهْتَدَى *to be directed aright*; اِسْتَسْقَى *to ask for drink*.

Concerning the vocalization of Derived Forms, it may be helpful to note that, in the perfect active, fatḥah is characteristic vowel of all: but in the imperfect active we find (except for IV having sukûn to the first radical) in Forms II III and IV

U A I . . . . يُسْلِمُ يُقَاتِلُ يُكَلِّمُ

in Forms V and VI

A A A A . . . . . . يَتَقَاتَلُ يَتَكَلَّمُ

and in Forms VII VIII and X (sukûn being duly noted)

A A I . . . . يَسْتَغْفِرُ يَفْتَرِقُ يَنْبَجِسُ

In the perfect passive we find

U I . . . . as أُسْلِمَ قُوتِلَ كُلِّمَ etc.

and in the imperfect passive

U A A . . . . as يُسْلَمُ يُقَاتَلُ يُكَلَّمُ etc.

NOTE. Nomina verbi are treated in §§ 195 to 212; while nomina agentis et patientis find place in §§ 229, 230, 236 sqq.

FIRST FORM OF THE STRONG VERB.

TABLE 1. ACTIVE.

Imperfect.				*Perfect.*	
Energ. I.	*Jussive.*	*Subj.*	*Indic.*		
يَكْلِمَنَّ	يَكْلِمْ	يَكْلِمَ	يَكْلِمُ	كَلَمَ	m. 3. Sing.
تَكْلِمَنَّ	تَكْلِمْ	تَكْلِمَ	تَكْلِمُ	كَلَمَتْ	f.
تَكْلِمَنَّ	تَكْلِمْ	تَكْلِمَ	تَكْلِمُ	كَلَمْتَ	m. 2.
تَكْلِمِنَّ	تَكْلِمِي	تَكْلِمِي	تَكْلِمِينَ	كَلَمْتِ	f.
أَكْلِمَنَّ	أَكْلِمْ	أَكْلِمَ	أَكْلِمُ	كَلَمْتُ	c. 1.
يَكْلِمَانِّ	يَكْلِمَا	يَكْلِمَا	يَكْلِمَانِ	كَلَمَا	m. 3. Dual
تَكْلِمَانِّ	تَكْلِمَا	تَكْلِمَا	تَكْلِمَانِ	كَلَمَتَا	f.
تَكْلِمَانِّ	تَكْلِمَا	تَكْلِمَا	تَكْلِمَانِ	كَلَمْتُمَا	c. 2.
يَكْلِمُنَّ	يَكْلِمُوا	يَكْلِمُوا	يَكْلِمُونَ	كَلَمُوا	m. 3. Plur.
يَكْلِمْنَانِّ	يَكْلِمْنَ	يَكْلِمْنَ	يَكْلِمْنَ	كَلَمْنَ	f.
تَكْلِمُنَّ	تَكْلِمُوا	تَكْلِمُوا	تَكْلِمُونَ	كَلَمْتُمْ	m. 2.
تَكْلِمْنَانِّ	تَكْلِمْنَ	تَكْلِمْنَ	تَكْلِمْنَ	كَلَمْتُنَّ	f.
نَكْلِمَنَّ	نَكْلِمْ	نَكْلِمَ	نَكْلِمُ	كَلَمْنَا	c. 1.

TABLE 1. (*continued.*)

Imperative.

Feminine	Common	Masculine	
إِكْلِمِي		إِكْلِمْ	2. Singular
	إِكْلِمَا		2. Dual
إِكْلِمْنَ		إِكْلِمُوا	2. Plural

VERBS WITH OTHER CHARACTERISTIC VOWELS.

We have seen however, in §§ 91, 92 and 93, that all strong verbs are not conjugated like the above; for instance,

Imperative	*Imperfect Indicative*	*Perfect*	
	يَقْتُلُ	قَتَلَ	m. 3. Singular
اُقْتُلْ.	تَقْتُلُ	قَتَلْتَ	m. 2.
	يَجْمَعُ	جَمَعَ	m. 3. Singular
اِجْمَعْ	تَجْمَعُ	جَمَعْتَ	m. 2.
	يَخْسَرُ	خَسِرَ	m. 3. Singular
اِخْسَرْ	تَخْسَرُ	خَسِرْتَ	m. 2.
	يَسْرُعُ	سَرُعَ	m. 3. Singular
اُسْرُعْ	تَسْرُعُ	سَرُعْتَ	m. 2.

FIRST FORM OF THE STRONG VERB.

TABLE 2. PASSIVE.

Imperfect.				*Perfect.*	
Energ. I.	*Jussive.*	*Subj.*	*Indic.*		
يُكْلَمَنَّ	يُكْلَمْ	يُكْلَمَ	يُكْلَمُ	كُلِمَ	m. 3. Sing.
تُكْلَمَنَّ	تُكْلَمْ	تُكْلَمَ	تُكْلَمُ	كُلِمَتْ	f.
تُكْلَمَنَّ	تُكْلَمْ	تُكْلَمَ	تُكْلَمُ	كُلِمْتَ	m. 2.
تُكْلَمِنَّ	تُكْلَمِي	تُكْلَمِي	تُكْلَمِينَ	كُلِمْتِ	f.
أُكْلَمَنَّ	أُكْلَمْ	أُكْلَمَ	أُكْلَمُ	كُلِمْتُ	c. 1.
يُكْلَمَانِّ	يُكْلَمَا	يُكْلَمَا	يُكْلَمَانِ	كُلِمَا	m. 3. Dual
تُكْلَمَانِّ	تُكْلَمَا	تُكْلَمَا	تُكْلَمَانِ	كُلِمَتَا	f.
تُكْلَمَانِّ	تُكْلَمَا	تُكْلَمَا	تُكْلَمَانِ	كُلِمْتُمَا	c. 2.
يُكْلَمُنَّ	يُكْلَمُوا	يُكْلَمُوا	يُكْلَمُونَ	كُلِمُوا	m. 3. Plur.
يُكْلَمْنَانِّ	يُكْلَمْنَ	يُكْلَمْنَ	يُكْلَمْنَ	كُلِمْنَ	f.
تُكْلَمُنَّ	تُكْلَمُوا	تُكْلَمُوا	تُكْلَمُونَ	كُلِمْتُمْ	m. 2.
تُكْلَمْنَانِّ	تُكْلَمْنَ	تُكْلَمْنَ	تُكْلَمْنَ	كُلِمْتُنَّ	f.
نُكْلَمَنَّ	نُكْلَمْ	نُكْلَمَ	نُكْلَمُ	كُلِمْنَا	c. 1.

DERIVED FORMS OF THE STRONG VERB.

TABLE 3.

PASSIVE.		ACTIVE.			
Indic.	*Perfect*	*Impera.*	*Indic.*	*Perfect*	
يُكَلَّمُ	كُلِّمَ	كَلِّمْ	يُكَلِّمُ	كَلَّمَ	II
يُقَاتَلُ	قُوتِلَ	قَاتِلْ	يُقَاتِلُ	قَاتَلَ	III
يُسْلَمُ	أُسْلِمَ	أَسْلِمْ	يُسْلِمُ	أَسْلَمَ	IV
يُتَكَلَّمُ	تُكُلِّمَ	تَكَلَّمْ	يَتَكَلَّمُ	تَكَلَّمَ	V
يُتَقَاتَلُ	تُقُوتِلَ	تَقَاتَلْ	يَتَقَاتَلُ	تَقَاتَلَ	VI
يُنْبَجَسُ	أُنْبُجِسَ	اِنْبَجِسْ	يَنْبَجِسُ	اِنْبَجَسَ	VII
يُفْتَرَقُ	اُفْتُرِقَ	اِفْتَرِقْ	يَفْتَرِقُ	اِفْتَرَقَ	VIII
		اِصْفَرِرْ	يَصْفَرُّ	اِصْفَرَّ	IX
يُسْتَغْفَرُ	اُسْتُغْفِرَ	اِسْتَغْفِرْ	يَسْتَغْفِرُ	اِسْتَغْفَرَ	X
		اِصْفَارِرْ	يَصْفَارُّ	اِصْفَارَّ	XI

FIRST FORM OF THE VERB WITH MIDDLE RADICAL DOUBLED.

TABLE 5. *a*. ACTIVE.

Imperfect.				*Perfect.*	
Energ. I.	*Jussive.*	*Subj.*	*Indic.*		
يَمُدَّنَّ	يَمْدُدْ	يَمُدَّ	يَمُدُّ	مَدَّ	m. 3. Sing.
تَمُدَّنَّ	تَمْدُدْ	تَمُدَّ	تَمُدُّ	مَدَّتْ	f.
تَمُدَّنَّ	تَمْدُدْ	تَمُدَّ	تَمُدُّ	مَدَدْتَ	m. 2.
تَمُدِّنَّ	تَمُدِّي	تَمُدِّي	تَمُدِّينَ	مَدَدْتِ	f.
أَمُدَّنَّ	أَمْدُدْ	أَمُدَّ	أَمُدُّ	مَدَدْتُ	c. 1.
يَمُدَّانِّ	يَمُدَّا	يَمُدَّا	يَمُدَّانِ	مَدَّا	m. 3. Dual
تَمُدَّانِّ	تَمُدَّا	تَمُدَّا	تَمُدَّانِ	مَدَّتَا	f.
تَمُدَّانِّ	تَمُدَّا	تَمُدَّا	تَمُدَّانِ	مَدَدْتُمَا	c. 2.
يَمُدُّنَّ	يَمُدُّوا	يَمُدُّوا	يَمُدُّونَ	مَدُّوا	m. 3. Plur.
يَمْدُدْنَانِّ	يَمْدُدْنَ	يَمْدُدْنَ	يَمْدُدْنَ	مَدَدْنَ	f.
تَمُدُّنَّ	تَمُدُّوا	تَمُدُّوا	تَمُدُّونَ	مَدَدْتُمْ	m. 2.
تَمْدُدْنَانِّ	تَمْدُدْنَ	تَمْدُدْنَ	تَمْدُدْنَ	مَدَدْتُنَّ	f.
نَمُدَّنَّ	نَمْدُدْ	نَمُدَّ	نَمُدُّ	مَدَدْنَا	c. 1.

TABLE 5. *a.* (*continued.*)

Imperative.

Feminine	Common	Masculine	
اُمْدُدِي		اُمْدُدْ	2. Singular
	اُمْدُدَا		2. Dual
اُمْدُدْنَ		اُمْدُدُوا	2. Plural

We find also in the Imperative مُدَّ, مُدِّ and مُدُّ; while the Jussive has also يَمُدَّ, يَمُدِّ and يَمُدُّ.

VERBS WITH OTHER CHARACTERISTIC VOWELS.

Attention is drawn in § 120 *b* to these verbs, which have other peculiarities beside those here noted:

Imperative.	*Imperfect.* *Jussive.*	*Imperfect.* *Indic.*	*Perfect.*	
	يَحْبِبْ يَحِبَّ يَحِبِّ	يَحِبُّ	حَبَّ	m. 3. Sing.
اِحْبِبْ حِبَّ حِبِّ	تَحْبِبْ تَحِبَّ تَحِبِّ	تَحِبُّ	حَبِبْتَ	m. 2.
	يَمْسُسْ يَمُسَّ يَمُسِّ يَمُسُّ	يَمُسُّ	مَسَّ	m. 3. Sing.
اُمْسُسْ مُسَّ مُسِّ مُسُّ	تَمْسُسْ تَمُسَّ تَمُسِّ تَمُسُّ	تَمُسُّ	مَسِسْتَ مِسْتَ	m. 2.

FIRST FORM OF THE VERB WITH MIDDLE RADICAL DOUBLED.

TABLE 5. *b*. PASSIVE.

Imperfect.				*Perfect.*
Energ. I.	*Jussive.*	*Subj.*	*Indic.*	
يُمَدَّنَّ	يُمْدَدْ	يُمَدَّ	يُمَدُّ	مُدَّ m. 3. Sing.
تُمَدَّنَّ	تُمْدَدْ	تُمَدَّ	تُمَدُّ	مُدَّتْ f.
تُمَدَّنَّ	تُمْدَدْ	تُمَدَّ	تُمَدُّ	مُدِدْتَ m. 2.
تُمَدِّنَّ	تُمَدِّي	تُمَدِّي	تُمَدِّينَ	مُدِدْتِ f.
أُمَدَّنَّ	أُمْدَدْ	أُمَدَّ	أُمَدُّ	مُدِدْتُ c. 1.
يُمَدَّانِّ	يُمَدَّا	يُمَدَّا	يُمَدَّانِ	مُدَّا m. 3. Dual
تُمَدَّانِّ	تُمَدَّا	تُمَدَّا	تُمَدَّانِ	مُدَّتَا f.
تُمَدَّانِّ	تُمَدَّا	تُمَدَّا	تُمَدَّانِ	مُدِدْتُمَا c. 2.
يُمَدُّنَّ	يُمَدُّوا	يُمَدُّوا	يُمَدُّونَ	مُدُّوا m. 3. Plur.
يُمْدَدْنَانِّ	يُمْدَدْنَ	يُمْدَدْنَ	يُمْدَدْنَ	مُدِدْنَ f.
تُمَدُّنَّ	تُمَدُّوا	تُمَدُّوا	تُمَدُّونَ	مُدِدْتُمْ m.
تُمْدَدْنَانِّ	تُمْدَدْنَ	تُمْدَدْنَ	تُمْدَدْنَ	مُدِدْتُنَّ f.
نُمَدَّنَّ	نُمْدَدْ	نُمَدَّ	نُمَدُّ	مُدِدْنَا c. 1.

DERIVED FORMS OF VERBS WITH MIDDLE RADICAL DOUBLED.

TABLE 5. *c.*

PASSIVE. *Indic.*	PASSIVE. *Perfect*	ACTIVE. *Impera.*	ACTIVE. *Indic.*	ACTIVE. *Perfect*	
يُمَدَّدُ	مُدِّدَ	مَدِّدْ	يُمَدِّدُ	مَدَّدَ	II
يُمَادَدُ يُمَادُّ	مُودِدَ	مَادِدْ	يُمَادِدُ يُمَادُّ	مَادَدَ مَادَّ	III
يُمَدُّ	أُمِدَّ	أَمْدِدْ أَمِدَّ	يُمِدُّ	أَمَدَّ	IV
يُتَمَدَّدُ	تُمُدِّدَ	تَمَدَّدْ	يَتَمَدَّدُ	تَمَدَّدَ	V
يُتَمَادَدُ يُتَمَادُّ	تُمُودِدَ	تَمَادَدْ	يَتَمَادَدُ يَتَمَادُّ	تَمَادَدَ تَمَادَّ	VI
يُنْجَرُّ	اُنْجُرَّ	اِنْجَرِرْ	يَنْجَرُّ	اِنْجَرَّ	VII
يُمْتَدُّ	اُمْتُدَّ	اِمْتَدِدْ اِمْتَدَّ	يَمْتَدُّ	اِمْتَدَّ	VIII
يُسْتَمَدُّ	اُسْتُمِدَّ	اِسْتَمْدِدْ اِسْتَمِدَّ	يَسْتَمِدُّ	اِسْتَمَدَّ	X

VERBS WITH INITIAL RADICAL HAMZATED.

TABLE 6.

PASSIVE.		ACTIVE.			
Indic.	*Perfect*	*Impera.*	*Indic.*	*Perfect*	
يُؤْدَبُ	أُدِبَ	اِيدِبْ	يَأْدِبُ	أَدَبَ	I
		اُودُبْ	يَأْدُبُ	أَدُبَ	I
يُؤْثَرُ	أُثِرَ	اُوثُرْ	يَأْثُرُ	أَثَرَ	I
يُؤْلَهُ	أُلِهَ	اِيلَهْ	يَأْلَهُ	أَلَهَ	I
يُؤْلَمُ	أُلِمَ	اِيلَمْ	يَأْلَمُ	أَلِمَ	I
يُؤَدَّبُ	أُدِّبَ	أَدِّبْ	يُؤَدِّبُ	أَدَّبَ	II
يُؤَامَرُ	أُومِرَ	آمِرْ	يُؤَامِرُ	آمَرَ	III
يُؤْسَفُ	أُوسِفَ	آسِفْ	يُؤْسِفُ	آسَفَ	IV
يُتَأَذَّنُ	تُؤُذِّنَ	تَأَذَّنْ	يَتَأَذَّنُ	تَأَذَّنَ	V
يُتَآمَرُ	تُـُومِرَ	تَآمَرْ	يَتَآمَرُ	تَآمَرَ	VI
يُتَوَامَرُ	تُوُومِرَ	تَوَامَرْ	يَتَوَامَرُ	تَوَامَرَ	VI
يُؤْتَجَرُ	اُوتُجِرَ	اِيتَجِرْ	يَأْتَجِرُ	اِيتَجَرَ	VIII
يُتَّجَرُ	اُتُّجِرَ	اِتَّجِرْ	يَتَّجِرُ	اِتَّجَرَ	VIII
يُسْتَأْذَنُ	اُسْتُؤْذِنَ	اِسْتَأْذِنْ	يَسْتَأْذِنُ	اِسْتَأْذَنَ	X

Form VII is not found.

VERBS WITH MIDDLE RADICAL HAMZATED.

TABLE 7.

PASSIVE. *Indic.*	PASSIVE. *Perfect*	ACTIVE. *Impera.*	ACTIVE. *Indic.*	ACTIVE. *Perfect*	
		اُبْؤُسْ	يَبْؤُسُ	بَؤُسَ	I
		اِبْأَسْ	يَبْأَسُ	بَئِسَ	
		اِبْئِسْ	يَبْئِسُ		
يُسْأَلُ	سُئِلَ	اِسْأَلْ	يَسْأَلُ	سَأَلَ	
يُسْئَلُ		اِسْئَلْ	يَسْئَلُ		
يُرَأَّسُ	رُئِّسَ	رَئِّسْ	يُرَئِّسُ	رَأَّسَ	II
يُلَاءَمُ	لُوئِمَ	لَائِمْ	يُلَائِمُ	لَاءَمَ	III
يُلْأَكُ	أُلْئِكَ	أَلْئِكْ	يُلْئِكُ	أَلْأَكَ	IV
يُتَرَأَّسُ	تُرُئِّسَ	تَرَأَّسْ	يَتَرَأَّسُ	تَرَأَّسَ	V
يُتَبَاءَسُ	تُبُوئِسَ	تَبَاءَسْ	يَتَبَاءَسُ	تَبَاءَسَ	VI
يُنْجَأَثُ	اُنْجُئِثَ	اِنْجَئِثْ	يَنْجَئِثُ	اِنْجَأَثَ	VII
يُبْتَأَسُ	اُبْتُئِسَ	اِبْتَئِسْ	يَبْتَئِسُ	اِبْتَأَسَ	VIII
يُسْتَشْأَمُ	اُسْتُشْئِمَ	اِسْتَشْئِمْ	يَسْتَشْئِمُ	اِسْتَشْأَمَ	X

VERBS WITH FINAL RADICAL HAMZATED.

TABLE 8.

PASSIVE.		ACTIVE.			
Indic.	*Perfect*	*Impera.*	*Indic.*	*Perfect*	
يُهْنَأُ	هُنِئَ	اِهْنِئْ	يَهْنِئُ	هَنَأَ	I
		اُدْنُؤْ	يَدْنُؤُ	دَنُؤَ	I
يُقْرَأُ	قُرِئَ	اِقْرَأْ	يَقْرَأُ	قَرَأَ	I
يُخْطَأُ	خُطِئَ	اِخْطَأْ	يَخْطَأُ	خَطِئَ	I
يُنَبَّأُ	نُبِّئَ	نَبِّئْ	يُنَبِّئُ	نَبَّأَ	II
يُقَارَأُ	قُورِئَ	قَارِئْ	يُقَارِئُ	قَارَأَ	III
يُقْرَأُ	أُقْرِئَ	أَقْرِئْ	يُقْرِئُ	أَقْرَأَ	IV
يُتَنَبَّأُ	تُنُبِّئَ	تَنَبَّأْ	يَتَنَبَّأُ	تَنَبَّأَ	V
يُتَخَاطَأُ	تُخُوطِئَ	تَخَاطَأْ	يَتَخَاطَأُ	تَخَاطَأَ	VI
يُنْسَبَأُ	اُنْسُبِئَ	اِنْسَبِئْ	يَنْسَبِئُ	اِنْسَبَأَ	VII
يُهْتَنَأُ	اُهْتُنِئَ	اِهْتَنِئْ	يَهْتَنِئُ	اِهْتَنَأَ	VIII
يُسْتَقْرَأُ	اُسْتُقْرِئَ	اِسْتَقْرِئْ	يَسْتَقْرِئُ	اِسْتَقْرَأَ	X

VERBS WITH و OR ي AS INITIAL RADICAL.

TABLE 9.

PASSIVE. Indic.	PASSIVE. Perfect	ACTIVE. Impera.	ACTIVE. Indic.	ACTIVE. Perfect	
يُوعَدُ	وُعِدَ	عِدْ	يَعِدُ	وَعَدَ	I
يُورَثُ	وُرِثَ	رِثْ	يَرِثُ	وَرِثَ	I
		اِيجَلْ	يَوْجَلُ	وَجِلَ	I
يُوسَرُ	يُسِرَ	اِيسِرْ	يَيْسِرُ	يَسَرَ	I
يُورَثُ	أُورِثَ	أَوْرِثْ	يُورِثُ	أَوْرَثَ	IV
يُوقَنُ	أُوقِنَ	أَيْقِنْ	يُوقِنُ	أَيْقَنَ	IV
يُتَّعَظُ	اُتُّعِظَ	اِتَّعِظْ	يَتَّعِظُ	اِتَّعَظَ	VIII
يُتَّسَرُ	اُتُّسِرَ	اِتَّسِرْ	يَتَّسِرُ	اِتَّسَرَ	VIII
يُسْتَوْقَعُ	اُسْتُوقِعَ	اِسْتَوْقِعْ	يَسْتَوْقِعُ	اِسْتَوْقَعَ	X
يُسْتَيْسَرُ	اُسْتُوسِرَ	اِسْتَيْسِرْ	يَسْتَيْسِرُ	اِسْتَيْسَرَ	X

Forms II, III, V and VI resemble strong verbs, and VII is not found

FIRST FORM OF THE VERB WITH و AS MIDDLE RADICAL.

TABLE 10. ACTIVE.

Imperfect.				*Perfect.*
Energ. I.	*Jussive.*	*Subj.*	*Indic.*	
يَقُولَنَّ	يَقُلْ	يَقُولَ	يَقُولُ	قَالَ m. 3. Sing.
تَقُولَنَّ	تَقُلْ	تَقُولَ	تَقُولُ	قَالَتْ f.
تَقُولَنَّ	تَقُلْ	تَقُولَ	تَقُولُ	قُلْتَ m. 2.
تَقُولِنَّ	تَقُولِي	تَقُولِي	تَقُولِينَ	قُلْتِ f.
أَقُولَنَّ	أَقُلْ	أَقُولَ	أَقُولُ	قُلْتُ c. 1.
يَقُولَانِّ	يَقُولَا	يَقُولَا	يَقُولَانِ	قَالَا m. 3. Dual
تَقُولَانِّ	تَقُولَا	تَقُولَا	تَقُولَانِ	قَالَتَا f.
تَقُولَانِّ	تَقُولَا	تَقُولَا	تَقُولَانِ	قُلْتُمَا c. 2.
يَقُولُنَّ	يَقُولُوا	يَقُولُوا	يَقُولُونَ	قَالُوا m. 3. Plur.
يَقُلْنَانِّ	يَقُلْنَ	يَقُلْنَ	يَقُلْنَ	قُلْنَ f.
تَقُولُنَّ	تَقُولُوا	تَقُولُوا	تَقُولُونَ	قُلْتُمْ m. 2.
تَقُلْنَانِّ	تَقُلْنَ	تَقُلْنَ	تَقُلْنَ	قُلْتُنَّ f.
نَقُولَنَّ	نَقُلْ	نَقُولَ	نَقُولُ	قُلْنَا c. 1.

TABLE 10. (*continued.*)

Imperative.

Feminine	Common	Masculine	
قُولِي		قُلْ	2. Singular
	قُولَا		2. Dual
قُلْنَ		قُولُوا	2. Plural.

TABLE 11.

Imperative.

Feminine	Common	Masculine	
سِيرِي		سِرْ	2. Singular
	سِيرَا		2. Dual
سِرْنَ		سِيرُوا	2. Plural

TABLE 11. *a.*

Imperative.

Feminine	Common	Masculine	
خَافِي		خَفْ	2. Singular
	خَافَا		2. Dual
خَفْنَ		خَافُوا	2. Plural

FIRST FORM OF THE VERB WITH ي AS MIDDLE RADICAL.

TABLE 11. (*continued from page* 124). ACTIVE.

Imperfect.				*Perfect.*	
Energ. I.	*Jussive.*	*Subj.*	*Indic.*		
يَسِيرَنَّ	يَسِرْ	يَسِيرَ	يَسِيرُ	سَارَ	m. 3. Sing.
تَسِيرَنَّ	تَسِرْ	تَسِيرَ	تَسِيرُ	سَارَتْ	f.
تَسِيرَنَّ	تَسِرْ	تَسِيرَ	تَسِيرُ	سِرْتَ	m. 2.
تَسِيرِنَّ	تَسِيرِي	تَسِيرِي	تَسِيرِينَ	سِرْتِ	f.
أَسِيرَنَّ	أَسِرْ	أَسِيرَ	أَسِيرُ	سِرْتُ	c. 1.
يَسِيرَانِّ	يَسِيرَا	يَسِيرَا	يَسِيرَانِ	سَارَا	m. 3. Dual
تَسِيرَانِّ	تَسِيرَا	تَسِيرَا	تَسِيرَانِ	سَارَتَا	f.
تَسِيرَانِّ	تَسِيرَا	تَسِيرَا	تَسِيرَانِ	سِرْتُمَا	c. 2.
يَسِيرُنَّ	يَسِيرُوا	يَسِيرُوا	يَسِيرُونَ	سَارُوا	m. 3. Plur.
يَسِرْنَانِّ	يَسِرْنَ	يَسِرْنَ	يَسِرْنَ	سِرْنَ	f.
تَسِيرُنَّ	تَسِيرُوا	تَسِيرُوا	تَسِيرُونَ	سِرْتُمْ	m. 2.
تَسِرْنَانِّ	تَسِرْنَ	تَسِرْنَ	تَسِرْنَ	سِرْتُنَّ	f.
نَسِيرَنَّ	نَسِرْ	نَسِيرَ	نَسِيرُ	سِرْنَا	c. 1.

FIRST FORM OF THE VERB WITH و KASRATED AS MIDDLE RADICAL.

TABLE 11. *a.* (*continued from page* 124). ACTIVE.

Imperfect. Energ. I.	Jussive.	Subj.	Indic.	*Perfect.*	
يَخَافَنَّ	يَخَفْ	يَخَافَ	يَخَافُ	خَافَ	m. 3. Sing.
تَخَافَنَّ	تَخَفْ	تَخَافَ	تَخَافُ	خَافَتْ	f.
تَخَافَنَّ	تَخَفْ	تَخَافَ	تَخَافُ	خِفْتَ	m. 2.
تَخَافِنَّ	تَخَافِي	تَخَافِي	تَخَافِينَ	خِفْتِ	f.
أَخَافَنَّ	أَخَفْ	أَخَافَ	أَخَافُ	خِفْتُ	c. 1.
يَخَافَانِّ	يَخَافَا	يَخَافَا	يَخَافَانِ	خَافَا	m. 3. Dual
تَخَافَانِّ	تَخَافَا	تَخَافَا	تَخَافَانِ	خَافَتَا	f.
تَخَافَانِّ	تَخَافَا	تَخَافَا	تَخَافَانِ	خِفْتُمَا	c. 2.
يَخَافُنَّ	يَخَافُوا	يَخَافُوا	يَخَافُونَ	خَافُوا	m. 3. Plur.
يَخَفْنَانِّ	يَخَفْنَ	يَخَفْنَ	يَخَفْنَ	خِفْنَ	f.
تَخَافُنَّ	تَخَافُوا	تَخَافُوا	تَخَافُونَ	خِفْتُمْ	m. 2.
تَخَفْنَانِّ	تَخَفْنَ	تَخَفْنَ	تَخَفْنَ	خِفْتُنَّ	f.
نَخَافَنَّ	نَخَفْ	نَخَافَ	نَخَافُ	خِفْنَا	c. 1.

FIRST FORM OF THE VERB WITH و OR ي AS MIDDLE RADICAL.

TABLE 12. PASSIVE.

Imperfect.				*Perfect.*
Energ. I.	*Jussive.*	*Subj.*	*Indic.*	
يُقَالَنَّ	يُقَلْ	يُقَالَ	يُقَالُ	قِيلَ m. 3. Sing.
تُقَالَنَّ	تُقَلْ	تُقَالَ	تُقَالُ	قِيلَتْ f.
تُقَالَنَّ	تُقَلْ	تُقَالَ	تُقَالُ	قِلْتَ m. 2.
تُقَالِنَّ	تُقَالِي	تُقَالِي	تُقَالِينَ	قِلْتِ f.
أُقَالَنَّ	أُقَلْ	أُقَالَ	أُقَالُ	قِلْتُ c. 1.
يُقَالَانِّ	يُقَالَا	يُقَالَا	يُقَالَانِ	قِيلَا m. 3. Dual
تُقَالَانِّ	تُقَالَا	تُقَالَا	تُقَالَانِ	قِيلَتَا f.
تُقَالَانِّ	تُقَالَا	تُقَالَا	تُقَالَانِ	قِلْتُمَا c. 2.
يُقَالُنَّ	يُقَالُوا	يُقَالُوا	يُقَالُونَ	قِيلُوا m. 3. Plur.
يُقَلْنَانِّ	يُقَلْنَ	يُقَلْنَ	يُقَلْنَ	قِلْنَ f.
تُقَالُنَّ	تُقَالُوا	تُقَالُوا	تُقَالُونَ	قِلْتُمْ m. 2.
تُقَلْنَانِّ	تُقَلْنَ	تُقَلْنَ	تُقَلْنَ	قِلْتُنَّ f.
نُقَالَنَّ	نُقَلْ	نُقَالَ	نُقَالُ	قِلْنَا c. 1.

DERIVED FORMS OF VERBS WITH و OR يِ AS MIDDLE RADICAL.

TABLE 13.

PASSIVE.		ACTIVE.			
Indic.	*Perfect*	*Impera.*	*Indic.*	*Perfect*	
يُصَوَّرُ	صُوِّرَ	صَوِّرْ	يُصَوِّرُ	صَوَّرَ	II
يُسَيَّرُ	سُيِّرَ	سَيِّرْ	يُسَيِّرُ	سَيَّرَ	
يُطَاوَعُ	طُووِعَ	طَاوِعْ	يُطَاوِعُ	طَاوَعَ	III
يُسَايَرُ	سُويِرَ	سَايِرْ	يُسَايِرُ	سَايَرَ	
يُحَاطُ	أُحِيطَ	أَحِطْ	يُحِيطُ	أَحَاطَ 3. m. Sing. أَحَطْتَ 2. m.	IV
يُتَقَوَّلُ	تُقُوِّلَ	تَقَوَّلْ	يَتَقَوَّلُ	تَقَوَّلَ	V
يُتَبَيَّنُ	تُبُيِّنَ	تَبَيَّنْ	يَتَبَيَّنُ	تَبَيَّنَ	
يُتَعَاوَنُ	تُعُووِنَ	تَعَاوَنْ	يَتَعَاوَنُ	تَعَاوَنَ	VI
يُتَسَايَرُ	تُسُويِرَ	تَسَايَرْ	يَتَسَايَرُ	تَسَايَرَ	
يُنْسَاقُ	اُنْسِيقَ	اِنْسَقْ	يَنْسَاقُ	اِنْسَاقَ 3. m. Sing. اِنْسَقْتَ 2. m.	VII
يُخْتَارُ	اُخْتِيرَ	اِخْتَرْ	يَخْتَارُ	اِخْتَارَ 3. m. Sing. اِخْتَرْتَ 2. m.	VIII
تُسْتَقَامُ	اُسْتُقِيمَ	اِسْتَقِمْ	يَسْتَقِيمُ	اِسْتَقَامَ 3. m. Sing. اِسْتَقَمْتَ 2. m.	X

FIRST FORM OF THE VERB WITH و AS FINAL RADICAL.

TABLE 14. ACTIVE.

Imperfect.				*Perfect.*	
Energ. I.	*Jussive.*	*Subj.*	*Indic.*		
يَرْجُوَنَّ	يَرْجُ	يَرْجُوَ	يَرْجُو	رَجَا	m. 3. Sing.
تَرْجُوَنَّ	تَرْجُ	تَرْجُوَ	تَرْجُو	رَجَتْ	f.
تَرْجُوَنَّ	تَرْجُ	تَرْجُوَ	تَرْجُو	رَجَوْتَ	m. 2.
تَرْجِنَّ	تَرْجِي	تَرْجِي	تَرْجِينَ	رَجَوْتِ	f.
أَرْجُوَنَّ	أَرْجُ	أَرْجُوَ	أَرْجُو	رَجَوْتُ	c. 1.
يَرْجُوَانِّ	يَرْجُوَا	يَرْجُوَا	يَرْجُوَانِ	رَجَوَا	m. 3. Dual
تَرْجُوَانِّ	تَرْجُوَا	تَرْجُوَا	تَرْجُوَانِ	رَجَتَا	f.
تَرْجُوَانِّ	تَرْجُوَا	تَرْجُوَا	تَرْجُوَانِ	رَجَوْتُمَا	c. 2.
يَرْجُنَّ	يَرْجُوا	يَرْجُوا	يَرْجُونَ	رَجَوْا	m. 3. Plur.
يَرْجُونَانِّ	يَرْجُونَ	يَرْجُونَ	يَرْجُونَ	رَجَوْنَ	f.
تَرْجُنَّ	تَرْجُوا	تَرْجُوا	تَرْجُونَ	رَجَوْتُمْ	m. 2.
تَرْجُونَانِّ	تَرْجُونَ	تَرْجُونَ	تَرْجُونَ	رَجَوْتُنَّ	f.
نَرْجُوَنَّ	نَرْجُ	نَرْجُوَ	نَرْجُو	رَجَوْنَا	c. 1.

TABLE 14. (*continued*).

Imperative.

Feminine	Common	Masculine	
اُرْجِي		اُرْجُ	2. Singular
	اُرْجُوَا		2. Dual
اُرْجُونَ		اُرْجُوا	2. Plural

TABLE 15.

Imperative.

Feminine	Common	Masculine	
اِهْدِي		اِهْدِ	2. Singular
	اِهْدِيَا		2. Dual
اِهْدِينَ		اِهْدُوا	2. Plural

TABLE 16.

Imperative.

Feminine	Common	Masculine	
اِرْضَيْ		اِرْضَ	2. Singular
	اِرْضَيَا		2. Dual
اِرْضَيْنَ		اِرْضَوْا	2. Plural

FIRST FORM OF THE VERB WITH ي AS FINAL RADICAL.

TABLE 15. (*continued from page* 130). ACTIVE.

Imperfect. Energ. I.	Jussive.	Subj.	Indic.	*Perfect.*	
يَهْدِيَنَّ	يَهْدِ	يَهْدِيَ	يَهْدِي	هَدَى	m. 3. Sing.
تَهْدِيَنَّ	تَهْدِ	تَهْدِيَ	تَهْدِي	هَدَتْ	f.
تَهْدِيَنَّ	تَهْدِ	تَهْدِيَ	تَهْدِي	هَدَيْتَ	m. 2.
تَهْدِنَّ	تَهْدِي	تَهْدِي	تَهْدِينَ	هَدَيْتِ	f.
أَهْدِيَنَّ	أَهْدِ	أَهْدِيَ	أَهْدِي	هَدَيْتُ	c. 1.
يَهْدِيَانِّ	يَهْدِيَا	يَهْدِيَا	يَهْدِيَانِ	هَدَيَا	m. 3. Dual
تَهْدِيَانِّ	تَهْدِيَا	تَهْدِيَا	تَهْدِيَانِ	هَدَتَا	f.
تَهْدِيَانِّ	تَهْدِيَا	تَهْدِيَا	تَهْدِيَانِ	هَدَيْتُمَا	c. 2.
يَهْدُنَّ	يَهْدُوا	يَهْدُوا	يَهْدُونَ	هَدَوْا	m. 3. Plur.
يَهْدِينَانِّ	يَهْدِينَ	يَهْدِينَ	يَهْدِينَ	هَدَيْنَ	f.
تَهْدُنَّ	تَهْدُوا	تَهْدُوا	تَهْدُونَ	هَدَيْتُمْ	m. 2.
تَهْدِينَانِّ	تَهْدِينَ	تَهْدِينَ	تَهْدِينَ	هَدَيْتُنَّ	f.
نَهْدِيَنَّ	نَهْدِ	نَهْدِيَ	نَهْدِي	هَدَيْنَا	c. 1.

FIRST FORM OF THE VERB WITH MIDDLE RADICAL KASRATED AND و OR ي AS FINAL RADICAL.

TABLE 16. (*continued from page* 130). ACTIVE.

Imperfect.				*Perfect.*	
Energ. I.	*Jussive.*	*Subj.*	*Indic.*		
يَرْضَيَنَّ	يَرْضَ	يَرْضَى	يَرْضَى	رَضِيَ	m. 3. Sing.
تَرْضَيَنَّ	تَرْضَ	تَرْضَى	تَرْضَى	رَضِيَتْ	f.
تَرْضَيَنَّ	تَرْضَ	تَرْضَى	تَرْضَى	رَضِيتَ	m. 2.
تَرْضَيِنَّ	تَرْضَيْ	تَرْضَيْ	تَرْضَيْنَ	رَضِيتِ	f.
أَرْضَيَنَّ	أَرْضَ	أَرْضَى	أَرْضَى	رَضِيتُ	c. 1.
يَرْضَيَانِّ	يَرْضَيَا	يَرْضَيَا	يَرْضَيَانِ	رَضِيَا	m. 3. Dual
تَرْضَيَانِّ	تَرْضَيَا	تَرْضَيَا	تَرْضَيَانِ	رَضِيَتَا	f.
تَرْضَيَانِّ	تَرْضَيَا	تَرْضَيَا	تَرْضَيَانِ	رَضِيتُمَا	c. 2.
يَرْضَوُنَّ	يَرْضَوْا	يَرْضَوْا	يَرْضَوْنَ	رَضُوا	m. 3. Plur.
يَرْضَيْنَانِّ	يَرْضَيْنَ	يَرْضَيْنَ	يَرْضَيْنَ	رَضِينَ	f.
تَرْضَوُنَّ	تَرْضَوْا	تَرْضَوْا	تَرْضَوْنَ	رَضِيتُمْ	m. 2.
تَرْضَيْنَانِّ	تَرْضَيْنَ	تَرْضَيْنَ	تَرْضَيْنَ	رَضِيتُنَّ	f.
نَرْضَيَنَّ	نَرْضَ	نَرْضَى	نَرْضَى	رَضِينَا	c. 1.

FIRST FORM OF THE VERB WITH و OR ي AS FINAL RADICAL.

TABLE 17. PASSIVE.

Imperfect.				Perfect.	
Energ. I.	*Jussive.*	*Subj.*	*Indic.*		
يُرْجَيَنَّ	يُرْجَ	يُرْجَى	يُرْجَى	رُجِيَ	m. 3. Sing.
تُرْجَيَنَّ	تُرْجَ	تُرْجَى	تُرْجَى	رُجِيَتْ	f.
تُرْجَيَنَّ	تُرْجَ	تُرْجَى	تُرْجَى	رُجِيتَ	m. 2.
تُرْجَيِنَّ	تُرْجَيْ	تُرْجَيْ	تُرْجَيْنَ	رُجِيتِ	f.
أُرْجَيَنَّ	أُرْجَ	أُرْجَى	أُرْجَى	رُجِيتُ	c. 1.
يُرْجَيَانِّ	يُرْجَيَا	يُرْجَيَا	يُرْجَيَانِ	رُجِيَا	m. 3. Dual
تُرْجَيَانِّ	تُرْجَيَا	تُرْجَيَا	تُرْجَيَانِ	رُجِيَتَا	f.
تُرْجَيَانِّ	تُرْجَيَا	تُرْجَيَا	تُرْجَيَانِ	رُجِيتُمَا	c. 2.
يُرْجَوُنَّ	يُرْجَوْا	يُرْجَوْا	يُرْجَوْنَ	رُجُوا	m. 3. Plur.
يُرْجَيْنَانِّ	يُرْجَيْنَ	يُرْجَيْنَ	يُرْجَيْنَ	رُجِينَ	f.
تُرْجَوُنَّ	تُرْجَوْا	تُرْجَوْا	تُرْجَوْنَ	رُجِيتُمْ	m. 2.
تُرْجَيْنَانِّ	تُرْجَيْنَ	تُرْجَيْنَ	تُرْجَيْنَ	رُجِيتُنَّ	f.
نُرْجَيَنَّ	نُرْجَ	نُرْجَى	نُرْجَى	رُجِينَا	c. 1.

DERIVED FORMS OF VERBS WITH و OR ي AS FINAL RADICAL.

TABLE 18.

Passive		Active			
Indic.	*Perfect*	*Impera.*	*Indic.*	*Perfect*	
يُعَدَّى	عُدِّيَ	عَدِّ	يُعَدِّي	عَدَّى	II
n. pat., m. مُعَدًّى f. مُعَدَّاةٌ		n. ag., m. مُعَدٍّ f. مُعَدِّيَةٌ			
يُعَاطَى	عُوطِيَ	عَاطِ	يُعَاطِي	عَاطَى	III
n. pat., m. مُعَاطًى f. مُعَاطَاةٌ		n. ag., m. مُعَاطٍ f. مُعَاطِيَةٌ			
يُرْجَى	أُرْجِيَ	أَرْجِ	يُرْجِي	أَرْجَى	IV
n. pat., m. مُرْجًى f. مُرْجَاةٌ		n. ag., m. مُرْجٍ f. مُرْجِيَةٌ			
يُتَجَلَّى	تُجُلِّيَ	تَجَلَّ	يَتَجَلَّى	تَجَلَّى	V
n. pat., m. مُتَجَلًّى f. مُتَجَلَّاةٌ		n. ag., m. مُتَجَلٍّ f. مُتَجَلِّيَةٌ			
يُتَعَالَى	تُعُولِيَ	تَعَالَ	يَتَعَالَى	تَعَالَى	VI
n. pat., m. مُتَعَالًى f. مُتَعَالَاةٌ		n. ag., m. مُتَعَالٍ f. مُتَعَالِيَةٌ			
يُنْجَلَى	أُنْجُلِيَ	اِنْجَلِ	يَنْجَلِي	اِنْجَلَى	VII
n. pat., m. مُنْجَلًى f. مُنْجَلَاةٌ		n. ag., m. مُنْجَلٍ f. مُنْجَلِيَةٌ			
يُهْتَدَى	أُهْتُدِيَ	اِهْتَدِ	يَهْتَدِي	اِهْتَدَى	VIII
n. pat., m. مُهْتَدًى f. مُهْتَدَاةٌ		n. ag., m. مُهْتَدٍ f. مُهْتَدِيَةٌ			
يُسْتَسْقَى	أُسْتُسْقِيَ	اِسْتَسْقِ	يَسْتَسْقِي	اِسْتَسْقَى	X
n. pat., m. مُسْتَسْقًى f. مُسْتَسْقَاةٌ		n. ag., m. مُسْتَسْقٍ f. مُسْتَسْقِيَةٌ			

PART III.

SYNTAX.

[*From section numbers below there must be subtracted* 400, *in order to ascertain the corresponding section of Wright's Arabic Grammar, vol. ii.*]

401. We have observed in § 77 that an Arabic verb has two States: of these the *Perfect* indicates,—

(*a*) an act completed at some time past, as نَزَعَ مُوسَى يَدَهُ *Moses plucked out his hand*;

(*b*) an act which has been already completed at the moment of speaking, and remains so, thus أَغَيْرَ ٱللّٰهِ أَبْغِيكُمْ إِلٰهًا وَهُوَ فَضَّلَكُمْ عَلَى ٱلْعَالَمِينَ *shall I seek for you an object of worship other than God, seeing that He has favoured you above all creatures?*

(*c*) a past action which still continues, as وَسِعَ كُرْسِيُّهُ ٱلسَّمٰوَاتِ *His throne comprises the heavens,* مَا أَصَابَ مِنْ مُصِيبَةٍ إِلَّا بِإِذْنِ ٱللّٰهِ *no mischance befalls except by permission of God*;

(*d*) an act just completed at the moment of speaking, as تُبْتُ إِلَيْكَ *I repent toward Thee*;

(*e*) in treaties, promises, bargains and the like, an act which, though future, is quite certain;

(*f*) something desired, as رَحِمَهُ ٱللّٰهُ *God have mercy upon him,* صَلَّى ٱللّٰهُ عَلَيْهِ وَسَلَّمَ *God bless him and grant him peace.*

REM. Europeans translate تَبَارَكَ ٱللّٰهُ رَبُّ ٱلْعَالَمِينَ *blessed be God the Lord of all creatures,* but the verb is declarative (see § 50, rem. *a*).

402. The perfect is often preceded by قَدْ (see § 362 *z*) to add assurance of completeness; which may lie

(*a*) in certainty, as قَدْ أَرْسَلْنَا نُوحًا *We sent Noah,* فَٱنْبَجَسَتْ مِنْهُ ٱثْنَتَا عَشْرَةَ عَيْنًا قَدْ عَلِمَ كُلُّ أُنَاسٍ مَشْرَبَهُمْ *so from it twelve springs gushed, every tribe assuredly knew their drinking-place*; or

(*b*) in being expected or contrary to expectation, as قَدْ جِئْتُكُمْ بِبَيِّنَةٍ *I have brought you evidence.*

NOTE. If preceded by affirmative لَ (see § 361 *c*) the influence of قَدْ is in no way affected.

403. The pluperfect is expressed,—

(*a*) by the simple perfect in a relative or conjunctive clause* which depends upon a clause in which the verb is perfect; thus تَمَّتْ كَلِمَتُ رَبِّكَ ٱلْحُسْنَى عَلَى بَنِي إِسْرَآئِيلَ بِمَا صَبَرُوا *the most gracious word of thy Lord was fulfilled to the sons of Israel by reason of what they had endured*; فَلَمَّا أَلْقَوْا سَحَرُوا أَعْيُنَ ٱلنَّاسِ *so when they had cast, they bewitched men's eyes*;

(*b*) by the perfect and قَدْ, with or without وَ, provided the preceding clause has its verb in the perfect, as وَلَمَّا رَأَوْا أَنَّهُمْ قَدْ ضَلُّوا *and when they saw that they had erred*;

(*c*) by كَانَ *to be* prefixed to the perfect;

---

* A relative or conjunctive clause is one coupled to its ruling clause by a relative pronoun or connective particle.

(*d*) by كَانَ and the perfect, with قَدْ interposed, or prefixed.

404. (*a*) When two correlative clauses follow لَوْ *if* (see §§ 367 *o* and 588) or any similar hypothetical particle, perfect verbs in both clauses may correspond with the English pluperfect subjunctive; as لَوْ شِئْتَ أَهْلَكْتَهُمْ مِنْ قَبْلُ *if Thou hadst wished Thou wouldst have destroyed them beforehand.*

405. After إِذَا *whenever, as often as* (see 367 *b*) a perfect is said to take the imperfect's meaning; and perfect verbs in two correlative clauses have either a present or future signification, provided the first clause extends its conversive influence to the verb of the second; thus فَإِذَا جَآءَتْهُمُ ٱلْحَسَنَةُ قَالُوا لَنَا هٰذِهِ *and whenever a boon comes to them they will say, This (boon) is due to us.* Sometimes إِذَا is followed by an imperfect, and sometimes preceded by كَانَ or the like.

Rem. *c.* So also with two perfect verbs after حَتَّى إِذَا (see § 415 *c*) as حَتَّى إِذَا أَقَلَّتْ سَحَابًا سُقْنَاهُ *until, when they (the winds) bear cloud, We drive it*; or in English idiom, *till they bear cloud, when We drive it.*

406. (*a*) After إِنْ *if* (see § 367 *f*) and words similarly of conditional meaning, the perfect is said to take a future sense and can be rendered by the English present; as, for instance, after مَنْ *who, whoever,* مَا *what,* مَهْمَا *whatever,* حَيْثُ *where,* and the like. Thus إِنْ كُنَّا نَحْنُ ٱلْغَالِبِينَ *if we be the victors,* مَنْ يُوقَ شُحَّ نَفْسِهِ *whoever is made to guard against his own covetousness,* إِلَّا مَا شَآءَ *except what he wishes,* كُلُوا حَيْثُ شِئْتُمْ *eat wherever ye wish.* In certain cases this rule applies to أَوْ *or.*

(*b*) If the words إِنْ etc. be followed by two clauses, the first expressing a condition and the second its result, both verbs may be perfect.

(*c*) If the perfect after إِنْ etc. is to keep its original sense, كَانَ or one of أَخَوَاتُ كَانَ *the sisters of the verb kâna* (see § 442) must stand in the protasis before the verb and فَ must mark the apodosis. Thus إِنْ كُنْتَ جِئْتَ بِآيَةٍ فَأْتِ بِهَا إِنْ كُنْتَ مِنَ ٱلصَّادِقِينَ *if thou hast brought a sign, produce it, if thou art of the truthful.*

(*d* and *e*) Other cases arise in the use of إِنْ and similar words.

Rem. *c*. When مَا etc. are interrogatives or simple relatives, and حَيْثُ a simple relative adverb, without any conditional signification, perfects dependent upon them keep their original sense.

407. After مَا *as long as* (see § 367 *p*) the perfect has a present or future signification; thus اِتَّقُوا ٱللّٰهَ مَا ٱسْتَطَعْتُمْ *fear God as far as ye are able.*

408. The *Imperfect Indicative* expresses no temporal definition, but indicates a state existing at any time. Hence it signifies ;—

(*a*) what is always taking, or may at any time take, place (the indefinite present); as يَخْرُجُ نَبَاتُهُ بِإِذْنِ رَبِّهِ *its (the land's) plants come forth by permission of its Lord*:

(*b*) an incomplete act, commenced and continuing (the definite present); as أَنْصَحُ لَكُمْ *I counsel you*:

(c) what will occur (the simple future), as كَذٰلِكَ نُخْرِجُ ٱلْمَوْتَى *thus shall We bring forth the dead*; اُذْكُرْ يَوْمَ يَجْمَعُكُمْ *make mention of the day whereon He shall assemble you.* The future sense may be made more distinct by using سَوْفَ (see § 364 *e*), thus فَسَوْفَ تَعْلَمُونَ *so ye shall know*; or سَ (see § 361 *b*), thus سَنَزِيدُ ٱلْمُحْسِنِينَ *We will give increase to the righteous.*

(d) When appended to the perfect without intervening particle, it expresses (either what is explained in the following subsection, or) an act which was future to the past time of which we speak; thus أَرْسَلَ يُعْلِمُهُ بِذٰلِكَ *he sent to inform him of this,* أَجْمَعَ يَمْكُرُ بِالْيَهُودِ *he determined to circumvent the Jews.*

(e) Under circumstances similar to those mentioned in the preceding subsection, the imperfect indicative frequently expresses an act which continues during the past time, and then it can be translated by the English present participle; thus أَخَذَ بِرَاسِ أَخِيهِ يَجُرُّهُ إِلَيْهِ *he grasped the head of his brother, dragging it towards himself*; وَرِثُوا ٱلْكِتَابَ يَأْخُذُونَ عَرَضَ هٰذَا ٱلْأَدْنَى وَيَقُولُونَ سَيُغْفَرُ لَنَا *they inherited the book, taking the vain goods of this nearer* (i.e. the present world) *and saying, We shall be pardoned.*

Rem. *a.* After لَا *not* the imperfect indicative retains its idea of incompleteness and duration, as ٱلَّذِي خَبُثَ لَا يَخْرُجُ إِلَّا نَكِدًا *as to that (land) which is bad (its plants) do not come forth except scantily.* After مَا *not* it has the present sense (see § 557), as مَا تَنْقِمُ مِنَّا *thou dost not take vengeance on us.*

409. By prefixing كَانَ to the imperfect indicative we point out a past act which continued or was repeated; thus بَطَلَ مَا كَانُوا يَعْمَلُونَ *worthless was what they were doing*, ٱلَّذِينَ كَانُوا يُسْتَضْعَفُونَ *who used to be esteemed weak.*

411. The *Subjunctive* mood has always a future sense after the adverb لَنْ *not* (see § 362 *hh*), as لَنْ تَرَانِي *thou shalt not see Me*; also after certain conjunctions, amongst which are أَنْ *that*, as يُرِيدُ أَنْ يُخْرِجَكُمْ *he wishes that he may expel you*; أَنْ لَا (pronounced أَلَّا see § 14 *b*, rem. *b*) *that not*, as حَقِيقٌ عَلَيَّ أَنْ لَا أَقُولَ عَلَى ٱللّٰهِ إِلَّا ٱلْحَقَّ (*it is*) *binding on me that I shall not speak concerning God except the truth*; and لِ *that, so that*, as أَتَذَرُ مُوسَى لِيُفْسِدَ فِي ٱلْأَرْضِ وَيَذَرَكَ وَآلِهَتَكَ *dost thou leave Moses so that he shall commit disorders in the land and shall leave thee and thy gods?* For further particulars see § 415.

412. The *Jussive* mood takes the perfect's meaning when preceded by لَمْ *not* (see § 362 *ff*) or لَمَّا *not yet*, as أَلَمْ يُؤْخَذْ عَلَيْهِمْ مِيثَاقُ ٱلْكِتَابِ *has not the covenant of the book been made with them?* See § 418.

413. The jussive after إِنْ *if* and words of conditional sense (see § 406) has the same meaning as the perfect in a similar situation; as إِنْ تُصِبْهُمْ سَيِّئَةٌ يَطَّيَّرُوا بِمُوسَى وَمَنْ مَعَهُ *if an evil befall them, they attribute their bad luck to Moses and those who are with him*; مَهْمَا تَأْتِنَا بِهِ مِنْ آيَةٍ لِتَسْحَرَنَا بِهَا *whatever sign thou bringest us in order that thou mayest bewitch us thereby.* When the first of two correlative clauses contains an imperative,

and the second a jussive, the latter has the same meaning as if the first clause contained a verb in the jussive preceded by إِنْ ; thus أُدْخُلُوا ٱلْبَابَ نَغْفِرْ لَكُمْ خَطِيئَاتِكُمْ *enter the gate* (*and*) *We will pardon to you your sins* meaning *if ye enter the gate We will pardon you.* See § 417 *c* ii.

414. The imperfect *Energetics* are future in sense, as لَأُقَطِّعَنَّ أَيْدِيَكُمْ وَأَرْجُلَكُمْ مِنْ خِلَافٍ ثُمَّ لَأُصَلِّبَنَّكُمْ *I will cut off your hands and feet on opposite sides, then I will crucify you.* See § 419.

---

415. The *Subjunctive* mood, which can occur only in a subordinate clause, indicates an act dependent upon, and future to, that mentioned in the previous clause: it is governed by certain particles, amongst which are the following.

(*a*) i. By أَنْ (see § 367 *e*) *that* after verbs expressing inclination, order, permission, necessity etc.; as also by أَنْ لَا *that not* and لَنْ *not* (see § 362 *hh*). Thus عَسَى رَبُّكُمْ أَنْ يُهْلِكَ عَدُوَّكُمْ *your Lord may perhaps destroy your enemies*; see also examples in § 411.

NOTE. When إِمَّا (see § 367 *f*) is used, the ruling verb may be understood, as قَالُوا يَا مُوسَى إِمَّا أَنْ تُلْقِيَ وَإِمَّا أَنْ نَكُونَ نَحْنُ ٱلْمُلْقِينَ *they said, O Moses* (*choose*) *either that thou or we throw.* We find أَنْ لَنْ as زَعَمَ ٱلَّذِينَ كَفَرُوا أَنْ لَنْ يُبْعَثُوا *the unbelievers have asserted that they shall not be raised* (*from the dead*): here أَنْ stands for أَنَّهُمْ, and this is common when the verb is negatived, as well as when the verb is strengthened with قَدْ, سَ or سَوْفَ.

ii. But if the ruling verb makes an assertion (without expectation, wish, or the like) and the verb following أَنْ is to express a past or present sense we use the perfect or imperfect indicative after أَنْ. Thus عَجِبْتُمْ أَنْ جَآءَكُمْ ذِكْرٌ *ye wonder that an admonition has come to you*, أَعْلَمُ أَنْ يَنَامُ *I know that he is sleeping.* It is however more usual in this case to employ a nominal proposition (see § 513) using أَنَّ with a pronoun; thus يَعْلَمُ أَنَّكَ تَقُومُ *he knows that thou standest*, أَلَمْ يَرَوْا أَنَّهُ لَا يُكَلِّمُهُمْ *could they not perceive that it (the calf) did not speak to them?* If the ruling verb expresses doubt or supposition concerning a thing future, أَنْ may govern the imperfect indicative or subjunctive; as ظَنُّوا أَنْ يَقَعُ عَلَيْهِمْ *they thought it was about to fall upon them.*

Rem. *a.* As regards أَنِ ٱلْمَصْدَرِيَّةُ *the 'an which with its verb is equivalent to a maçdar*, see § 488.

(*b*) By لِ *in order that* (see § 366 *c* ii) and its compounds; thus إِنَّ هٰذَا لَمَكْرٌ مَكَرْتُمُوهُ فِي ٱلْمَدِينَةِ لِتُخْرِجُوا مِنْهَا أَهْلَهَا *verily this is a plot which ye have contrived in the city in order that ye may drive out of it its people.*

Rem. *a.* Originally لِ was a preposition (see § 356 *c*), and when a conjunction it stands for لِأَنْ *for that*, as is seen in the negative لِئَلَّا (for لِأَنْ لَا): we cannot say لِلَا.

(*c*) By حَتَّى *till* (also originally a preposition, see § 358 *b*): but if no intention or expectation of the agent be implied, there follows the indicative, or as in § 405, rem. *c*, the perfect.

(*d*) By فَ *so that* when it introduces a clause giving the result or effect of a preceding clause which expresses a wish; thus عَسَى رَبُّكُمْ أَنْ يَسْتَخْلِفَكُمْ فِي ٱلْأَرْضِ فَيَنْظُرَ كَيْفَ تَعْمَلُونَ *your Lord may perhaps make you successors in the land, so that He may see how ye act.* There are other conditions under which فَ governs a subjunctive.

416. The Indicative must be used in all clauses except those governed by أَنْ or other particle with sense of أَنْ; as كَذٰلِكَ نُصَرِّفُ ٱلْآيَاتِ لِقَوْمٍ يَشْكُرُونَ *thus We diversify the signs to a grateful people*; أَعْلَمُ مِنَ ٱللّٰهِ مَا لَا تَعْلَمُونَ *I know from God what ye know not*; تُضِلُّ مَنْ تَشَآءُ وَتَهْدِي مَنْ تَشَآءُ *Thou causest to err whomsoever Thou dost wish, and Thou leadest aright whom Thou dost will*; لَعَلَّهُمْ يَذَّكَّرُونَ *perhaps they will take warning*; إِذَا هُمْ يَنْكُثُونَ *lo, they break their promise*; إِذْ يَعْدُونَ فِي ٱلسَّبْتِ *when they transgress on the Sabbath.*

417. The *Jussive* usually conveys an order, being connected in form with the imperative.

(*a*) It is used with لِ prefixed (the li of command, see § 366 *c* i) in place of the imperative; and if وَ or فَ be also employed, we may write لْ: thus عَلَى ٱللّٰهِ فَلْيَتَوَكَّلِ ٱلْمُؤْمِنُونَ *upon God then let the believers rely* (as to this verb's final vowel, see § 20 *d*). We seldom find لِ thus used except with the 3rd person, which is wanting to the imperative.

(*b*) With the adverb لَا (see § 362 *dd*) we use it to express a prohibition, or a wish that something be not done; as لَا تُفْسِدْ *do not thou* (masc.) *commit disorders*; لَا تُشْمِتْ بِيَ ٱلْأَعْدَآءَ وَلَا

تَجْعَلْنِي مَعَ ٱلْقَوْمِ ٱلظَّالِمِينَ *do not thou make mine enemies to rejoice at my trouble, and do not place me with the wrongdoers.*

(*c*) i. Also we find jussives in the protasis and apodosis of correlative conditional clauses, which depend upon إِنْ or any particle having the sense of إِنْ (see §§ 406 and 413): in the protasis, when the verb is without كَانَ and is imperfect; in the apodosis, when without فَ and having an imperfect verb. Thus إِنْ يَرَوْا سَبِيلَ ٱلْغَيِّ يَتَّخِذُوهُ سَبِيلًا *if they see the path of error, they will adopt it for their path*; إِنْ تَأْتِهِ عَرَضٌ مِثْلُهُ يَأْخُذْهُ *if worthless gain come to him like it* (the former) *he accepts it* (*also*); مَنْ يُؤْمِنْ بِٱللّٰهِ يَهْدِ قَلْبَهُ *whosoever believes in God, He shall direct his heart.* If however فَ marks the apodosis, we must use an indicative; as مَنْ يُؤْمِنْ بِرَبِّهِ فَلَا يَخَافُ *whosoever believes in his Lord, does not fear.*

ii. The jussive may appear in apodosis when the protasis contains an imperative verb; as فَخُذِ ٱلْأَلْوَاحَ بِقُوَّةٍ وَأْمُرْ قَوْمَكَ يَأْخُذُوا بِأَحْسَنِهَا *and thereupon* (*We said*) *Take the tables with force, and command thy people* (*so*) *shall they grasp the best part thereof*; أَرْسِلْ حَاشِرِينَ يَأْتُوكَ بِكُلِّ سَاحِرٍ عَلِيمٍ *send gatherers* (*and*) *they shall bring thee every skilled magician*; أَرِنِي أَنْظُرْ إِلَيْكَ *show me* (*Thyself, and*) *I shall look upon thee.* This construction is explained in § 413.

Rem. *b.* The conditional sentence whose apodosis must be introduced by فَ is further treated in § 587.

Rem. *c.* When (1) the apodosis has a jussive, connected with a following imperfect by فَ or وَ, we usually employ the jussive again; thus إِنْ تُقْرِضُوا ٱللّٰهَ قَرْضًا حَسَنًا يُضَاعِفْهُ لَكُمْ وَيَغْفِرْ لَكُمْ *if ye lend to God a fair loan, he will multiply it to you and will pardon you*: so when (2) the protasis has a jussive, connected with the following imperfect by فَ or وَ; as إِنْ تَعْفُوا وَتَصْفَحُوا وَتَغْفِرُوا فَإِنَّ ٱللّٰهَ غَفُورٌ رَحِيمٌ *if ye condone and pardon and forgive, surely God is forgiving and merciful.* Here also مَنْ يُؤْمِنْ بِٱللّٰهِ وَيَعْمَلْ صَالِحًا يُكَفِّرْ عَنْهُ سَيِّئَاتِهِ وَيُدْخِلْهُ جَنَّاتٍ *whoso believes in God and does right, He shall efface from him his misdeeds and shall cause him to enter gardens (of Paradise).*

418. The jussive is also used with the perfect's meaning, as we have seen in § 412, after لَمْ *not* or لَمَّا *not yet*; but in these cases we have the jussive's form and not its sense. Thus أَلَمْ يَأْتِكُمْ نَبَأٌ *has there not reached you a story?*

NOTE. When إِنْ *if* precedes, we observe § 406 *a*; thus إِنْ لَمْ يَرْحَمْنَا رَبُّنَا *if our Lord do not show us mercy.*

419. The imperfect *Energetic* (see § 414) has several uses, amongst which are the following:—

(*a*) With لَ *verily* (see § 361 *c*) prefixed to it in a simple asseveration, thus تَأَذَّنَ رَبُّكَ لَيَبْعَثَنَّ عَلَيْهِمْ مَنْ يَسُومُهُمْ سُوءَ ٱلْعَذَابِ *thy Lord proclaimed (that) he would surely send against them one who should afflict them with woeful torment*; and in asseverations strengthened by an oath, thus قُلْ بَلَى وَرَبِّي لَتُبْعَثُنَّ ثُمَّ لَتُنَبَّؤُنَّ بِمَا عَمِلْتُمْ *say, On the contrary, by my Lord, ye shall be raised (from the dead), then ye shall be informed of what ye have done.*

(*c*) With لَ in the apodosis of correlative conditional clauses in which case لَ must be prefixed to the protasis also, as لَئِنْ لَمْ يَغْفِرْ لَنَا رَبُّنَا لَنَكُونَنَّ مِنَ ٱلْخَاسِرِينَ *verily if our Lord do not pardon us, we shall surely be of those who suffer loss.*

420. The *Imperative* cannot be used in negative sense: instead we must employ the jussive as in § 417 *b*. Thus هُدْ *repent thou*, لَا تَهُدْ *do not (thou) repent*; كَلِّمْنَا بِٱلْعَرَبِيَّةِ وَلَا تُكَلِّمْنَا بِٱلْإِنْكِلِيزِيَّةِ *speak Arabic to us, do not speak in English.*

---

421. The verb may govern a noun in its accusative (or oblique) case, and by help of a preposition a noun which we then put in the dependent (or oblique) case. We shall have frequent examples of this government, not only by States and Moods, but also by nomina actionis, agentis, et patientis and by other nouns possessing verbal force. Sometimes the verb is understood; or it may lie concealed in a particle.

422. The *accusative* of a noun is governed by the verb, either

(*a*) as an objective complement, assigning a limit; or

(*b*) as an adverbial complement, see § 440 et seq.

423. Most *transitive* verbs take their objective complement in the accusative, as لَا تَتَّبِعْ سَبِيلَ ٱلْمُفْسِدِينَ *do not thou follow the path of the transgressors*; many however govern the object by help of a preposition, as لَمَّا وَقَعَ عَلَيْهِمُ ٱلرِّجْزُ *when the plague fell upon them*; some govern in both ways with the same meaning, thus كَذَّبُوهُ *they accused him of lying*, and أَغْرَقْنَا ٱلَّذِينَ كَذَّبُوا بِآيَاتِنَا *We drowned those who charged with falsehood Our signs.* More frequently a verb which governs in both ways has

different meanings, thus مَسَّكَهُ *he perfumed it with musk*, مَسَّكَ بِهِ *he held it fast*; and diverse significations may attach to the same verb if used with different prepositions, thus رَغِبَ ـَ *to desire*, which is transitive and intransitive, has رَغِبَ فِي *to like*, رَغِبَ عَنْ *to dislike*, and رَغِبَ إِلَى *to supplicate*.

Rem. *a*. Amongst ٱلْأَفْعَالُ ٱلْمُتَعَدِّيَةُ *the transitive verbs* (see § 75) we include those which govern by help of a preposition alike with those whose object is in the accusative. Besides being transitive as وَقَعَ عَلَى *to fall upon*, the same verb may be intransitive as وَقَعَ *to befall, come to pass*, thus فَوَقَعَ ٱلْحَقُّ *so the truth was established*.

Rem. *b*. Dictionaries will teach a student how each verb may be employed. Be it observed that, in Arabic, verbs *to come* govern the accusative and require no intervening preposition, thus أَتَيْتُهُ *I came to him*, أَتَيْتُهَا بِهِ *I came to her with it*, i.e. I brought it to her, جَآءَ ٱلسَّحَرَةُ فِرْعَوْنَ *the magicians came to Pharaoh*, جَآؤُوا بِسِحْرٍ عَظِيمٍ *they brought a mighty enchantment* (see § 456 *b*).

Rem. *c*. A sentence may stand as objective complement, thus دَمَّرْنَا مَا كَانَ يَصْنَعُ *We destroyed what he was making* (see § 514). As regards قَالَ *to say* and its derivatives we may note, that when followed by حِكَايَةٌ *a narration* one uses قَالَ إِنَّ, thus قُلْ إِنِّي رَسُولُ ٱللّٰهِ إِلَيْكُمْ *say thou, Verily I am God's apostle to you*, and what follows it is commonly a quotation, as قَالَ إِنَّكُمْ قَوْمٌ تَجْهَلُونَ *he said, Certainly ye are an ignorant people*. Very sparingly, if at all, is it permitted to use قَالَ أَنَّ.

424. Two objective complements in the accusative may follow certain verbs, of which there are two sorts.

(*a*) Those whose objects are unconnected, they being causatives of which the ground form is transitive and governs an accusative (see § 41 and § 45); thus أُبَلِّغُكُمْ رِسَالَاتِ *I bring you messages*, يُغْشِي ٱللَّيْلَ ٱلنَّهَارَ *He causes the night to cover the day*, خُذُوا مَا آتَيْنَاكُمْ *take what We have given you*, سَأُرِيكُمْ دَارَ ٱلْفَاسِقِينَ *I will show you the dwelling of the impious*, يُورِثُهَا مَنْ يَشَآءُ مِنْ عِبَادِهِ *He causes whom He will of His servants to inherit it*: also some other verbs of causative nature, meaning *to give*, *lend*, etc. as كُلُوا مَا رَزَقْنَاكُمْ *eat what We have provided for you*, اِهْدِنَا ٱلصِّرَاطَ ٱلْمُسْتَقِيمَ *direct us* (*in*) *the straight road*, لَا يَهْدِيهِمْ سَبِيلًا *it* (*the calf*) *did not direct them* (*in*) *a* (*right*) *path*, يَسُومُونَكُمْ سُوٓءَ ٱلْعَذَابِ *they lay upon you the evil of punishment*, وَاعَدْنَا مُوسَى ثَلَاثِينَ لَيْلَةً *We appointed with Moses* (*a period of*) *thirty nights*.

(*b*) Those whose objects stand to one another in the relation of subject and predicate; being (i) verbs signifying *to make*, *adopt*, *name*, *appoint*, etc., as جَعَلَهُ دَكًّا *he made it* (*into*) *atoms*, قَطَّعْنَاهُمْ أُمَمًا *We divided them into nations*; or (ii) أَفْعَالُ ٱلْقَلْبِ *the verbs of the heart*, which are so called because their action is mental; for instance رَأَى *to see*, *think*, *know* and its IV passive أُرِيَ *to think*, *believe*, عَلِمَ *to know*, زَعَمَ *to deem*, قَالَ *to think*, etc.; thus ظَنَنْتُهَا صَبُورًا *I thought her patient*, يَجِدُونَهُ مَكْتُوبًا *they find him mentioned* (lit. written).

REM. *b*. Verbs like رَأَى and وَجَدَ must also be reckoned among أَفْعَالُ ٱلْحِسِّ *verbs of* (*the organs of*) *sense*.

REM. *d.* Three accusatives are governed by أَفْعَالُ ٱلْقَلْبِ in their fourth form, as سَيُرِيكُمْ أَعْمَالَكُمْ خَبِيثَةً *he will make you think your actions foul.*

426. All verbs, transitive and intransitive, active and passive, may take their own مَصَادِرُ *infinitives* (see § 195), or their deverbal nouns of the classes nomina vicis et speciei*, as objective complements in the accusative. Thus ضَرَبَهُ ضَرْبًا *he gave him a beating,* طَمِعَ طَمَعًا *he desired eagerly,* ضُرِبَ ضَرْبًا *he received a beating,* إِسْتَكْبَرُوا إِسْتِكْبَارًا *they were puffed with arrogant pride.* This accusative is called اَلْمَفْعُولُ ٱلْمُطْلَقُ *the absolute object* or اَلْمَصْدَرُ, and it may appear, or be مَحْذُوفٌ *eliminated*: thus يَعْمَلُ صَالِحًا *he does right* for يَعْمَلُ عَمَلًا صَالِحًا, also يَطْلُبُهُ حَثِيثًا for يَطْلُبُهُ طَلَبًا حَثِيثًا *he follows it in swift search.* We have given (§ 202 Note) عَذَابٌ as derivative of the second form to which it serves as maçdar, thus أُعَذِّبُهُمْ عَذَابًا شَدِيدًا *I will chastise them very severely*; but the maçdar of a different form may be employed, or even of a different verb provided it be synonymous.

NOTE. Verbal nouns (nomina actionis agentis et patientis, etc.) can like finite verbs take اَلْمَفْعُولُ ٱلْمُطْلَقُ; thus اَللّٰهُ مُعَذِّبُهُمْ عَذَابًا شَدِيدًا *God is their very severe chastiser.*

427. It has been observed of nomina verbi (in § 195 and § 421) that, when infinitives from verbs which govern an objective complement in the accusative case, they can govern an accusative instead of a dependent. This is especially the case if one or more

* Nomina vicis et speciei are treated in Wright's Grammar, vol. I. §§ 219, 220.

words divide an object from its governing infinitive, because a dependent case cannot be separated from the word which governs it. Also, when an infinitive is defined by the article, its object must stand in the accusative, because the noun so defined cannot take after it a dependent.

Rem. *c.* Beside infinitives (nomina actionis) there are verbal nouns of similar force and significance which govern in the same way.

428. With rare exceptions, infinitives govern by help of a preposition, when from verbs which are transitive in that manner.

429. Frequently however an infinitive governs its objective complement in the dependent with لِ (see § 453) instead of in the accusative. Thus كَتَبْنَا تَفْصِيلًا لِكُلِّ شَيْءٍ *We wrote an exposition of every thing.* So it is with certain other verbal nouns.

430. Nomina agentis can, like infinitives, govern a noun in the accusative, as ٱللّٰهُ مُعَذِّبٌ ٱلْقَوْمَ *God is a chastiser of the people,* or in the dependent, as ٱللّٰهُ مُهْلِكُ ٱلْقَوْمِ *God is the destroyer of the people.*

Note. When derived from verbs which are transitive by help of a preposition, nomina agentis must govern in the same way. Thus إِنَّا إِلَى رَبِّنَا مُنْقَلِبُونَ *verily to our Lord shall we return;* كَذَّبُوا بِآيَاتِنَا وَكَانُوا عَنْهَا غَافِلِينَ *they denied Our signs, and were neglectors of them;* ظَنُّوا أَنَّهُ وَاقِعٌ عَلَيْهِمْ *they thought it to be falling upon them;* أُلَائِكَ أَصْحَابُ ٱلنَّارِ خَالِدِينَ فِيهَا *these are the people of Hell-fire, abiding therein.*

431. What has been said in § 429 concerning لِ after an infinitive, applies equally to a nomen agentis.

REM. When by rhetorical transposition a finite verb, which is transitive without help from a preposition, follows its object, we may use the accusative, as مَا ظَلَمُونَا وَلٰكِنْ كَانُوا أَنْفُسَهُمْ يَظْلِمُونَ *they did not injure Us, but they were injuring themselves*; or we may employ لِ, as اَلَّذِينَ لِرَبِّهِمْ يَرْهَبُونَ *those who fear their Lord.* In like case a nomen agentis cannot govern an accusative but requires لِ, thus أَنْتُمْ لَهَا كَارِهُونَ *ye dislike her.* If the transposed object be a pronominal suffix, إِيَّا may with the finite verb be employed instead of لِ as in § 189 *b*.

433. Beside the nomina agentis, some other verbal adjectives govern either an accusative case or لِ with the dependent.

NOTE. When derived from verbs which are transitive by help of a preposition, these adjectives govern in the same way. Thus حَقِيقٌ عَلَيَّ *binding upon me,* هُوَ عَلَى كُلِّ شَيْءٍ قَدِيرٌ *He is able for everything,* اَللّٰهُ بِكُلِّ شَيْءٍ عَلِيمٌ *God is acquainted with everything.*

435. Frequently the accusative depends upon a verb which is مَحْذُوفٌ *eliminated* :—

(*a*) In phrases of command, exclamations, etc. we must supply the verb to which the accusative noun serves as اَلْمَفْعُولُ اَلْمُطْلَقُ (see § 426). Thus مَهْلًا *gently!* for أَمْهِلْ مَهْلًا *deal gently,* سَمْعًا وَطَاعَةً *hearing and obeying* for أَسْمَعُ سَمْعًا وَأُطِيعُ طَاعَةً *I hear well and implicitly obey.*

NOTE. The Arabian grammarians represent that سُبْحَانَكَ stands for أُسَبِّحُ سُبْحَانَكَ *I praise Thine absolute perfection* (see § 41, rem. *c*).

(*b*) In other cases the verb must be conjectured, as أَهْلًا وَسَهْلًا where we may supply أَتَيْتَ *thou hast come to people and a plain*, i.e. to friends and a smooth place; مَرْحَبًا بِكَ that is وَجَدْتَ *thou hast found for thyself roominess* (see § 27 Note); رِجْلَكَ that is قِ (see § 178) *guard thy foot*; وَرَاءَكَ that is أُنْظُرْ *look behind thee.*

436. The adverb إِنَّ and the conjunction أَنَّ take the following noun or pronoun in the accusative case instead of in the nominative (as one expects the subject of a sentence to be) because, so it is said, these particles embody the verb *to see*; thus إِنَّ رَبَّكُمُ ٱللّٰهُ *verily* (i.e. see) *your Lord* (*He*) *is God*, أَوَلَا يَعْلَمُونَ أَنَّ ٱللّٰهَ يَعْلَمُ مَا يُسِرُّونَ وَمَا يُعْلِنُونَ *do they not know that God knows what they conceal and what they reveal?* So in case of their compounds لٰكِنَّ and وَلٰكِنَّ (see § 362 *ee* and § 584 *b*) *but, yet,* كَأَنَّ *as though* (see § 367 *g*), and when coupled with a preposition, as بِأَنَّ and لِأَنَّ; thus وَلٰكِنَّ أَكْثَرَهُمْ لَا يَعْلَمُونَ *but most of them do not know,* كَأَنَّهُ ظُلَّةٌ *as though it were a canopy,* أَلَمْ يَعْلَمْ بِأَنَّ ٱللّٰهَ يَرَى *does he not know that God sees?* In the above examples the subject immediately follows إِنَّ etc. and under such circumstances لَ (see § 361 *c*) may be prefixed to the predicate; thus إِنَّا لَنَرَاكَ فِي ضَلَالٍ *verily we perceive thee* (*to be*) *in error*; إِنَّ رَبَّكَ لَسَرِيعُ ٱلْعِقَابِ وَإِنَّهُ لَغَفُورٌ رَحِيمٌ *surely*

thy Lord is prompt with chastisement and certainly He is forgiving and merciful. There may however be a separation, between إِنَّ etc. and the subject, caused by an adverb of time and place or by a preposition with its complement; thus إِنَّ مِنْ أَزْوَاجِكُمْ وَأَوْلَادِكُمْ عَدُوًّا لَكُمْ *verily enemies of you are* (*to be found*) *amongst your spouses and children*: when this separation occurs لَ may be prefixed to the subject of إِنَّ or أَنَّ, as أَئِنَّ لَنَا لَأَجْرًا *shall there indeed be to us a reward?* If the predicate be negative we must not use لَ, thus إِنَّهُ لَا يُحِبُّ ٱلْمُعْتَدِينَ *surely He doth not love the transgressors*; إِنَّا لَا نُضِيعُ أَجْرَ ٱلْمُصْلِحِينَ *verily We will not allow to be lost the reward of the righteous*: and so if the verb be a perfect without قَدْ, thus إِنَّ ٱلْقَوْمَ ٱسْتَضْعَفُونِي وَكَادُوا يَقْتُلُونَنِي *surely the people despised me and were just on the point of slaying me.*

Rem. *a.* These particles, together with those given in rem. *f*, are named إِنَّ وَأَخَوَاتُهَا *'inna and its sisters.* The word governed is called their اِسْمٌ *noun* (see § 525 rem.) and the predicate خَبَرٌ.

Rem. *b.* If the predicate is placed between إِنَّ or أَنَّ and its noun, the logical emphasis falls upon the latter, thus إِنَّ مَعَكَ صَاحِبَكَ *your* friend *is with you*; but if the predicate follows the noun, it receives the logical emphasis itself, as إِنَّ صَاحِبَكَ مَعَكَ *your friend is* with *you.*

Rem. *d.* In § 353* we have mentioned مَا ٱلْكَافَّةُ *the hindering mâ*, which when appended to إِنَّ, أَنَّ, كَأَنَّ and لٰكِنَّ is followed by a nominative; thus إِنَّمَا أَوْلَادُكُمْ فِتْنَةٌ *your children are only* *a temptation,* وَٱعْلَمُوا أَنَّمَا أَمْوَالُكُمْ فِتْنَةٌ *know that your riches are a temptation.* The same influence is exercised by ضَمِيرُ ٱلشَّأْنِ (see § 362 *m* and § 367 *g*) as إِنَّهُ كِرَامٌ قَوْمُكَ *truly thy people are generous.*

REM. *e.* A lightened form of these particles may be used.

REM. *f.* The words لَيْتَ *would that* and عَلَّ or لَعَلَّ *perhaps* govern an accusative like إِنَّ etc., thus لَعَلَّكُمْ تَذَكَّرُونَ *perhaps ye will take warning.*

438. An interjection usually precedes the person or thing called; while for vocative case we must use the nominative or accusative.

(*a*) As has been noted in § 368 يَا *O!* takes its following noun without the article.

(i) We use the nominative—in the singular without tanwin—when a particular person or thing is addressed by the speaker directly and without explanatory term; thus يَا مُحَمَّدُ *O Muḥammad!* يَا رَجُلُ *O man!* or *Sir,* قَالَ مُوسَى يَا فِرْعَوْنُ *Moses said, O Pharaoh!*

(ii) We use the accusative when the person or thing called is indefinite and not directly addressed, يَا رَجُلًا *somebody!*; as also when an explanatory term is appended, thus يَا بَنِي إِسْرَائِيلَ *O sons of Israel!* يَا إِخْوَتَنَا *O brothers of ours!*

REM. *a.* These rules hold good in the absence of an interjection, as رَبَّنَا أَفْرِغْ عَلَيْنَا صَبْرًا *O our Lord, pour upon us patience.*

REM. *b.* In the vocative ـِي is usually shortened into ـِ (see § 317, rem. *b*), thus يَا قَوْمِ *O my people!* رَبِّ *O my Lord!*

but this abbreviation is not permitted with derivatives ending in ـِيُ or ـٍ from verbs whose final radical is و or ي. Beside ـِي and ـِ there are other forms possible, as قَالَ ٱبْنَ أُمَّ *he (Aaron) said, O son of my mother!*

REM. *d.* One word only, viz. ٱللّٰهُ, may retain the article and follow يَا; thus يَا ٱللّٰهُ *O God!* or irregularly يَا أَللّٰهُ.

(*b*) The noun following أَيُّهَا or يَا أَيُّهَا, whether singular, dual or plural, must be nominative and defined by the article; thus أَيُّهَا ٱلنَّاسُ *O people!* يَا أَيُّهَا ٱلَّذِينَ آمَنُوا *O ye who believe!*

439. When لَا is immediately followed by an indefinite object and denies its existence we make the noun accusative and, if possible, we omit tanwîn; as ٱللّٰهُ لَا إِلٰهَ إِلَّا هُوَ *God, there is no god but He.* Should an explanatory term follow, tanwîn is retained; as لَا حَافِظًا لِلْقُرْآنِ عِنْدَكُمْ *there is no one knowing the Corân by heart amongst you.*

440. We have been treating objective complements since § 422 and shall now consider the adverbial complement. This sort of accusative depends (*a*) when expressed by كَانَ *to be, exist* (and by certain similar verbs, see § 442) on the idea of existence or being, which is limited and determined by the accusative; and (*b*) on circumstances detailed in § 443 et seq.

441. When employed as the *logical copula كَانَ is called كَانَ ٱلنَّاقِصَةُ *the incomplete kâna* because to complete the sense

---

* In logic the copula is a word which unites the subject and predicate of a proposition; it is known as اَلرَّابِطَةُ *the fastening.*

there is required an attribute, which we must put in the accusative. Thus كَانُوا قَوْمًا مُجْرِمِينَ *they were guilty people,* اِتَّخَذُوهُ وَكَانُوا ظَالِمِينَ *they took it (the calf for their god) and were wrong doers,* قُلْنَا لَهُمْ كُونُوا قِرَدَةً خَاسِئِينَ *We said to them, Be ye* i.e. Become *abject apes.* Also we may note كُنْ مِنَ ٱلشَّاكِرِينَ *be thou (one) of the grateful,* which is equivalent (see § 448 *f*) to كُنْ شَاكِرًا. But when the idea of existence is attributed by كَانَ to its subject we can only employ the nominative, as كَانَ قِرْدٌ *there was an ape*: here the verb is كَانَ ٱلتَّامَّةُ *the complete kâna,* because it contains the attribute and requires no other, for كَانَ قِرْدًا would mean *he was an ape.*

REM. *a.* The subject is called اِسْمُ كَانَ and the predicate خَبَرُ كَانَ, while the natural sequence (see § 518) is verb, subject, predicate; this order may however be varied if sense allow.

REM. *b.* Sometimes كَانَ is مَحْذُوفٌ *eliminated,* as اِسْمَعُوا وَأَطِيعُوا وَأَنْفِقُوا خَيْرًا لِأَنْفُسِكُمْ *hear ye, and obey, and give alms,* it will be *better for your souls,* where يَكُنْ is understood.

442. The same construction appertains to أَخَوَاتُ كَانَ *the sisters of kâna* which are often used as synonyms of كَانَ without relation to time, though they add some modification to the simple idea of existence. In this class are دَامَ ـُ *to continue,* بَقِيَ ـَ *to remain,* صَارَ ـِ *to become,* ظَلَّ ـَ *to be* or *do all day* and not a few others, most of which may be تَامَّةٌ: while لَيْسَ *not to be,* which is always نَاقِصَةٌ, expresses the negation of existence; thus لَيْسَ بِي ضَلَالَةٌ *in me is no error.*

REM. *g*. Instead of an accusative or a preposition with its dependent أَخَوَاتُ كَانَ may take as attribute a verb in the imperfect, thus following the analogy of كَانَ (see § 408 *d* and *e*, and § 409). With this construction we can connect that of أَفْعَالُ ٱلْمُقَارَبَةِ *verbs of appropinquation*, which are of two kinds. (1) Amongst those which indicate simple proximity of the predicate is كَادَ ـَ (see § 157) *to be just on the point of*: commonly its predicate is an imperfect indicative, thus كَادُوا يَقْتُلُونَنِي *they were on the point of killing me*. (2) Amongst those which indicate a hope of the predicate's occurrence is عَسَى *perhaps*: commonly it is construed with أَنْ and the subjunctive, as عَسَى رَبُّكُمْ أَنْ يُهْلِكَ عَدُوَّكُمْ *your Lord may perhaps destroy your enemy*; but it can take as accusative a pronominal suffix like لَعَلَّ (see § 436, rem. *f*).

443. Brief allusion has been made in § 440 *b* to other adverbial accusatives which determine and limit the subject, verb, or predicate of a sentence, and sometimes the sentence as a whole. These adverbial accusatives are of different sorts and indicate :—

444. (*a*) The time in or during which an act occurs; as خَالِدُونَ فِيهَا أَبَدًا *abiding in them (the gardens) perpetually*, إِذْ تَأْتِيهِمْ حِيتَانُهُمْ يَوْمَ سَبْتِهِمْ *when their fish came to them on the day of their sabbath*.

(*b*) Locality, direction, and extension, may in certain cases take the accusative; as نَظَرَ يَمِينًا وَيَسَارًا *he looked right and left*. Of this sort are the words given as prepositions in § 359.

Rem. *a.* We must use فِي *in*, when the place is definitely specified, as أَقَمْتُ فِي مَقْتَلِ ٱلْحُسَيْنِ *I stopped at the place where al Ḥusain was killed.* But with a verb meaning *to remain* or the like مَكَانٌ, and similar vague nouns of place, are employed without preposition and therefore in the accusative; thus إِنِ ٱسْتَقَرَّ مَكَانَهُ *if it stand firm in its place.*

Note. Certain substantives signifying time or place can be مُضَافٌ *annexed* (see § 475 and § 478) to a verbal sentence, but only in the accusative case; thus يَوْمَ لَا يَسْبِتُونَ لَا تَأْتِيهِمْ حِيتَانٌ *on the day on which they did not keep sabbath, fish did not come to them.*

Rem. *b.* The accusative of time and place, illustrated in above examples of this section, is called اَلظَّرْفُ *the vessel* (see § 221, rem. *a*) or اَلْمَفْعُولُ فِيهِ *that in which the act is done.*

(*c*) The most important however of adverbial accusatives is called اَلْحَالُ *the state* or *condition*, i.e. of the subject or object or of both, while the act is happening. Thus لَمَّا رَجَعَ مُوسَى إِلَى قَوْمِهِ غَضْبَانَ أَسِفًا *when Moses returned to his people angry, afflicted* i.e. in a state of affliction and anger; هُوَ ٱلَّذِي يُرْسِلُ ٱلرِّيَاحَ بُشْرًا بَيْنَ يَدَيْ رَحْمَتِهِ *He it is who sends the winds, heralds of His mercy* lit. *between the two hands of His mercy* i.e. in advance of rain; أُلْقِيَ ٱلسَّحَرَةُ سَاجِدِينَ *the magicians were thrown down prostrate* (*adoring*).

Rem. *a.* The ḥâl is فَضْلَةٌ *a redundancy*; thus اُدْعُوا رَبَّكُمْ تَضَرُّعًا وَخُفْيَةً *call upon your Lord humbly and in secret.* Here the command to pray is of itself a sentence; and the conditions, grammatically superfluous, reply to كَيْفَ *how?* as the accusative called اَلْحَالُ must always do.

Rem. *b.* The ḥâl depends upon a regent (عَامِلُ ٱلْحَالِ) which may be (1) a verb, as خَرَّ مُوسَى صَعِقًا *Moses fell down thunderstruck*; or (2) a deverbal adjective, as إِنِّي رَسُولُ ٱللّٰهِ إِلَيْكُمْ جَمِيعًا *verily I am God's apostle to you all,* where رَسُول is accounted a deverbal adjective, إِنِّي رَسُولٌ being equivalent to أُرْسِلْتُ *I have been sent*; or (3) a demonstrative pronoun or other expression having verbal force, as أُلَآئِكَ أَصْحَابُ ٱلنَّارِ خَالِدِينَ فِيهَا *these are the people of the fire, dwelling continually therein,* where أُلَآئِكَ is equivalent to يُشَارُ إِلَيْهِمْ *they are pointed out as.*

Rem. *c.* The ḥâl is (1) usually صِفَةٌ *an adjective* expressing a transitory state, as تَأْتِيهِمْ حِيتَانُهُمْ شُرَّعًا *their fish came to them manifestly*: though the adjective may express a permanent state, thus رَبَّنَا تَوَفَّنَا مُسْلِمِينَ *O our Lord, receive us dying, as those who are resigned to Thy will*; خَلَقَ ٱلشَّمْسَ وَٱلْقَمَرَ وَٱلنُّجُومَ مُسَخَّرَاتٍ بِأَمْرِهِ *He created the sun and the moon and the stars, held in (a state of) subjection by His command.* Sometimes however (2) it is an infinitive with the meaning of a participial adjective, as أَخَذْتُ ذٰلِكَ مِنْهُ سَمْعًا *I received that from him by hearing*; or even (3) a concrete substantive, as فَأَرْسَلْنَا عَلَيْهِمُ ٱلطُّوفَانَ وَٱلْجَرَادَ وَٱلْقُمَّلَ وَٱلضَّفَادِعَ وَٱلدَّمَ آيَاتٍ مُفَصَّلَاتٍ *so We sent upon them the deluge and locusts and lice and frogs and blood (in the nature of) signs, separated by intervals.* Lastly (4) ḥâl may be a proposition, as in § 583. There may be more than one ḥâl, with or without وَ *and* between them, as can be seen above.

REM. *e.* In all our examples ḥâl is نَكِرَةٌ *indefinite,* and this is most usual.

REM. *f.* We call the subject or object to which a ḥâl refers صَاحِبُ ٱلْحَالِ or ذُو ٱلْحَالِ, and it is usually مَعْرِفَةٌ *definite* as happens in all our examples.

NOTE. Occasionally صَاحِبُ ٱلْحَالِ is eliminated, as ٱلَّذِي خَبُثَ لَا يَخْرُجُ إِلَّا نَكِدًا *as to that* (*land*) *which was bad* its herbage *does not come forth except scantily,* where نَبَاتُهُ must be supplied as çâhib to نَكِدًا.

REM. *g.* Also it will be observed that in all our examples the ḥâl is placed after its regent: as a rule it occupies this position.

(*d*) The accusative may express an agent's motive and object in the act, its cause and reason; as أُدْعُوهُ خَوْفًا وَطَمَعًا *call ye upon Him out of fear and eager desire.* Definition by the article is unusual, this accusative being indefinite except when in construct state (see § 475).

REM. Only مَصْدَرٌ قَلْبِيٌّ *a mental or intellectual infinitive* can be employed in this way; thus, in Koran, VII. 164 مَعْذِرَةً (*we warn them*) *by way of excusing* (*ourselves*). Reply is given to the question لِمَ *why?* (see § 351, rem.).

(*e*) Other determinations and limitations of the predicate may be expressed by an accusative called ٱلتَّمْيِيزُ *the specification;* thus طَابَ دَاوُدُ نَفْسًا *David is cheerful in spirit.*

REM. *a.* Like ٱلْحَالُ this accusative is فَضْلَةٌ see (*c*) rem. *a.* It must be an indefinite substantive.

Rem. *b*. We have mentioned in §§ 322 and 323 the accusative which follows cardinal numbers from 11 to 99 inclusive: it is of this sort, being called تَمْيِيزُ ٱلْعَدَدِ *the specification of number*, and is most usually singular, see § 499.

---

446. Relations of time and place are designated by *prepositions*, as also are many ideal conceptions. We shall treat those mentioned in § 447 as indicating motion from, in § 450 motion towards, and in § 454 rest at a place; while in § 470 compound prepositions will be found, over and above those detailed by § 355 et seq.

447. The prepositions indicating motion from or away from a place, are مِنْ *out of*, *from*, and عَنْ *away from*.

448. We designate by help of مِنْ

(*a*) the local point of departure from a place; as أَخْرَجَكُمْ مِنْ أَرْضِكُمْ *he expelled you from your land*, فَأَرْسَلْنَا عَلَيْهِمْ رِجْزًا مِنَ ٱلسَّمَآءِ *so We sent upon them a plague from heaven*, مِنْ خِلَافٍ *from a contrary* i.e. on opposite sides. Hence it is used with verbs which indicate liberating, preserving, warning, etc. as أَنْجَيْنَاكُمْ مِنْ آلِ فِرْعَوْنَ *We delivered you from Pharaoh's people*, مَوْعِظَةٌ مِنْ كُلِّ شَيْءٍ *a warning from* i.e. against *everything*.

(*b*) The temporal point of departure; as مِنَ ٱلْهِجْرَةِ *from the Hegira* i.e. from 622 A.D.

Rem. *a* When used in any of the above significations, we say that مِنْ is employed لِلِابْتِدَآءِ *to denote the beginning*.

(*c*) The causal point of departure, the origin and source of a thing; as أَعْلَمُهُ مِنَ ٱللّٰهِ *I know it from God*, جَآءَكُمْ ذِكْرٌ مِنْ رَبِّكُمْ *an admonition has come to you from your Lord*, مِنْ أَزْوَاجِكُمْ عَدُوٌّ *from among your wives originate enemies*, مَا تَنْقِمُ مِنَّا إِلَّا أَنْ آمَنَّا بِآيَاتِ رَبِّنَا لَمَّا جَآءَتْنَا *thou dost not resent anything of which we are the origin except that we believed the signs of our Lord when they came to us.*

Rem. *a*. Here مِنْ is employed لِلتَّعْلِيلِ *to assign the reason*.

(*d*) The distance from anything, especially after words signifying proximity, when in English we must render مِنْ *to*; thus إِنَّ رَحْمَةَ ٱللّٰهِ قَرِيبٌ مِنَ ٱلْمُحْسِنِينَ *surely the mercy of God is near to the righteous.*

(*e*) The difference between two things when compared: hence the use of مِنْ with an elative (see § 234) when comparative; thus أَحْسَنُ مِنْهُ *handsomer than he.*

Rem. *a*. Sometimes مِنْ with its complement is omitted; as ٱلدَّارُ ٱلْآخِرَةُ خَيْرٌ لِلَّذِينَ يَتَّقُونَ *the last abode is better* than this world *for those who take heed to themselves*, where مِنَ ٱلدُّنْيَا may be supplied.

(*f*) The relationship between part and whole, between species and genus; thus قَالَ نَعَمْ وَإِنَّكُمْ لَمِنَ ٱلْمُقَرَّبِينَ *he said, Yes, and ye shall be of those who are brought near* (*me*), ٱلْمَلَأُ مِنْ قَوْمِ فِرْعَوْنَ *the chiefs of Pharaoh's people*, أُسْكُنُوا هٰذِهِ ٱلْقَرْيَةَ وَكُلُوا مِنْهَا *inhabit this village and eat therefrom*, ٱلسُّفَهَآءُ مِنَّا *the fools among us.*

REM. *a.* Preceding a definite noun, which is usually plural, مِن may indicate an indefinite quantity or number; as كُلُوا مِنَ ٱلطَّيِّبَاتِ *eat of the good things.* Together with an indefinite dependent مِنْ may be subject of a sentence as in the following: مَا أَصَابَ مِنْ مُصِيبَةٍ إِلَّا بِإِذْنِ ٱللّٰهِ *no mischance befalls except by permission of God.*

REM. *b.* Governing an indefinite noun after a negative particle, مِنْ gives the clause an absolute and general sense; thus مَا لَكُمْ مِنْ إِلٰهٍ *ye have no god whatever.*

REM. *e.* In these examples مِنْ is used لِلتَّبْعِيضِ *to indicate division into parts,* as also in أَخْرَجْنَا مِنْ كُلِّ ٱلثَّمَرَاتِ *We produced all sorts of fruit*; sometimes it is employed لِلتَّرْكِيبِ *to indicate composition.*

(*g*) After indefinite مَا and مَهْمَا *whatever* we must use مِنْ before the explanatory word; thus مَهْمَا تَأْتِنَا بِهِ مِنْ آيَةٍ *whatever thou bringest us of a sign*: in this case we have a general term rendered more definite, as also when مِنْ indicates the material of which an article has been made; thus عِجْلٌ مِنْ حُلِيِّهِمْ *a calf (made) out of their ornaments.*

REM. Here مِنْ is employed لِلْبَيَانِ *to explain.*

(*h*) Another use of مِنْ is called اَلتَّمْيِيزُ *the specification*; thus لَقَدْ أَخَذْنَا آلَ فِرْعَوْنَ بِٱلسِّنِينَ وَنَقْصٍ مِنَ ٱلثَّمَرَاتِ *We visited the people of Pharaoh with years (of barrenness) and with diminution of fruit.*

NOTE. There is yet another use of مِنْ in فَٱنْتَقَمْنَا مِنْهُمْ *so We took vengeance on them.*

449. By help of عَنْ we designate distance from, motion away from, and the like: hence it is used

(*a*) after verbs which denote setting free, forbidding, etc. as يَضَعُ عَنْهُمْ إِصْرَهُمْ *he puts away from them their burden,* يَنْهَاهُمْ عَنِ ٱلْمُنْكَرِ *he forbids them from the disapproved.*

(*b*) After verbs which imply the removal of a covering, as asking etc., thus وَٱسْأَلْهُمْ عَنِ ٱلْقَرْيَةِ *and ask them concerning the village,* كَشَفْتَ عَنَّا ٱلرِّجْزَ *thou hast removed from us the plague.*

(*c*) After verbs which imply turning away, as كَانُوا عَنْهُ غَافِلِينَ *they were neglectors of it,* يُكَفِّرْ عَنْهُ سَيِّئَاتِهِ *He effaces from him his misdeeds,* لَمَّا سَكَتَ عَنْ مُوسَى ٱلْغَضَبُ *when the anger became still (so as to be) away from Moses,* سَأَصْرِفُ عَنْ آيَاتِي *I will cause to turn away from (the direction of) my signs,* عَتَوْا عَمَّا عَتَا *they disdainfully turned away from that from which he turned disdainfully,* رَغِبَ عَنْهُ *he avoided it.*

450. The prepositions indicating motion to or towards a place are إِلَى *to,* حَتَّى *up to,* and لِ *to.*

451. Opposed to مِنْ and عَنْ is إِلَى which signifies

(*a*) motion or direction to or towards a place; thus أَرْسَلْنَا نُوحًا إِلَى قَوْمِهِ *We sent Noah unto his people,* إِلَيْهِ ٱلْمَصِيرُ *to Him is the returning,* وَلٰكِنِ ٱنْظُرْ إِلَى ٱلْجَبَلِ *but look toward the mountain,* أَوْحَيْنَا إِلَى مُوسَى *We revealed* i.e. indicated *to Moses.* Hence, because inclination is implied, إِلَى follows verbs of excusing and repenting; thus تُبْتُ إِلَيْكَ *I repent toward Thee,* مَعْذِرَةً إِلَى رَبِّكُمْ *it is an excuse to your Lord.*

(*b*) In respect of time إِلَى usually indicates during a continuance; as إِلَى أَجَلٍ *until a fixed term,* إِلَى يَوْمِ ٱلْقِيَامَةِ *during all the time till the day of judgement.*

REM. When used in the above significations, we say that إِلَى is employed لِلْاِنْتِهَآءِ *to designate the limit.*

(*c*) To show that one thing is added to another we use إِلَى and hence إِلَى آخِرِهِ (see § 23, rem. *d*) *to its end,* which is definite but serves for *etcetera.*

452. In addition to implying like إِلَى motion towards an object, حَتَّى must indicate arrival.

REM. *c.* When حَتَّى is a conjunction (see § 367 *k*) it exercises no governing power upon nouns.

453. Whenever possible لِ must be so translated as to indicate abstract relations, those that are concrete being expressed by إِلَى; thus إِلَى بَلَدٍ مَيِّتٍ *to a dead country,* but سُقْنَاهُ لِبَلَدٍ مَيِّتٍ *We drove it for the use of a dead country.* This distinction cannot always be preserved as is shown by §§ 429 et seq. where لِ indicates an action's relation to the direct object which stands in place of an accusative; thus أَنْصَحُ لَكُمْ or أَنْصَحُكُمْ *I advise you* (see § 423). More often however we employ لِ

(*a*) for passing on the action to an indirect object; as قَالَ مُوسَى لِقَوْمِهِ *Moses said to his people,* اِجْعَلْ لَنَا *make for us,* يُضَاعِفْهُ لَكُمْ *he multiplies it to you,* اِغْفِرْ لَنَا وَٱرْحَمْنَا *pardon (the sin) to us and have mercy upon us*: so with reflexive verbs, which govern *self* as their direct object; thus لَمَّا تَجَلَّى رَبُّهُ لِلْجَبَلِ *when his Lord manifested Himself to the mountain,* and we find the sense of تجلّى in إِذَا هِيَ بَيْضَآءُ لِلنَّاظِرِينَ *lo, it is white to the beholders*; also by taking *praise* as the direct object, we may place here يُسَبِّحُ لِلّٰهِ مَا فِي ٱلسَّمٰوَاتِ *whatsoever is in heaven gives praise to God*; and unless wholly idiomatic آمَنَ لَكَ *he believed in thee.* In these cases لِ and its dependent are not essential to the clause, whereas it is different in

(*b*) the dative (i) of possession; as لَهُ ٱلْمُلْكُ وَلَهُ ٱلْحَمْدُ *to Him belong the dominion and the praise,* لَهُ خُوَارٌ *which lows* lit. *to it is the* (*power of*) *lowing,* يَعْكُفُونَ عَلَى أَصْنَامٍ لَهُمْ *they cling to their idols,* خَيْرٌ لِي *better for me,* بِنْتٌ لِلْمَلِكِ *a daughter of the king* (see § 492): (ii) of permission or right; as يُحِلُّ لَهُمُ ٱلطَّيِّبَاتِ *he makes lawful to them the good things,* آذَنُ لَكَ *I give thee permission*: (iii) of advantage, contrasting with عَلَى (see § 459 *b*); as أُدْعُ لَنَا رَبَّكَ *pray on behalf of us to thy Lord* but دَعَا عَلَيْهِ *he cursed him*; also هُدًى وَرَحْمَةٌ لِلَّذِينَ *a guidance and a mercy for the benefit of those who,* وَٱكْتُبْ لَنَا فِي هٰذِهِ ٱلدُّنْيَا حَسَنَةً وَفِي ٱلْآخِرَةِ *and do Thou write for us* i.e. place to credit of our account *advantage in this world and in the next,* لَنَا هٰذِهِ *this is owing to us.*

Rem. *b.* By use of لِ we express the verb *to have,* as مَا لِي أَخٌ *I have no brother.*

(*c*) Attention is drawn by لِ to the purpose or cause of an act; thus لِمَ *for what reason?* (see § 351, rem.), وَإِذْ قَالَتْ أُمَّةٌ مِنْهُمْ لِمَ تَعِظُونَ ٱلْقَوْمَ *and when a section of them asked, Why do ye warn the people?* كِتَابٌ لِلطُّلَّابِ *a book for the use of students,*

نُصَرِّفُ ٱلْآيَاتِ لِقَوْمٍ *We diversify the signs for the use of a people,* اُذْكُرْ يَوْمَ يَجْمَعُكُمْ لِيَوْمِ ٱلْجَمْعِ *make mention of the day whereon He shall gather you for the sake of (what is in) the day of assemblage (of the angels)* i.e. the day of judgement*.

REM. Here لِ is employed لِلتَّعْلِيلِ *to indicate the cause.*

(*e*) Also لِ marks the time of an occurrence; as وَلَمَّا جَآءَ مُوسَى لِمِيقَاتِنَا *and when Moses had come to Our appointed time,* لِأَوَّلِ لَيْلَةٍ مِنْ مُحَرَّمٍ *on Moslem new year's day* lit. *at a point of time when a night has passed from Muḥarram*†.

NOTE. Many verbs indicating a state of mind, friendly or hostile, advantageous or disadvantageous, take لِ of the person towards whom the feeling is directed; thus عَدِيتُ لَهُ *I hate him.*

454. The prepositions indicating rest at a place are فِي *in, into,* بِ *at, in, by, with,* مَعَ *with, along with,* لَدُنْ or لَدَى *with, beside, near,* and عَلَى *over, above, upon.*

455. We designate by help of فِي

(*a*) rest in a place or during a time, and motion into a place, as لَهُ مَا فِي ٱلسَّمٰوَاتِ وَمَا فِي ٱلْأَرْضِ *to Him belongs whatsoever is in heaven and earth,* خَلَقَهَا فِي سِتَّةِ أَيَّامٍ *He created them in six days,* كَتَبْنَاهَا لَهُ فِي ٱلْأَلْوَاحِ *We wrote it for his benefit upon the tables,* لَمَّا سُقِطَ فِي أَيْدِيهِمْ *when a falling took place into*

* This rendering is in accordance with Baiḍâwî.

† Further explanation of dates will be found in Wright's Grammar, vol. II. §§ 110 and 111.

their hands i.e. when they grievously repented, اُذْكُرْ مَا فِيهِ *remember what is in it,* فِي ٱلسَّبْتِ *on the sabbath day,* أَرْسِلْ فِي ٱلْمَدَائِنِ حَاشِرِينَ *send gatherers into the cities.* This meaning applies also to less concrete relations, as اِغْفِرْ لِي وَلِأَخِي وَأَدْخِلْنَا فِي رَحْمَتِكَ *pardon (the sin) to me and my brother and cause us to enter into Thy mercy.*

(*b*) By rights فِي means *in the midst of* as may well be seen with a plural or collective; thus قَالَ مُوسَى لِأَخِيهِ هٰرُونَ ٱخْلُفْنِي فِي قَوْمِي وَأَصْلِحْ *Moses said to his brother Aaron, Do thou act as my deputy among my people, and behave uprightly.*

(*c*) We use فِي to state the subject of thought, conversation, or writing; thus اَلْكِتَابُ ٱلْأَوَّلُ فِي ٱللُّغَةِ ٱلْعَرَبِيَّةِ *The first book treating of the Arabic language.*

(*d*) Further فِي is employed with verbs of desire, as رَغِبَ فِيهِ *he liked it.*

REM. We say that فِي is used لِلظَّرْفِيَّةِ *to indicate time and place.*

NOTE. The phrase ٱلْأَرْضُ ٱلَّتِي بَارَكْنَا فِيهَا *the land which We blessed* is equivalent to اَلَّتِي بَارَكْنَاهَا.

456. Whereas فِي indicates *amongst* we more often express with بِ mere proximity; thus مَرَرْتُ بِرَجُلٍ *I passed by a man,* بَعَثْنَا مُوسَى بِآيَاتِنَا *We sent Moses with Our signs,* خُذْهَا بِقُوَّةٍ *take it with force,* يَطَّيَّرُوا بِمُوسَى *they associate bad luck with Moses,* لَيْسَ بِي ضَلَالَةٌ *there is in me no error,* خَلَقَ ٱلسَّمٰوَاتِ وَٱلْأَرْضَ بِٱلْحَقِّ *He created the heavens and the earth rightly.* Accordingly verbs with certain meanings govern بِ and its dependent in place of an accusative; thus بَصُرْتُ بِمَا لَمْ يَبْصُرُوا بِهِ *I saw that which they saw not,* لَا يُحِيطُونَ بِشَيْءٍ مِنْ عِلْمِهِ *they do not comprehend anything of His knowledge,* ثُمَّ لَتُنَبَّؤُنَّ بِمَا عَمِلْتُمْ *then ye shall be informed of what ye have done,* ٱلَّذِينَ يُمَسِّكُونَ بِٱلْكِتَابِ *those who hold fast to the book,* أَبْتَدِئُ بِسْمِ ٱللّٰهِ *I begin with the name of God*; and بِ with its dependent may take the place of a second accusative, thus لَا تُشْمِتْ بِيَ ٱلْأَعْدَآءَ *do not cause mine enemies to attach ignominy to me,* ذَكِّرْهُمْ بِأَيَّامِ ٱللّٰهِ *remind them of the days of God.* Sometimes a verb governs in both ways with the same meaning (see § 423); thus أَخَذَ بِرَأْسِ أَخِيهِ *he seized the head of his brother,* and لَا تَأْخُذُهُ سِنَةٌ وَلَا نَوْمٌ *drowsiness does not seize Him nor sleep*; اِسْتَعِينُوا بِٱللّٰهِ *ask assistance of God,* and إِيَّاكَ نَعْبُدُ وَإِيَّاكَ نَسْتَعِينُ *Thee only do we worship and of Thee alone we ask assistance*; ظَلَمُوا بِهَا *they treated it unjustly,* and مَا ظَلَمُونَا *they did not injure Us.* Under this general idea of contact are represented the following.

(*a*) The relation between subject and predicate, especially in negative propositions; as مَا نَحْنُ بِمُؤْمِنِينَ *we are not believers.*

(*b*) The relation between an act and its object, especially after ٱلْأَفْعَالُ ٱللَّازِمَةُ *intransitive verbs*; thus يَأْمُرُهُمْ بِٱلْمَعْرُوفِ *he commands the approved to them*; آمَنَّا *we have believed,* but آمَنَّا بِرَبِّ ٱلْعَالَمِينَ *we have believed the Lord of the worlds*: we notice this particularly after those indicating motion, which must then be translated by transitive verbs (see § 423, rem. *b*); thus ذٰلِكَ بِأَنَّهُ كَانَتْ تَأْتِيهِمْ رُسُلُهُمْ بِٱلْبَيِّنَاتِ *this was because their apostles used to bring them proofs*, جَاوَزْنَا بِبَنِي إِسْرَائِيلَ ٱلْبَحْرَ *We caused the children of Israel to traverse the sea.*

(*c*) The relation between an act and its instrument or reason; thus ذٰلِكَ بِأَنَّ ٱللّٰهَ مَوْلَى ٱلَّذِينَ آمَنُوا *this shall be because God is the patron of those who believe*, أَنْزَلْنَا بِسَحَابٍ ٱلْمَاءَ فَأَخْرَجْنَا بِهِ مِنْ كُلِّ ٱلثَّمَرَاتِ *We caused to descend by means of cloud the water, and we produced by means of it (the rain) all sorts of fruits*, بِإِذْنِ ٱللّٰهِ *by God's permission*, مُسَخَّرَاتٌ بِأَمْرِهِ *held in subjection by His command*, وَأَوْحَيْنَا إِلَى مُوسَى إِذِ ٱسْتَسْقَاهُ قَوْمُهُ أَنِ ٱضْرِبْ بِعَصَاكَ ٱلْحَجَرَ *and We revealed to Moses, when his people asked drink of him, saying* (see § 367 *e*) *Strike the stone with thy rod*, كَذٰلِكَ نَبْلُوهُمْ بِمَا كَانُوا يَفْسُقُونَ *thus We try them by reason of that in which they were impious*, وَاعَدْنَا مُوسَى ثَلَاثِينَ لَيْلَةً وَأَتْمَمْنَاهَا بِعَشْرٍ *We appointed with Moses (a period of) thirty nights and We completed them by means of ten (more)*, إِنِّي ٱصْطَفَيْتُكَ عَلَى ٱلنَّاسِ بِرِسَالَاتِي وَبِكَلَامِي *verily I have chosen thee above (all) men by reason of (My putting thee in charge of) My messages and because of My speaking (to thee).*

REM. *c.* To express *without* we can use بِغَيْرِ; thus ٱلَّذِينَ يَتَكَبَّرُونَ فِي ٱلْأَرْضِ بِغَيْرِ ٱلْحَقِّ *those who behave proudly in the earth without justice.*

REM. *d.* Some would place in this sub-section بِسْمِ ٱللّٰهِ *by the name of God* while others supply أَبْتَدِئُ as above.

REM. *e.* Arabian grammarians have divers expressions to denote the uses of بِ.

NOTE. We find بِ used in the sense of عَلَى, thus ظَنُّوا أَنَّهُ وَاقِعٌ بِهِمْ *they thought that it was falling upon them.*

457. By help of مَعَ (or مَعْ) *with, along with,* we indicate association and connection in time or place; thus أَرْسِلْهُ مَعِي *send him with me*: there are also less usual meanings.

459. We employ عَلَى *over, upon, above*

(*a*) in its local sense; thus وَظَلَّلْنَا عَلَيْهِمُ ٱلْغَمَامَ *and We spread for shade over them the cloud,* ثُمَّ ٱسْتَوَى عَلَى ٱلْعَرْشِ *then He established Himself upon the throne*: and a similar sense may be discerned in لَمَّا وَقَعَ عَلَيْهِمُ ٱلرِّجْزُ *when the plague fell upon them,* وَأَنْزَلْنَا عَلَيْهِمُ ٱلْمَنَّ وَٱلسَّلْوَى *and We sent down upon them manna and quail,* أَخَافُ عَلَيْكُمْ عَذَابًا *I fear in your case a punishment,* عَلَى ٱللهِ فَلْيَتَوَكَّلِ ٱلْمُؤْمِنُونَ *upon God then let the believers rely,* ٱلَّذِينَ أَنْعَمْتَ عَلَيْهِمْ *those upon whom Thou hast shed blessings.*

(*b*) As implying disadvantage (see § 453 *b* iii); thus غَضِبَ ٱللهُ عَلَيْهِ *God was angry with him,* بَعَثَهُ عَلَيْهِمْ *he sent him against them.* Also we use عَلَى after words signifying *difficulty* and the opposite; thus يُحَرِّمُ عَلَيْهِمُ ٱلْخَبَائِثَ *he makes unlawful to them the foul things,* ذٰلِكَ عَلَى ٱللهِ يَسِيرٌ *this for God is easy.*

(*c*) To express an obligation; thus عَلَى رَسُولِنَا ٱلْبَلَاغُ ٱلْمُبِينُ

distinct delivery is incumbent upon Our apostle, أَلَمْ يُؤْخَذْ عَلَيْهِمْ مِيثَاقُ ٱلْكِتَابِ *is not the covenant of the book taken upon them,* حَقِيقٌ عَلَيَّ *it is binding upon me.*

(*d*) To show superiority in one over another; thus فَضَّلَكُمْ عَلَى ٱلْعَالَمِينَ *He has favoured you above all creatures,* وَهُوَ عَلَى كُلِّ شَيْءٍ قَدِيرٌ *and He is all-powerful over everything.*

(*e*) To give the condition serving as basis upon which a person rests; thus كَانَ عَلَى دِينِ ٱلْمَسِيحِ *he followed the Christian religion.*

(*f*) To indicate the subject spoken of; thus أَنْ لَا يَقُولُوا عَلَى ٱللّٰهِ إِلَّا ٱلْحَقَّ *that they should not say concerning God other than the truth.*

REM. *a.* Other uses exist; as جَآءَكُمْ ذِكْرٌ عَلَى رَجُلٍ مِنْكُمْ *an admonition has come to you through one of yourselves.*

462. With an oath (قَسَمٌ) we employ وَ *by* provided a substantive follows and there is no verb of swearing. The complement (جَوَابُ ٱلْقَسَمِ) may be an affirmative verbal proposition, and the verb may be imperfect, in which case لَ is prefixed to the energetic form; thus وَرَبِّي لَتُبْعَثُنَّ *by my Lord, ye shall be raised.*

463. While commonly reckoned among prepositions كَ *as, like* is a substantive and synonymous with مِثْلٌ *likeness* (see § 482 *f*). We find it in كَذَا *thus,* كَذٰلِكَ *in like manner, so,* and كَأَنَّ *as though.*

NOTE. Attached to كَ we find مَا ٱلْكَافَّةُ *the hindering mā* (see § 353*), thus اِجْعَلْ لَنَا إِلٰهًا كَمَا لَهُمْ آلِهَةٌ *make for us a god like their gods.*

466. To signify *at the side of* we employ عِنْدَ; thus وَٱللّٰهُ عِنْدَهُ أَجْرٌ عَظِيمٌ *and with God there is great reward,* بِمَا عَهِدَ عِنْدَكَ *by virtue of the covenant He has made with thee,* يَجِدُونَهُ مَكْتُوبًا عِنْدَهُمْ فِي ٱلتَّوْرَاةِ وَٱلْإِنْجِيلِ *they find him written down with them* i.e. mentioned *in the Old Testament and Gospel,* أَلَا إِنَّمَا طَائِرُهُمْ عِنْدَ ٱللّٰهِ *verily the cause of their good and ill luck lies hidden in the counsels of God.* When used of time عِنْدَ may indicate a particular moment, thus أَيْقَنْتُ عِنْدَ كِتَابِهَا *I felt sure at the time of writing it.*

467. Signifying *between* بَيْنَ indicates an intervening space, thus بَيْنَ ٱلطُّوفَانِ وَبَيْنَ ٱلْهِجْرَةِ *between the Flood and the Hegira.* Of common occurrence is بَيْنَ يَدَيْهِ *between his two hands* i.e. in his presence, and بَيْنَ أَيْدِيهِمْ *between their hands* i.e. before them; thus بَيْنَ يَدَيْ رَحْمَتِهِ *before his mercy.*

468. Signifying *beneath* تَحْتَ indicates the lower part; thus تَحْتَ ٱلشَّجَرَةِ *under the tree.*

REM. *b.* Its opposite is فَوْقَ *above*; as وَهُوَ ٱلْقَاهِرُ فَوْقَ عِبَادِهِ *and He is all-powerful over His servants.*

469. Signifying *below* دُونَ often indicates something inferior, and

(*e*) that a quality belonging to one is not possessed by

another; thus مِنْهُمُ ٱلصَّالِحُونَ وَمِنْهُمْ دُونَ ذٰلِكَ *the good are among them and those who are not that are among them.*

Rem. Beside عِنْدَ, بَيْنَ, تَحْتَ and دُونَ, there are other nouns in the accusative (see §§ 359 and 444 *b*) which are employed as prepositions: for instance,

(*a*) قَبْلَ *before* of time; thus أَآمَنْتُمْ بِهِ قَبْلَ أَنْ آذَنَ لَكُمْ *have ye believed Him before that I gave you permission.* Its opposite is بَعْدَ *after*; thus لَا تُفْسِدُوا فِي ٱلْأَرْضِ بَعْدَ إِصْلَاحِهَا *do not ye commit disorders in the earth after its ordering.*

(c) وَرَآءَ *behind*, thus اُنْظُرْ وَرَآءَكَ *look behind thee*: equivalent is خَلْفَ, thus يَعْلَمُ مَا بَيْنَ أَيْدِيهِمْ وَمَا خَلْفَهُمْ *He knows what is before them and what behind* i.e. what is and shall be.

470. Compound prepositions have usually مِنْ as the first part, and the second part must be in dependent case. Thus

(*b*) مِنْ تَحْتِ; as وَيُدْخِلُهُ جَنَّاتٍ تَجْرِي مِنْ تَحْتِهَا ٱلْأَنْهَارُ *and He shall cause him to enter gardens under which flow the runnels of water.*

(*c*) مِنْ قَبْلِ and مِنْ بَعْدِ; as مِنْ قَبْلِ إِتْيَانِكَ إِيَّانَا *before thy coming to us*, ثُمَّ بَعَثْنَا مِنْ بَعْدِهِمْ مُوسَى *then after them* (the aforesaid) *We sent Moses*, بِئْسَمَا خَلَفْتُمُونِي مِنْ بَعْدِي *evil have ye wrought in mine absence after my departure*, ٱلَّذِينَ عَمِلُوا ٱلسَّيِّئَاتِ ثُمَّ تَابُوا مِنْ بَعْدِهَا *those who do evil things* (*and*) *then after that repent.*

Rem. *e.* The construction may sometimes be made more

concise by omission of a preposition; thus وَٱخْتَارَ مُوسَى قَوْمَهُ سَبْعِينَ رَجُلًا لِمِيقَاتِنَا instead of مِنْ قَوْمِهِ *and Moses chose from his people seventy men for Our appointed time.*

---

471. The *infinitive* (see §§ 195 and 426 to 429) like other nouns is indefinite unless defined by the article or otherwise; thus فِي ذٰلِكُمْ بَلَآءٌ مِنْ رَبِّكُمْ عَظِيمٌ *therein, O you, is a great trial from your Lord*; إِنَّ ٱلَّذِينَ ٱتَّخَذُوا ٱلْعِجْلَ سَيَنَالُهُمْ غَضَبٌ مِنْ رَبِّهِمْ وَذِلَّةٌ فِي ٱلْحَيَاةِ ٱلدُّنْيَا *verily those who chose the calf* (*as a god*), *wrath shall overtake them from their Lord, and ignominy in this present life*; قَالُوا مَعْذِرَةً إِلَى رَبِّكُمْ *they said, It is a way of excusing* (*ourselves*) *to your Lord.*

472. The rection* of nomina agentis has been treated in §§ 430, 431. They and nomina patientis (originally adjectives, see § 80) are frequently used as *concrete verbal nouns*, designating a person or thing to which the verbal idea closely attaches itself, while remaining immovable. The Imperfect is nearly akin but being part of a finite verb indicates motion or renewal.

Note. We retain Professor Wright's term *nomen concretum verbale*, though it might perhaps be as well to employ the word *participle*, here and elsewhere.

473. For a specific indication of time we must look to some other word in the sentence; thus قَالَ سَنُقَتِّلُ أَبْنَآءَهُمْ وَنَسْتَحْيِي نِسَآءَهُمْ وَإِنَّا فَوْقَهُمْ قَاهِرُونَ *he answered, We will massacre their*

---

* By a word's rection, we mean its influence in regard to construction, requiring that another word be in a particular case: the corresponding term is عَمَلٌ *action of government.*

sons and we will save alive their daughters (lit. women) *and verily we shall be subduers over them,* where سَ gives a future sense to all three clauses.

(*a*) In a clause which is not circumstantial the concrete verbal noun refers to a present or future time; thus فَلَمَّا كَشَفْنَا عَنْهُمُ ٱلرِّجْزَ إِلَى أَجَلٍ هُمْ بَالِغُوهُ *but when We removed from them the plague until a fixed term, which they were about to attain*; إِنَّ هَاؤُلَآءِ مُتَبَّرٌ مَا هُمْ فِيهِ وَبَاطِلٌ مَا كَانُوا يَعْمَلُونَ *as to these people destroyed is that (religion) in which they were, and vain is what they were making*; هُوَ ٱلَّذِي خَلَقَكُمْ فَمِنْكُمْ كَافِرٌ وَمِنْكُمْ مُؤْمِنٌ *He it is who created you, and one of you is an unbeliever, and one of you a believer*; قَالُوا مَهْمَا تَأْتِنَا بِهِ مِنْ آيَةٍ فَمَا نَحْنُ لَكَ بِمُؤْمِنِينَ *they said, Whatever sign thou bringest to us we do not believe in thee.*

(*b*) But the concrete verbal noun in a circumstantial clause refers to the same period of time as the ruling verb; see § 583. The Imperfect Indicative will be found used in nearly the same way; see § 408 *e*.

474. When attached to a verb as adverbial accusative (see § 444 *c*) a concrete verbal noun refers to the same period of time as the verb itself; thus ادْخُلُوا ٱلْبَابَ سُجَّدًا *enter the gate prostrating yourselves*; يُدْخِلُهُمْ جَنَّاتٍ خَالِدِينَ فِيهَا *He shall make them enter gardens to abide therein*, an instance of حَالٌ مُقَدَّرٌ *ḥāl indicating the future.*

475. A noun, when governing another noun in the dependent case, is called by the Arabians مُضَافٌ *annexed*, and is said by European grammarians to be in *construct state.* It is shortened in pronunciation by omission of tanwin or of the terminations نِ and نَ, in order that the speaker may pass quickly to the governed word, which is called ٱلْمُضَافُ إِلَيْهِ *that to which annexation is made.* Their relationship is known as إِضَافَةٌ *annexation.*

Rem. There are two kinds of annexation اَلْإِضَافَةُ ٱلْحَقِيقِيَّةُ *the proper annexation* and اَلْإِضَافَةُ غَيْرُ ٱلْحَقِيقِيَّةِ *the improper annexation*: in the former اَلْمُضَافُ may be مَعْرِفَةٌ *defined* or نَكِرَةٌ *undefined*; in the latter it can only be نَكِرَةٌ, except when the article is prefixed, see § 489.

476. In the construct state of a governing noun, followed immediately by the dependent of a governed, can be represented all ideas which we express in English with the preposition *of.* Thus سُورَةُ ٱلْبَقَرَةِ *the chapter of the cow*, حَاضِرَةُ ٱلْبَحْرِ *in presence of the sea* i.e. situated by the sea, إِنْ يَرَوْا سَبِيلَ ٱلرُّشْدِ *if they see the path of true direction.* A word may be governing and governed; as مَالِكِ يَوْمِ ٱلدِّينِ *the Ruler of the day of the judgement*, مِيقَاتُ رَبِّهِ *the appointed time of his Lord*, أَعَجِلْتُمْ أَمْرَ رَبِّكُمْ *have ye hastened the affair of your Lord?*

478. (*a*) The governed word (اَلْمُضَافُ إِلَيْهِ) in proper annexation may be nomen substantivum*, a pronoun or other word

* We use nomen substantivum here as in § 190, to include primitive nouns, infinitives, and simple substantives.

regarded as a substantive, or an entire clause (see § 488). Thus سُورَةُ ٱلتَّغَابُنِ *the chapter of the overreaching,* مُوسَى وَقَوْمُهُ *Moses and his people,* وَٱلَّذِينَ كَذَّبُوا بِآيَاتِنَا وَلِقَاءِ ٱلْآخِرَةِ حَبِطَتْ أَعْمَالُهُمْ *and those who deny Our signs and the meeting of the last (dwelling), vain are their works,* كُلُوا مِنْ طَيِّبَاتِ مَا رَزَقْنَاكُمْ *eat of the good things which we have provided for you,* نَبَأُ ٱلَّذِينَ كَفَرُوا *the story of those who disbelieved.*

(*b*) The governing word (ٱلْمُضَافُ i.e. the one in construct state) must in proper annexation be nomen substantivum* in which category are accounted prepositions, as بَعْدَ إِصْلَاحِهَا *after its ordering*; so also are numerals, for which see § 496 et seq. Thus رَبُّ هٰرُونَ *the Lord of Aaron,* ذَاقُوا وَبَالَ أَمْرِهِمْ *they tasted the mischief of their doing,* وَٱللّٰهُ عَلِيمٌ بِذَاتِ ٱلصُّدُورِ *and God is well acquainted with what is in possession of the breasts.* An adjective in construct state is improperly annexed (see § 489) unless, as in the following examples, standing in the position of a defined noun so as to have the force of a substantive; thus حَسَنُ ٱلْوَجْهِ *the handsome (part) of the face* or even *the handsome face,* عَالِمُ ٱلْغَيْبِ وَٱلشَّهَادَةِ *the Knower of the hidden and of the manifest.* As regards superlatives, see §§ 486 and 493.

REM. *a.* In proper annexation the article أَلْ can never be prefixed to ٱلْمُضَافُ, in the improper it may (see § 489).

NOTE. The annexed word can be governed by a verb مَحْذُوفٌ *eliminated,* as يَوْمَ يَجْمَعُكُمْ لِيَوْمِ ٱلْجَمْعِ ذٰلِكَ يَوْمُ ٱلتَّغَابُنِ make mention of *the day whereon He shall gather you for the day of*

* We use nomen substantivum here as in § 190, to include primitive nouns, infinitives, and simple substantives.

assembly, this will be the day of general deception: here we must prefix اُذْكُرْ.

480. Instead of having an adjective attached to it, a noun may be in construct state qualified by another noun; as رَجُلُ صِدْقٍ *a sincere man*: this is common in specifying the material, as عِجْلُ حُلِيٍّ *a calf (made) of ornaments.*

482. The following substantives are used to express the whole, the part, the like, and the different, by being annexed (مُضَافٌ) to a dependent.

(*a*) كُلٌّ *the totality, the whole.* If the leading substantive is defined and signifies something single and indivisible, كُلٌّ means *whole* as كُلُّ ٱلْبَيْتِ *the whole house*; if it is definite but plural or collective, we must render كُلٌّ *all*, as كُلُّ ٱلثَّمَرَاتِ *all the fruits*, كُلُّ ٱلْبَقَرِ *all the cattle*; if it is indefinite كُلٌّ means *each*, *every*, as إِنْ يَرَوْا كُلَّ آيَةٍ لَا يُؤْمِنُوا بِهَا *if they see each sign they will not believe in it*, رَحْمَتِي وَسِعَتْ كُلَّ شَيْءٍ *My mercy comprises everything.* In § 402 *a* will be found كُلُّ أُنَاسٍ *every tribe*: here, as may be learned from the context, أُنَاس is collective (see § 305, rem. *e*) but is used as a singular.

(*b*) جَمِيعٌ *the totality, the whole*, much resembles كُلٌّ; we may however say إِلَيْكُمْ جَمِيعًا *to you all* (see § 444 *c*, rem. *b* 2) but not إِلَيْكُمْ كُلًّا.

(*d*) غَيْرٌ *something different* may usually be translated *other than*: thus اُعْبُدُوا ٱللّٰهَ مَا لَكُمْ مِنْ إِلٰهٍ غَيْرُهُ *worship God, ye have no god other than Him*; أَغَيْرَ ٱللّٰهِ أَبْغِيكُمْ إِلٰهًا *shall I seek for you a god other than God?* بَدَّلَ ٱلَّذِينَ ظَلَمُوا مِنْهُمْ قَوْلًا غَيْرَ ٱلَّذِي قِيلَ لَهُمْ *the wrongdoers among them substituted a word, other than that which was told them.* For بِغَيْرِ *without* see § 456, rem. *c*.

Rem. *a*. We employ غَيْر as a negative, thus غَيْرُ مُمْكِنٍ *impossible*; but if repetition be needed we must after the first negative use لَا followed alike by a dependent, thus صِرَاطُ ٱلَّذِينَ أَنْعَمْتَ عَلَيْهِمْ غَيْرِ ٱلْمَغْضُوبِ عَلَيْهِمْ وَلَا ٱلضَّالِّينَ *the way of those upon whom Thou hast shed blessing, other than those who are the objects of (Thine) anger and are in error.*

(*f*) مِثْلٌ *likeness, like*, as مِثْلُهُ *the like of it, like it.*

Rem. *a*. Similar in sense to مِثْلٌ, but without case signs, is كَ see § 463.

486. Properly annexed, in construct state, are found deverbal adjectives expressing the superlative, of form أَفْعَلُ (see § 234) or فَعْلٌ (see § 242, note 1); thus وَأَنْتَ أَرْحَمُ ٱلرَّاحِمِينَ *and Thou art the most merciful of the merciful,* وَأَنْتَ خَيْرُ ٱلْغَافِرِينَ *and Thou art the best of those who pardon.* Here one item is made to stand prominently out of a whole designated by the dependent; and being in this annexation definite substantives (see § 478 *b*) أَفْعَلُ and فَعْلٌ need not vary in gender or number (see § 493, rem. *a*), thus أَكْبَرُ ٱلْمَدَائِنِ *the greatest of the cities,* أَحْسَنُهَا *the best thing that is in it.*

REM. *a.* Being superlative أَوَّلُ *first* stands in annexation of the same sort, thus أَنَا أَوَّلُ ٱلْمُؤْمِنِينَ *I am the first of the believers.* The other ordinal numbers ought not so to be used, for they are nomina agentis from transitive verbs, see § 328.

488. When أَنْ governs a verb (see § 415 *a*) it is أَنِ ٱلْمَصْدَرِيَّةُ *the 'an which with its verb is equivalent to a maçdar* (see § 195) and the same construction appertains to the indefinite مَا (see § 353*). Thus أُوذِينَا مِنْ قَبْلِ أَنْ تَأْتِيَنَا وَمِنْ بَعْدِ مَا جِئْتَنَا *we were afflicted before that thou camest to us and after that thou hast come,* which is equivalent to مِنْ قَبْلِ إِتْيَانِكَ إِيَّانَا وَمِنْ بَعْدِ مَجِيئِكَ إِيَّانَا *before thy coming to us and after thy coming to us.* Clauses of this sort frequently stand as ٱلْمُضَافُ إِلَيْهِ (the second member of an annexation, see § 478 *a*) in lieu of a dependent.

489. When improperly annexed the noun in construct state must be an adjective, thus حَسَنُ ٱلْوَجْهِ *handsome of face,* سَرِيعُ ٱلْعِقَابِ *prompt of chastisement.* Here the dependent though always defined by the article exercises no defining influence upon its governing word, which remains نَكِرَةٌ (see § 475, rem.) and can be defined by the article, thus اَللّٰهُ ٱلسَّرِيعُ ٱلْعِقَابِ *God the prompt to punish**.

490. Except by poetic licence, nothing can intervene between a noun in construct state and its following dependent, consequently an adjective qualifying the first member must be placed

* This sort of annexation is treated in Wright's Grammar, vol. II. § 80.

after the second; thus ٱلْحَمْدُ لِلّٰهِ رَبِّ ٱلْعَالَمِينَ ٱلرَّحْمٰنِ ٱلرَّحِيمِ praise belongs to God, the Lord of the worlds, the compassionate and merciful.

492. In proper annexation if the second member be indefinite the first is the same, as إِنِّي أَخَافُ عَلَيْكُمْ عَذَابَ يَوْمٍ عَظِيمٍ *verily I fear in your case a punishment of a great day.* But if the second member be definite so is the first, as أَوْرَثْنَا ٱلْقَوْمَ مَشَارِقَ ٱلْأَرْضِ وَمَغَارِبَهَا *We caused the people to inherit the eastern parts of the land and the western parts of it.* If we desire that the first noun be indefinite while the second is definite we must employ the preposition لِ, thus اِبْنٌ لِلرَّجُلِ *a son of the man* (see § 453 *b*, i): certain words of wide signification may however remain indefinite even when followed by a definite dependent.

493. The examples in § 486 have each its dependent (ٱلْمُضَافُ إِلَيْهِ) definite and therefore partitive: if indefinite the dependent must be explicative, as هُنَّ أَفْضَلُ نِسَآءٍ *they are most excellent women,* اَللّٰهُ خَيْرُ حَافِظٍ *God is the best preserver.* After the superlatives أَوَّلُ *first* and آخِرُ *last* the indefinite dependent is likewise explicative; thus أَوَّلُ آيَةٍ *the first verse,* آخِرُ يَوْمٍ *the last day.*

Rem. *a.* If the dependent be definite the noun in construct state (ٱلْمُضَافُ) may resume its characteristic attribute as an adjective and conform in number and gender to the object or objects mentioned; thus هِيَ كُبْرَى ٱلْمَدَآئِنِ *it is the largest of the cities,* هُنَّ كُبْرَيَاتُ ٱلْمَدَآئِنِ *they are the largest of the cities.*

494. Attention has been drawn in § 480 to a way of specifying the material from which any thing is made: this also may be done by putting the material in apposition to the object, both being either definite or indefinite; thus وَٱتَّخَذَ قَوْمُ مُوسَى مِنْ بَعْدِهِ عِجْلًا جَسَدًا *and the people of Moses after his departure took for themselves (as god) a calf of red gold.*

495. Of two things which are identical, the second may be in dependent case and the first in construct state.

(*b*) This happens when a specific noun is preceded by a substantive designating the genus, as سُورَةُ فَاتِحَةِ ٱلْكِتَابِ equivalent to اَلسُّورَةُ ٱلَّتِي هِيَ فَاتِحَةُ ٱلْكِتَابِ *the chapter which is the opener of the book.*

---

496. It has been mentioned in § 321 that *cardinal numbers* from 3 to 10, when in apposition to the things numbered, agree with them in case; but when placed in annexation before them (see § 478 *b*) govern a plural dependent. A plural of paucity (see § 307) must be employed if the substantive have one; thus خَلَقَ ٱلسَّمٰوَاتِ وَٱلْأَرْضَ فِي سِتَّةِ أَيَّامٍ *He created the heavens and the earth in six days.*

Rem. *a.* Exceptional is مِائَةٌ *one hundred* which, in dependent singular, always follows the governing numeral, see § 325.

Rem. *b.* Should جَمْعُ ٱلْقِلَّةِ *the plural of paucity* not be in common use, there must perforce be employed جَمْعُ ٱلْكَثْرَةِ *the plural of abundance.*

Rem. *c.* We must remember that a sound plural is plural of

paucity, thus آيُهَا سَبْعُ آيَاتٍ *its verses are seven in number*; (آيٌ is a generic noun which forms a nomen unitatis, being also a plural of abundance, see § 304, No. 28 and § 306, rem. *a*). If however an adjective specifies the objects numbered, مِنْ must be employed as in § 448 *f*; or the noun must be put in apposition to the numeral, thus أَرْبَعَةٌ مُسْلِمُونَ *four Moslems*, سِتٌّ مُؤْمِنَاتٌ *six believing women.*

499. We have seen § 444 *e*, rem. *b*, that cardinal numbers from 11 to 99 take their objects numbered in the accusative singular; thus اخْتَارَ مُوسَى قَوْمَهُ سَبْعِينَ رَجُلًا *Moses chose from his people seventy men*, سُورَةٌ مَكِّيَّةٌ وَهِيَ ثَمَانِ عَشْرَةَ آيَةً *A chapter written at Mecca and it (has) eighteen verses.* Very rarely they are followed by an accusative plural, as اثْنَتَا عَشْرَةَ أُمَمًا *twelve nations.* In gender the tens (عِشْرُونَ, ثَلَاثُونَ, etc.) are common; but units conform to the gender of the noun denoting the objects numbered, thus انْبَجَسَتِ ٱثْنَتَا عَشْرَةَ عَيْنًا *twelve springs gushed out* (عَيْنٌ being feminine, see § 290 *a*).

506. Cardinal numbers agree in gender with nouns denoting the objects numbered according to the following rules; there being constantly borne in mind the peculiarity explained at § 319.

(*a*) The numeral agrees in gender with the singular of the substantive denoting the objects numbered, even if the plural is of different gender; as خَمْسُ سِنِينَ *five years* (the singular

سَنَةٌ being feminine), تِسْعَةُ رَمَضَانَاتٍ *nine Ramaḍans* (the singular رَمَضَانُ being masculine), ثَمَانِيَةَ عَشَرَ رَجُلًا *eighteen men.*

(*b*) When the objects numbered are designated by a noun of general signification, its grammatical gender is usually followed by the numeral; as اِثْنَا عَشَرَ أَسْبَاطًا *twelve tribes* (the sing. سِبْطٌ being masculine). But if another substantive be attached which determines more precisely the real gender of the objects, then the numeral agrees with the second noun; thus قَطَّعْنَاهُمُ ٱثْنَتَيْ عَشْرَةَ أَسْبَاطًا أُمَمًا *We divided them into twelve tribes* (i.e.) *nations* (the sing. أُمَّةٌ being feminine).

---

512. To every جُمْلَةٌ *totality, sentence* there must be a subject and a predicate, the latter being called اَلْمُسْنَدُ *that which is supported, the attribute.* The subject is called اَلْمُسْنَدُ إِلَيْهِ *that by which* (*the attribute*) *is supported,* and the relation between them is termed اَلْإِسْنَادُ *the act of supporting or causing to lean, attribution.*

513. The subject may be a noun substantive, as قَالَ ٱلْمَلَأُ مِنْ قَوْمِهِ *the chieftains of his people answered*; or an expressed pronoun, as هُوَ ٱلْهُدَى وَٱلْفُرْقَانُ *it is the guidance and the criterion,* هِيَ مَعْذِرَةٌ *it is an excuse*; or a pronoun مُسْتَتِرٌ *concealed* in the verb*, as أَغْرَقْنَاهُمْ فِي ٱلْيَمِّ *We drowned them in the sea,* يُحْيِي وَيُمِيتُ *He giveth life and causeth to die*; or a conjunctive

* Tables of these pronouns, prefixed and suffixed, are given in Wright's Grammar, vol. I. § 89.

clause (see § 572), as يُسَبِّحُ لِلّٰهِ مَا فِي ٱلسَّمٰوَاتِ وَمَا فِي ٱلْأَرْضِ *there praises God whatsoever is in heaven and in earth,* زَعَمَ ٱلَّذِينَ كَفَرُوا *the unbelievers have asserted*; or a preposition with its dependent, as دُونَ ذٰلِكَ in مِنْهُمُ ٱلصَّالِحُونَ وَمِنْهُمْ دُونَ ذٰلِكَ *the good are among them, and those who are not that are among them.* The predicate may be a noun (substantive or adjective), as وَلٰكِنِّي رَسُولٌ مِنْ رَبِّ ٱلْعَالَمِينَ *but I am an apostle from the Lord of the worlds,* هُوَ ٱلْعَزِيزُ ٱلْحَكِيمُ *He is the potent, the wise*; or a verb, as فَلَمَّا أَفَاقَ مُوسَى *so when Moses awoke*; or a preposition with its dependent, as هُمْ فِيهِ *they are in it*; or an adverb, as أَنَا هُنَا *I am here*; or a conjunctive clause, as هُوَ ٱلَّذِي خَلَقَكُمْ *He is your Creator,* هٰذَا مَا فَعَلَهُ *this is what did it* or *this is what he did.* Be the predicate what it may, every sentence beginning with its subject is جُمْلَةٌ ٱسْمِيَّةٌ *a nominal sentence* (which may be simple or compound, see §§ 519 and 520), thus هُوَ ٱلْعَلِيُّ ٱلْعَظِيمُ *He is the sublime, the mighty,* إِنَّ ٱلْأَرْضَ لِلّٰهِ *surely the earth belongs to God,* مُوسَى أَفَاقَ *Moses awoke.* On the other hand we call جُمْلَةٌ فِعْلِيَّةٌ *a verbal sentence* (simple or compound) any one in which the predicate is a verb preceding its subject, thus ٱسْتَغْنَى ٱللّٰهُ *God is self-sufficing,* لَا يَؤُودُهُ حِفْظُهُمَا *the guarding of them both does not weary Him*; or in which the verb represents both subject and predicate, thus تَوَلَّوْا *they turned aside.* The subject of a nominal sentence is termed ٱلْمُبْتَدَأُ *the inchoative* (except when put in the accusative by a preceding إِنَّ, for it is then known as ٱسْمُ إِنَّ see § 525 rem.) and its predicate

اَلْخَبَرُ *the enunciative*; while the subject of a verbal sentence is called اَلْفَاعِلُ *the agent*, and its predicate اَلْفِعْلُ *the action* or *verb*.

Rem. *b*. Here Professor de Goeje adds the following:—

The difference between verbal and nominal sentences, to which the native grammarians attach no small importance, is properly this, that the former relates an act or event, the latter gives a description of a person or thing, either absolutely, or in the form of a clause descriptive of state (see § 583 *a*). This is the constant rule in good old Arabic, unless the desire to emphasize a part of the sentence be the cause of a change in its position.

514. A verb with أَنْ or مَا (then called maçdarîyah, see § 488) may serve as subject either to a nominal or to a verbal sentence; thus حَقِيقٌ عَلَيَّ أَنْ أَقُولَ *that I say* so and so *is incumbent upon me*.

515. The predicate may (see § 513) be a preposition with its dependent, and when the subject precedes we have a nominal sentence; thus اَلْعَاقِبَةُ لِلْمُتَّقِينَ *the result is to the devout*. If however the preposition and dependent stand first, thus إِلَيْهِ اَلْمَصِيرُ *the returning is to Him* (see also next section), we may call the phrase جُمْلَةٌ ظَرْفِيَّةٌ *a local sentence* (see §§ 221, rem. *a* and 527 *a*).

Rem. The logical emphasis falls upon the later word as in § 436, rem. *b*.

516. If the predicate be an adverb or a preposition with its dependent, and the subject an indefinite substantive or a clause (see § 514) containing a finite verb governed by أَنْ, then the

predicate must precede, thus أَخَذَ ٱلْأَلْوَاحَ وَفِي نُسْخَتِهَا هُدًى وَرَحْمَةٌ *he took the tables and in their inscription were guidance and mercy,* لَهُ خُوَارٌ *it lows* lit. *a lowing is to it*: but either order is permitted if the indefinite substantive carries with it an adjective, expressed or implied, thus لَهُمْ عَذَابٌ أَلِيمٌ or عَذَابٌ أَلِيمٌ لَهُمْ *to them is a painful punishment.* In case of a sentence expressing a wish, however, its subject if indefinite must precede, as سَلَامٌ عَلَيْكُمْ *peace be unto you*; and should the subject follow, it must be defined, thus عَلَيْكُمُ ٱلسَّلَامُ.

517. The subject also necessarily follows its predicate in a nominal sentence, (*a*) when the مُبْتَدَأ contains a pronoun making reference to a word in the خَبَر, as فِي ٱلدَّارِ صَاحِبُهَا *its master is in the house*; (*b*) when the مُبْتَدَأ is restricted by إِنَّمَا or إِلَّا, as أَطِيعُوا ٱللّٰهَ وَأَطِيعُوا ٱلرَّسُولَ فَإِنْ تَوَلَّيْتُمْ فَإِنَّمَا عَلَى رَسُولِنَا ٱلْبَلَاغُ ٱلْمُبِينُ *obey God and obey the apostle, but if ye turn aside, then only the clear delivery (of his message) is incumbent upon Our apostle,* مَا لَنَا إِلَّا ٱتِّبَاعُهُ *we have nothing* (*to do*) *but to follow him* (see §§ 585 and 586); (*c*) when the خَبَر is an interrogative, as مَنْ هُوَ *who is he?* مَا هِيَ *what is it?* (see § 570).

518. In a verbal sentence the agent (i.e. subject) must always follow its verb (i.e. predicate); thus كَلَّمَهُ رَبُّهُ *his Lord spoke to him,* يَخْرُجُ نَبَاتٌ *plants spring up*: this it is held to do where a verb represents both subject and predicate; thus أَلْقَى ٱلْأَلْوَاحَ *he threw down the tables.*

519. In addition to simple sentences, nominal and verbal, we find *compound*, each consisting of an inchoative with a clause as enunciative. In one sort of compound nominal sentence, a noun (substantive or pronoun) is transposed to the first place and followed by a verb, thus رَحْمَتِي وَسِعَتْ كُلَّ شَيْءٍ (*as to*) *My mercy* (*it*) *comprises everything.* Here the agent of the clause (اَلْفَاعِلُ) is a concealed pronoun, which corresponds in gender and number with the inchoative of the sentence; and the inchoative contrasts (tacitly or expressly) with another inchoative having a different predicate, thus مُوسَى أَفَاقَ وَهٰرُونُ نَائِمٌ *Moses awoke while Aaron was* (*still*) *sleeping*, إِنَّا هُدْنَا إِلَيْكَ *verily as for us, we repent toward Thee*, وَلٰكِنَّ أَكْثَرَهُمْ لَا يَعْلَمُونَ *but most of them do not know*, بِأَنَّهُمْ كَذَّبُوا بِآيَاتِنَا *because they denied Our signs*, لَعَلَّكُمْ تُرْحَمُونَ *perchance ye may be mercifully dealt with*, لَعَلَّكُمْ تَهْتَدُونَ *perhaps ye may be guided aright.*

520. There are also compound sentences in which a pronominal suffix called اَلرَّابِطُ *the connecter* replaces the noun transposed. They may be (*a*) compound nominal, thus اَللّٰهُ عِنْدَهُ أَجْرٌ عَظِيمٌ *with God there is great reward*; or (*b*) compound verbal, thus اَلْبَلَدُ ٱلطَّيِّبُ يَخْرُجُ نَبَاتُهُ (*as to*) *the good land its herbage comes forth*, عَذَابِي أُصِيبُ بِهِ مَنْ أَشَآءُ (*as to*) *My punishment I strike with it whom I will.*

521. We may regard as verbal a sentence consisting of a

deverbal adjective and following noun, thus كَرِيمٌ قَوْمُكَ *thy people are generous* (see § 552 *b* ii).

522. There does not exist in Arabic a substantive verb, i.e. one which would unite subject and predicate in a nominal sentence without connoting the idea of existence; for كَانَ though occasionally supplying the place of logical copula, ascribes to its subject the attribute of existence; and being attributive, its predicate and those of أَخَوَاتُ كَانَ must be in the accusative case (see §§ 441 and 442).

523. The absence of logical copula expressed by or contained in a finite verb constitutes the essential characteristic of a (simple) nominal sentence (see § 513); so that when a definite noun (substantive or pronoun) and an indefinite adjective stand in juxtaposition we have a complete nominal sentence. The fact of the former being defined (no matter how) and the latter undefined, shows them to occupy the positions of subject and predicate; for, as will be seen in § 536, a descriptive epithet must agree with its noun in respect of definition as well as in gender, number and case. Thus اَللّٰهُ غَنِيٌّ حَمِيدٌ *God is self-sufficing (and) worthy to be praised,* سُورَةُ ٱلْأَعْرَافِ مَكِّيَّةٌ *the chapter of the uppermost parts is Meccan.*

524. If both subject and predicate are defined, we can make sure of their relative position being recognized, by inserting between them ضَمِيرُ ٱلْفَصْلِ *the pronoun of separation*; thus أُلَآئِكَ هُمُ ٱلْمُفْلِحُونَ *those are the prosperous.*

525. If the predicate be a nominative and the subject placed in the accusative after إِنَّ or the like, a pronoun of separation is unnecessary; thus إِنَّ رَبَّكُمُ ٱللّٰهُ *verily your Lord is God*: there may however be inserted such pronoun of the same person as اِسْمُ إِنَّ (see § 436, rem. *a*); thus إِنَّكَ أَنْتَ وَلِيُّنَا *truly Thou art our protector.*

Rem. A noun governed by إِنَّ etc. is not called مُبْتَدَأٌ *inchoative* by Arabian grammarians.

527. As a general rule the subject of a nominal sentence must, if not exactly defined, be specialized. No information is conveyed by "A horse is grey"; but we can say فَرَسٌ أَصْفَرُ هُوَ أَحْسَنُ مِنْ غَيْرِهِ *a grey horse is handsomest*, where فَرَسٌ though نَكِرَةٌ *indefinite* is specialized by its adjective; so also there is obviously a partial determination in رَغْبَةٌ فِي ٱلشَّرِّ شَرٌّ *a desire to do evil is bad*, and in عَذَابُ يَوْمٍ عَظِيمٍ مَخُوفٌ *a punishment of a great day is to be feared* (see § 492). These examples differ from true definition, which is only attained by use of the article لِلتَّعْرِيفِ *in order to distinguish* (see § 345), or by annexation to a defined noun (see § 475 et seq.): there are other cases where the subject of a nominal clause can be indefinite, among which are the following:—

(*a*) In a clause called at § 515 ẓarfīyah (i) when the predicate stands first, as مِنَ ٱلْقَوْمِ أُمَّةٌ *there is a section of the people*; and (ii) when the subject is preceded by an interrogative or negative particle, as هَلْ مَآءٌ فِي ٱلْبِئْرِ *is there water in the cistern?* مَا شُرْبٌ لَنَا *we have no drink.*

(*e*) When the sentence expresses a wish, as سَلَامٌ عَلَيْكُمْ *peace be unto you*; see § 516.

(*f*) Words containing the conditional meaning of إِنْ *if* (see § 406), though indefinite by their nature, serve as inchoative; thus مَنْ يُؤْمِنْ بِٱللّٰهِ *if any one believes God*, مَنْ يُوقَ شُحَّ نَفْسِهِ *whoever is made to guard against his own covetousness.*

529. A pronoun of separation is sometimes omitted if the meaning remains clear, as ذٰلِكَ ٱلْفَوْزُ ٱلْعَظِيمُ *this is the great prize.*

530. To give emphasis and occasion contrast ضَمِيرُ ٱلتَّوْكِيدِ أَوِ ٱلتَّأْكِيدِ *the pronoun of corroboration* may be introduced; it being wholly different from the pronoun of separation treated in § 524 et seq. Commonly it follows the subject, or a verb which represents both subject and predicate; thus ٱلَّذِينَ هُمْ لِرَبِّهِمْ يَرْهَبُونَ *those only who fear their Lord*, إِنْ كُنَّا نَحْنُ ٱلْغَالِبِينَ *if WE be the victors*; see also نَكُونَ نَحْنُ at § 415 *a* i, Note.

Note. The pronoun of corroboration may follow conjunctive pronouns in an oblique case, thus لِلَّذِينَ هُمْ بِآيَاتِنَا يُؤْمِنُونَ *for those especially who believe in Our signs.*

531. If however in the description of persons or things (see § 513, rem. *b*) a nominal clause lacks precision, we may use كَانَ or one of its sisters (see § 442). When so employed the imperfect has its usual meanings: but a perfect, beside examples like those in § 441, may express the present, as يَضَعُ عَنْهُمْ إِصْرَهُمْ وَٱلْأَغْلَالَ ٱلَّتِي كَانَتْ عَلَيْهِمْ *he puts away from them their burden and the*

fetters which are upon them; especially is this the case after an interrogative, or مَا *not*, as مَا كُنْتُ لِأَحْكُمَ بَيْنَكُمْ حَتَّى ٱلَخ *I am not ready to judge between you until etc.* (see § 557).

533. We have observed in § 73 that passive verbs must often be translated impersonally: commonly a 3rd person singular masculine is used to avoid specifying the subject, thus إِذْ قِيلَ لَهُمْ *when it was said to them.* In case of غَفَرَ — which governs only an accusative of the sin, we render سَيُغْفَرُ لَنَا *we shall be pardoned,* for *it will be pardoned to us* gives too explicit a subject. Nomina patientis of verbs which are transitive by help of a preposition (see § 423) can only appear in the masculine singular, changes of gender and number being marked by an alteration of the pronoun; thus هُوَ مَغْضُوبٌ عَلَيْهِ *he is an object of anger,* هِيَ مَغْضُوبٌ عَلَيْهَا *she is an object of anger,* ٱلْمَغْضُوبُ عَلَيْهِمْ *the objects of anger.* The neuter plural of adjectives is sometimes expressed by the feminine sound plural, and sometimes by a broken plural, but never by the masculine sound plural; thus وَبَلَوْنَاهُمْ بِٱلْحَسَنَاتِ وَٱلسَّيِّئَاتِ *and We tested them by means of good and evil things,* يُحِلُّ لَهُمُ ٱلطَّيِّبَاتِ وَيُحَرِّمُ عَلَيْهِمُ ٱلْخَبَآئِثَ *he makes lawful to them the pleasant things and makes unlawful to them the foul things.*

Rem. *a.* The passive of directly transitive verbs may be used personally or impersonally, thus غُلِبَ *he was overcome* or *there was a victory.*

534. To the subject and predicate *complements* are joined by subordination (the accusative or a preposition with its dependent), or by coordination which is more usually called apposition.

535. Pronominal suffixes may have a *reflexive* meaning when attached to a verb's object, but not when attached to the verb itself; consequently for this purpose we must employ نَفْسٌ *soul* or the like, thus كَانُوا أَنْفُسَهُمْ يَظْلِمُونَ *they were injuring themselves*: to this rule however verbs of the heart (see § 424 *b* ii) supply exceptions.

536. Complements coordinated with a subject or predicate are called تَوَابِعُ *appositives* (see § 304, No. 16), the usual apposition being of noun to noun and the more rare (see § 540) of verb to verb. There stands first اَلْمَتْبُوعُ *that which is followed* and then اَلتَّابِعُ *the follower*.

(*a*) After this fashion the *adjective* is joined to its substantive; they agreeing in gender, number and case, as well as (see § 523) by definition or by being undefined: thus ضَلَالٌ مُبِينٌ *manifest error*, إِلَى ٱلْبَلَدِ ٱلْمَيِّتِ *to the dead country*, رَأَيْتُ مَسْجِدَهُمُ ٱلْجَامِعَ *I saw their congregational mosque* or *their mosque which collects*, لِقَآءَ ٱلدَّارِ ٱلْآخِرَةِ *the meeting of the last abode*. A noun may of course have two or more adjectives connected with it, thus بِسْمِ ٱللّٰهِ ٱلرَّحْمٰنِ ٱلرَّحِيمِ *in the name of God the merciful (and) compassionate*: sometimes a nomen verbi (nomen actionis or other) takes the place of an adjective, thus حَالٌ نَكِرَةٌ *an indefinite ḥâl*, اِسْمٌ مَعْرِفَةٌ *a defined noun*. In the above examples all words are *singular*, and concords in case of the *dual* are equally simple: but with *plurals* the matter becomes difficult, though the rule as to definition is happily unalterable. A substantive (i) in *masculine sound* plural representing rational creatures must be followed by an adjective in the plural, thus بَنُونَ ضَالُّونَ *erring sons*, مُؤْمِنُونَ كِرَامٌ (see § 304, No. 5) *noble believers*, كَافِرُونَ مَلَاعِينُ (see § 305, No. 2) *accursed unbelievers*; while a substantive (ii) in *feminine sound* plural may be followed by an adjective, singular feminine as رِسَالَاتٌ حَسَنَةٌ *gracious messages*, or plural, either broken as جَنَّاتٌ كَرَائِمُ (see § 304, No. 17) *noble gardens*, بَقَرَاتٌ بِيضٌ (see § 304, No. 2) *white cattle*, or feminine sound as آيَاتٌ مُفَصَّلَاتٌ *signs separated by intervals.* A substantive in *broken* plural if (iii) denoting rational beings may be followed by an adjective in the singular feminine, thus اَلطُّلَّابُ ٱلْإِنْكِلِيزِيَّةُ *the English students*, رِجَالٌ مُسْلِمَةٌ *Moslem men*, نِسَآءٌ مُسْلِمَةٌ *Moslem women*, مُلُوكٌ شَدِيدَةٌ *strong kings*, جَوَارٍ شَدِيدَةٌ *strong girls*; it is however better, if the sex be indicated, to employ an appropriate sound plural, thus رِجَالٌ مُسْلِمُونَ and نِسَآءٌ مُسْلِمَاتٌ. But if the broken plural (iv) denotes objects other than rational beings, no matter what their gender in the singular, its adjective may be feminine, singular as حِيتَانٌ كَبِيرَةٌ *great fishes*, or plural as صُوَرٌ حَسَنَاتٌ *beautiful forms*; or else a broken plural, thus رِيَاحٌ عِزَازٌ *powerful winds*, جِبَالٌ كِرَامٌ *noble mountains.* Next as regards *collectives* which are treated in §§ 292 and 306 rem.: those (v) denoting rational beings usually take an adjective in that sound plural which corresponds by natural gender with the beings, thus اَلْقَوْمُ ٱلظَّالِمُونَ *the wrong-doers*, إِنَّهُمْ كَانُوا قَوْمًا عَمِينَ *truly they were a blind people*, حَرِيمُ مَحْمُودٍ ٱلْكَثِيرَاتُ *Maḥmûd's numerous family*; but the adjective may be singular and agree with the collective's grammatical gender, thus خَلْفٌ حَسَنٌ *excellent posterity,* أُمَّةٌ فَاسِقَةٌ *an impious nation.* Collective nouns (vi) which do not form a nomen unitatis and denote living objects destitute of reason (see § 290 *a*) are, in respect of concord with adjectives, similar to (see iv) broken plurals denoting irrational creatures: those (vii) which form a nomen unitatis, and denote objects other than rational, may take a feminine sound plural, as جَرَادٌ طَيَّارَاتٌ *flying locusts*; or a feminine singular, as قَمْلٌ آكُولَةٌ *voracious lice*; or a masculine singular, as اَلثَّمَرُ ٱلطَّيِّبُ *the fresh fruit*; or a broken plural, as سَحَابٌ ثِقَالٌ *heavy cloud.*

(*b*) Being definite by their nature and regarded as substantives, the demonstrative pronouns (see §§ 340, 341) must be coupled with a defined appositive: if this definition is caused by the article we usually find the demonstrative preceding, thus ذٰلِكَ ٱلْفَوْزُ *this prize,* هٰذِهِ ٱلْقَرْيَةَ *this village*; but if the substantive be definite in its nature or defined by a following dependent, it must precede, as مَحْمُودٌ هٰذَا *this Maḥmûd.*

Note. We find in Corân, Sûraȟ 7, verse 166 كُونُوا قِرَدَةً خَاسِئِينَ *become abject apes*: here the appositive is in masculine sound plural because human beings are addressed.

537. Sometimes we find the adjective أَجْمَعُ *all* following a substantive or pronoun and agreeing with it in gender, number and case; thus لَأُصَلِّبَنَّكُمْ أَجْمَعِينَ *I will crucify you all.*

539. In addition to its use at § 535 نَفْسٌ can signify *self*

without reflexive meaning, thus رَأَيْتُ نَفْسَهُ *I have seen himself*: if a plural be needed, أَنْفُسٌ must be employed.

REM. *a.* There is a class of appositives called اَلتَّوْكِيدُ or اَلتَّأْكِيدُ having two divisions; (1) اَلتَّوْكِيدُ ٱلْمَعْنَوِيُّ *the corroboration in meaning* which includes كُلٌّ, جَمِيعٌ, أَجْمَعُ and نَفْسٌ with a few other words; and (2) اَلتَّوْكِيدُ ٱللَّفْظِيُّ *the verbal corroboration*, when any word is repeated, thus نَعَمْ نَعَمْ *yes, yes.*

REM. *b.* Three more classes of appositives are in use. (1) اَلصِّفَةُ *the qualificative* which may refer to its مَتْبُوعٌ (see § 536) directly, in which case it is a simple adjective, thus اَللّٰهُ ٱلْحَيُّ ٱلْقَيُّومُ *the living and everlasting God*; or indirectly, applying to a following word and with it forming a qualificative clause. (2) اَلْبَدَلُ *the permutative* of which the most usual kind is بَدَلُ ٱلْكُلِّ مِنَ ٱلْكُلِّ *the substitution of the whole for the whole*; thus اِهْدِنَا ٱلصِّرَاطَ ٱلْمُسْتَقِيمَ صِرَاطَ ٱلَّذِينَ أَنْعَمْتَ عَلَيْهِمْ غَيْرِ ٱلْمَغْضُوبِ عَلَيْهِمْ *direct us (in) the straight road, the road of those upon whom thou hast shed blessing, other than those who are the objects of (Thine) anger.* Here صراط is badal of صراط, and غير of الذين. (3) عَطْفُ ٱلْبَيَانِ *the explicative connection*, being a substantive which explains its مَتْبُوعٌ; thus اَلرَّسُولُ ٱلنَّبِيُّ *the apostle the prophet*, قَالَ مُوسَى لِأَخِيهِ هٰرُونَ *Moses said to his brother Aaron*, عِجْلٌ جَسَدٌ *a calf a body*, i.e. a calf in bodily shape.

REM. *c.* One verb may be substituted for another by بَدَلُ ٱلْإِشْتِمَالِ *the comprehensive substitution*, i.e. the permutative explaining something involved in the previous verb; thus يَسُومُونَكُمْ سُوٓءَ ٱلْعَذَابِ يُقَتِّلُونَ أَبْنَآءَكُمْ وَيَسْتَحْيُونَ نِسَآءَكُمْ *they lay upon you the evil of punishment, killing your sons and saving alive your daughters.*

540. Two verbs used asyndetically (i.e. used without a conjunction) are regarded as in apposition, thus قَامَ سَجَدَ *he arose and prostrated himself,* سَجَدَ أَطَالَ *he continued long in prostration*; but the insertion of فَ is better.

---

541. As regards *concord in gender and number* between the parts of a sentence, the following rules hold good. We shall treat in § 552 of nominal sentences, and at present confine our attention to verbal sentences (see § 518); premising that a masculine singular subject can only be preceded (or followed) by a masculine singular verb, thus قَالَ فِرْعَوْنُ *Pharaoh said,* and that the equivalent of a plural subject (such as a relative sentence, etc.) takes a preceding verb in the singular, thus زَعَمَ ٱلَّذِينَ كَفَرُوا *the unbelievers have asserted.*

542. (*a*) If the subject be a singular substantive, feminine according to § 290 *a*, and (i) immediately following its verb, the verb must be feminine singular, thus اِمْتَدَّتْ يَدٌ *a hand became extended*: but (ii) if one or more words intervene, while the feminine is better, the masculine is permissible, thus بَصُرَ بِهَا ٱلْعَيْنُ *the eye saw it.*

(*b*) If the subject be a singular substantive, feminine according to § 290 *b* or § 291 the verb may precede in either gender, though preferably in the feminine if the subject follows immediately, thus تَمَّتْ كَلِمَتُ رَبِّكَ *the word of thy Lord was fulfilled*: but we find فَٱنْظُرْ كَيْفَ كَانَ عَاقِبَةُ ٱلْمُفْسِدِينَ *so look how was the end of the transgressors.*

Rem. The concord usually remains if, in negative or interrogative sentences, the subject be preceded by مِنْ; but in Corân, Sûrah 64, verse 11 we have مَا أَصَابَ مِنْ مُصِيبَةٍ *no mischance has befallen.*

(*d*) The verbs نِعْمَ and بِئْسَ take preferably the masculine form, be the subject's gender what it may; see § 183.

543. If the subject be a masculine sound plural the preceding verb is with rare exceptions singular masculine, thus عَلَى ٱللهِ فَلْيَتَوَكَّلِ ٱلْمُؤْمِنُونَ *upon God then let the believers rely.*

Rem. *b.* When meaning *family* or *tribe* بَنُونَ, the sound plural of اِبْنٌ *son*, may be preceded by a feminine singular verb; thus آمَنَتْ بِهِ بَنُو إِسْرَائِيلَ *the tribe of Israel believed Him.*

544. If the subject be a broken plural the preceding verb again with rare exceptions is singular, and of either gender no matter which, thus حَبِطَتْ أَعْمَالُهُمْ (from عَمَلٌ masc.) *their works are vain,* قُطِعَ ٱلْأَرْجُلُ (from رِجْلٌ fem.) *the feet were cut off.* But if the broken plural denote male persons the verb is better masculine, thus أَتُهْلِكُنَا بِمَا فَعَلَ ٱلسُّفَهَاءُ مِنَّا *wilt Thou destroy us on account of what the fools among us have done*; though we sometimes find the feminine, as كَانَتْ تَأْتِيهِمْ رُسُلٌ *apostles used to come to them.*

545. If the subject be a collective or other noun mentioned in § 292 the preceding verb must be singular but may be of either gender; thus قَالَ ٱلْمَلَأُ *the chiefs said*, ٱسْتَسْقَاهُ قَوْمُهُ *his people asked drink of him*, وَإِذْ قَالَتْ أُمَّةٌ مِنْهُمْ *and when a section of them said*.

546. If the subject be a feminine sound plural the preceding verb must be singular but may be of either gender, unless denoting female persons, in which case the feminine is preferable.

548. When the subject has been mentioned in a preceding clause, the verb must agree with it in gender and number according to the following rules. A masculine or feminine singular verb follows a like subject; and a masculine plural verb follows a masculine sound plural, thus سَفَرَ ٱلْمُسْلِمُونَ وَأَتَوْا *the Moslems journeyed and came*, as also the plural of pronouns, thus فَإِذَا جَآءَتْهُمُ ٱلْحَسَنَةُ قَالُوا *and when the boon came to them they said*. In case of broken plurals the following verb must be feminine, singular or plural, thus يُرْسِلُ ٱلرِّيَاحَ وَأَقَلَّتْ سَحَابًا *He sends the winds and they bear cloud* where أَقْلَلْنَ might also have been used: if however male persons are indicated the verb in masculine plural is used, thus جَآءَ ٱلسَّحَرَةُ فِرْعَوْنَ وَقَالُوا *the magicians came to Pharaoh and said*; or if female persons the verb is in feminine plural. Following a collective noun which indicates a predominance of male persons the verb is naturally in masculine plural, thus مِنْ قَوْمِ مُوسَى أُمَّةٌ يَهْدُونَ بِٱلْحَقِّ وَبِهِ يَعْدِلُونَ *among the people of Moses there is a section who direct (others) by the truth and by means of it do justice*, خَلَفَ خَلْفٌ وَرِثُوا ٱلْكِتَابَ *a posterity succeeded who inherited the Book*: other collectives treated in § 292 are followed by a singular verb of either gender. Lastly if the subject be a feminine sound plural the verb would naturally follow in feminine plural though the feminine singular occurs, thus آمَنَّا بِآيَاتِ رَبِّنَا لَمَّا جَاءَتْنَا *we believed the signs of our Lord, when they came to us*: but when female persons are indicated the concord must be strictly kept.

551. A verb sometjmes agrees in gender with the logical subject, i.e. a dependent annexed to the grammatical subject; this is most usual with words explained in § 482, thus وَلَوْ جَاءَتْهُمْ كُلُّ آيَةٍ *even though every sign come to them.*

552. In nominal sentences the concord of gender and number between subject and predicate closely resembles that in verbal sentences.

(*a*) When the predicate, being verb or adjective, follows its subject, they must agree strictly in gender and number; thus اَللّٰهُ أَعْلَمُ مِنْ غَيْرِهِ *God knows best* lit. *is more knowing than any other*, فَإِذَا هِيَ تَتَلَقَّفُ مَا يَأْفِكُونَ *so behold it swallows up what they cause to put on a false appearance*, هُمْ بَالِغُوهُ *they are attainers of it*, لَعَلَّهُمْ يَرْجِعُونَ *perhaps they may repent*, لَعَلَّكُمْ تَتَّقُونَ *perchance ye will take heed to yourselves*; but a broken plural may be followed by a feminine singular, as اَلْحِيتَانُ كَبِيرَةٌ *the fishes are large.*

(*b*) When the predicate precedes its subject, as in negative and interrogative sentences, (i) they must in a nominal sentence agree (see *c*) but (ii) in a verbal sentence (see § 251) the predicate ought to be singular, thus أَمِينٌ ٱلصَّادِقُونَ *the truthful are trustworthy.*

(*c*) If a subject be collective its predicate may follow in the plural, thus اَلْأَهْلُ جَاهِلُونَ *the people are ignorant.* Similarly, when a verb is placed after a collective subject, thus أَبَشَرٌ يَهْدُونَنَا *shall men direct us?*

(*d*) A predicate frequently agrees in gender with the logical subject, i.e. a dependent annexed to the grammatical subject, compare § 551.

---

553. In *negative and prohibitive* sentences a negation may apply to any part of the sentence—the predicate, the subject (see § 439), the object, the circumstantial expression (اَلْحَالُ) etc.

554. The negative most often immediately precedes that part of the sentence which it denies, but this is not necessarily so.

555. (*a*) The predicate of a verbal sentence in the imperfect with present sense may be denied by لَا (see § 362 *dd*), as لَا يَؤُودُهُ حِفْظُهُمَا *the guarding of them both does not weary Him*; or with the future sense, as إِنَّا لَا نُضِيعُ أَجْرَ ٱلْمُصْلِحِينَ *surely We will not allow to be lost the reward of the righteous*; or with a past sense, when preceded by a verb which expresses the past, as أَلَمْ يَرَوْا أَنَّهُ لَا يُكَلِّمُهُمْ *did they not perceive that it could not speak to them?*

(*b*) We rarely find لَا attached to a verb in the perfect, except when used with وَ to continue a previous negation.

556. The particle لَنْ (for لَا أَنْ see § 362 *hh*) is a very strong negation of the future, as can be seen in §§ 411 and 415 *a* i.

Rem. For لَمْ and لَمَّا see §§ 412 and 418.

557. The particle مَا *not* (see § 362 *kk*) denies the perfect when the latter has one of the meanings treated in § 401 *a* to *d*; when joined to the imperfect it denies the present, as is noted in § 408 *e*, rem. *a*.

NOTE. An instance of مَا denying كَانَ is given in § 531.

558. The particle إِنْ *not* (see § 362 *k*) beside being found in nominal sentences, thus إِنْ هِيَ إِلَّا فِتْنَتُكَ *this is only Thy temptation*, may be used before the imperfect indicative and the perfect of a verb.

559. The verb لَيْسَ (see §§ 182 and 442) which usually expresses the indefinite or definite present (see § 408 *a*, *b*) is commonly نَاقِصَةٌ *incomplete*, as لَسْتُ نَاظِرًا or لَسْتُ بِنَاظِرٍ *I am not an onlooker*; though it may be تَامَّةٌ *complete*. It is also employed as an indeclinable particle, denying more strongly than لَا that part of the sentence to which it is prefixed.

560. When a sentence containing one of the negatives مَا, لَمْ, لَمَّا, لَنْ or لَيْسَ is followed by another negative sentence, with وَ *and* to connect the two, (*a*) the second sentence is negatived by لَا when no special emphasis attaches to the form of negation, and (*b*) the first negative is repeated when the independence of the second sentence is emphasized; but (*c*) when the two verbs are conceived of as forming parts of one action, no second negative is required, thus إِنْ لَمْ يَرْحَمْنَا رَبُّنَا وَيَغْفِرْ لَنَا *if our Lord had not been merciful to us and pardoned us*.

REM. *a*. As regards the use of لَا instead of repeating غَيْر, see § 482 *d*, rem. *a*.

563. The prohibitive لَا governs the jussive, as may be seen in §§ 417 *b* and 420: this happens also with the energetic.

---

564. All *interrogative clauses* take the direct form, thus أَتَكْتُبُ ٱللُّغَةَ ٱلْعَرَبِيَّةَ *canst thou write Arabic?* سَأَلَ أَتَكْتُبُ ٱللُّغَةَ ٱلْعَرَبِيَّةَ *he inquired whether thou couldst write Arabic*; the difference between direct and indirect questions being ignored, both in the arrangement of words and in the moods of the verb.

565. Spoken questions may be indicated merely by the tone of voice: but written inquiries are usually introduced by one of the following particles, viz. أَ, أَلَا or هَلْ; unless provided with an interrogative adverb, such as أَيْنَ *where?* كَيْفَ *how?* or the like (see §§ 361 to 364).

566. The simplest interrogative is أَ thus أَعَجِلْتُمْ أَمْرَ رَبِّكُمْ *have ye hastened the affair of your Lord?* This particle may be prefixed to إِنَّ, وَ, فَ or ثُمَّ; thus أَئِنَّ لَنَا لَأَجْرًا (see § 361 *a*, rem.) *shall there indeed be to us a reward?* أَوَعَجِبْتُمْ *do ye wonder?* أَفَلَا تَعْقِلُونَ *do ye not therefore understand?*

567. The interrogative هَلْ introduces questions of a more lively sort, thus هَلْ يُجْزَوْنَ إِلَّا مَا كَانُوا يَعْمَلُونَ *shall they be rewarded otherwise than with what they have been accustomed to do.* Upon the use of this particle there are certain restrictions.

568. The particle أَلَا (originally meaning *is it not the case that?*) affirms a certainty, thus أَلَا لَهُ ٱلْخَلْقُ *truly to Him belongs the (whole) creation.* It is frequently followed by a

further asseverative, e.g. إِنَّمَا, thus أَلَا إِنَّمَا طَآئِرُهُمْ عِنْدَ ٱللّٰهِ *verily their luck* (or fate) *is in the hands of God only.*

570. The interrogative pronouns مَنْ *who?* and مَا *what?* (see § 351) may stand in any one of the three cases, nominative, dependent, or accusative. To render the interrogative more vigorous we append the demonstrative pronoun ذَا (see § 340) thus فَمَا ذَا تَأْمُرُونَ *so what do ye enjoin?* and this may happen when الذي follows, thus مَنْ ذَا ٱلَّذِي يَشْفَعُ عِنْدَهُ *who is he that shall intercede with Him?* The pronouns مَنْ and مَا are always used substantively, but cannot govern a dependent or be followed by a substantive in apposition.

Rem. *d.* As to مَ for مَا, see § 351, rem.

---

572. There are two kinds of *relative sentences*; (*a*) that called صِفَةٌ *a qualificative* which is immediately attached to an indefinite substantive without intervening pronoun, and (*b*) that called صِلَةٌ *a conjunctive*, where introduction is made by a pronoun which is definite in its nature The conjunctive pronoun (see § 346) is called اَلْمَوْصُولُ *that which is joined*, i.e. joined to اَلصِّلَةُ *the conjunctive clause.* As examples (*a*) the following are indefinite clauses; أُمَّةٌ يَهْدُونَ بِٱلْحَقِّ وَبِهِ يَعْدِلُونَ *a nation who direct* (*others*) *by means of the truth and who by it do justice,* فَأَتَوْا عَلَى قَوْمٍ يَعْكُفُونَ عَلَى أَصْنَامٍ لَهُمْ *so they came upon a people who clung to their idols*: (*b*) the following clauses are definite; وَٱسْأَلْهُمْ عَنِ ٱلْقَرْيَةِ ٱلَّتِي كَانَتْ حَاضِرَةَ ٱلْبَحْرِ *and ask them concerning the village which is situated by the sea,*

اَلَّذِينَ يَتَّقُونَ وَيُؤْتُونَ ٱلزَّكَاةَ *those who take heed to themselves and give the appointed alms,* مُوسَى وَمَنْ مَعَهُ *Moses and he who is* (or *those who are*) *with him,* اُدْعُ لَنَا رَبَّكَ بِمَا عَهِدَ عِنْدَكَ *entreat thy Lord on our behalf by virtue of that which he has covenanted with thee.*

Rem. *a.* When the antecedent substantive is indefinite we cannot in Arabic employ a conjunctive pronoun; for اَلَّذِي is (see § 347) always definite, while مَنْ and مَا though sometimes indefinite (see §§ 353* and 527 *f*) are always used substantively.

Rem. *b.* follows the next section.

Rem. *c.* Among qualificative clauses may be accounted those mentioned in § 539, rem. *b* 1.

573. The qualificative clause (اَلصِّفَةُ) necessarily contains a pronoun (called اَلْعَائِدُ), referring to the qualified noun and connecting it with the said qualificative clause. This 'â'id, in case the clause be verbal, is a pronoun concealed (see § 513) in the verb; as حَاشِرُونَ يَأْتُونَكَ *gatherers who* (*they*) *come to thee,* خَلَفَ خَلْفٌ وَرِثُوا ٱلْكِتَابَ *a posterity followed who* (*they*) *inherited the Book*: in case the clause be nominal, a separate pronoun is employed; as نَبِيٌّ هُوَ صَاحِبُكَ *a prophet who* (*he*) *is thy companion.* Frequently the 'â'id appears as a suffix in the accusative, thus هٰذَا مَكْرٌ مَكَرْتُمُوهُ *this is a plot which ye have contrived*; or in the dependent, as قَوْمٌ ٱللّٰهُ مُهْلِكُهُمْ *a people of whom God is the destroyer,* إِلَى أَجَلٍ هُمْ بَالِغُوهُ *until a fixed term which they were about to attain.* If however no 'â'id is needed to make clear the meaning, it may be omitted; thus يَوْمَ يَجْمَعُكُمْ

(*make mention of*) *the day on which He shall assemble you*, whence فِيهِ is eliminated.

Rem. In theory a 'â'id ought to be of the 3rd person, but in practice it often agrees with the subject to which the qualified substantive is predicate; thus إِنَّكُمْ قَوْمٌ تَجْهَلُونَ *verily ye are a people who* (*ye*) *are ignorant*. Compare § 575, rem. *a*.

574. The conjunctive clause (اَلصِّلَةُ) must begin with a conjunctive pronoun. Now it has been shown in § 346 et seq. that, like مَنْ and مَا when definite, اَلَّذِي is used substantively to mean *he who, that which*; thus اَلَّذِي خَبُثَ *that which was bad*, اَلَّذِينَ يَتَّبِعُونَ ٱلرَّسُولَ ٱلنَّبِيَّ ٱلْأُمِّيَّ *those who follow the apostle, the illiterate prophet*. Only اَلَّذِي can be used adjectively, and then like all adjectives it agrees with its antecedent, a definite substantive, in gender, number and case, its agreement in case being best shown by the dual which has case-endings: thus أَرِنَا ٱلشَّيْطَانَيْنِ ٱللَّذَيْنِ أَضَلَّانَا *show us the two devils who led us astray*, where اَللَّذَيْنِ is oblique (for the accusative) agreeing with اَلشَّيْطَانَيْنِ; again أَرِنَا ٱلشَّيْطَانَيْنِ ٱللَّذَيْنِ هُمَا مُضِلَّانَا *show us the two devils who lead us astray*. In both these examples the real subject in the relative clause is the pronoun called 'â'id, as will next be explained.

Note. Whether used substantively or adjectively اَلَّذِينَ can only apply to masculine rational creatures, compare § 302, rem. *a*.

575. The preceding section shows that Arabic conjunctive pronouns are not used quite like our English relative pronouns; for the case in which they are put is independent of the con-

junctive clause. If standing first as substantives and forming the subject of an independent sentence, they are in the nominative; as is اَلَّذِي when attached adjectively to a substantive in the nominative. But in every other instance, though at the beginning of a conjunctive clause, they are subject to government by an antecedent, whether noun, verb or particle: consequently they are in the particular case which their position requires, viz. either, that case occupied by the demonstrative-pronoun implied in them, thus بِمَا فَعَلَ *by reason of THAT which he has done*; or, the same case as the antecedent substantive with which they agree, thus فَآمِنُوا بِٱلنُّورِ ٱلَّذِي أَنْزَلْنَا *so believe the light which We have sent down.* To elucidate this difficult matter we have employed in the first instance two examples which do not display اَلضَّمِيرُ ٱلْعَائِدُ *the pronoun which refers back*, and we now propose showing to what use it serves in (*a*) the nominative case, (*b*) the accusative, and (*c*) the dependent.

(*a*) If a 'â'id stand in the nominative as subject, it is represented (i) in a verbal sentence by the personal pronoun concealed in the verb, thus بَعَثَ مَنْ ضَرَبَهُمْ *he sent him who struck them,* اِتَّبَعُوا ٱلنُّورَ ٱلَّذِي أُنْزِلَ مَعَهُ *they followed the light which has been sent down with him,* أَنْجَيْنَا ٱلَّذِينَ يَنْهَوْنَ عَنِ ٱلسُّوءِ وَأَخَذْنَا ٱلَّذِينَ ظَلَمُوا بِعَذَابٍ بَئِيسٍ *We delivered those who were forbidding the evil and We visited with grievous punishment those who were unjust.* But (ii) in a nominal sentence the 'â'id is expressed by a separate pronoun, as مَا هُوَ طَيِّبٌ *that which is sweet smelling* or *whatever is sweet smelling.* The separate pronoun however (iii) is not required in a nominal sentence when the predicate is an adverb, as ضَرَبْتُ مَنْ هُنَا *I struck the one who is here*; or a preposition with its dependent, as دَرَسُوا مَا فِيهِ *they studied what is in it*, فَأَنْجَيْنَاهُ وَٱلَّذِينَ مَعَهُ فِي ٱلْفُلْكِ *so We saved him and those who were with him in the ark.*

(*b*) If the 'â'id be an objective complement in the accusative, it is appended as suffix to its verb, thus ٱلَّذِي يَجِدُونَهُ *he whom they find*, خُذْ مَا آتَيْنَاهُ لِلنَّبِيِّ *take what we have given to the prophet.* The suffix however is very frequently eliminated, thus مَنْ أَشَآءُ *whom I wish* for مَنْ أَشَآءُهُ *he* (or مَنْ أَشَآءُهُمْ *they*) *whom I wish*, مَا كَانُوا يَعْرِشُونَ *what they were constructing*, ٱللّٰهُ بِمَا تَعْمَلُونَ بَصِيرٌ *God is able to see what ye do.*

(*c*) When in dependent case the 'â'id represents our relative pronouns, standing in cases other than the nominative and accusative. Thus ٱلَّذِينَ أَنْعَمْتَ عَلَيْهِمْ *those upon whom Thou hast shed blessings*, ٱلَّذِي لَهُ مُلْكُ ٱلسَّمٰوَاتِ وَٱلْأَرْضِ *He to Whom belongs the dominion over heaven and earth*, فَلَمَّا نَسُوا مَا ذُكِّرُوا بِهِ *and when they forgot that of which they had been reminded*, مَا هُمْ فِيهِ *that in which they are.* There are occasions on which a 'â'id may be omitted, as for instance when it and the preceding conjunctive pronoun are governed by the same preposition, as عَتَوْا عَمَّا عَتَا *they turned in disdain from that from which he turned in disdain* where عَنْهُ is eliminated; but omission is not permissible if the preposition be used in two senses, or if it follow different verbs, thus فَلَمَّا عَتَوْا عَمَّا نُهُوا عَنْهُ *so when they turned in disdain from that from which they were forbidden.*

Rem. *a.* In theory a 'â'id after اَلَّذِي ought to be of the 3rd person but it is not so always: compare § 573, rem.

Note. In relation to a 'â'id مَهْمَا exactly resembles مَا, thus مَهْمَا تَأْتِنَا بِهِ مِنْ آيَةٍ *whatever thou bringest us of a sign.*

---

576. *Copulative sentences* require وَ or فَ (see § 366) of which the former is used to connect words and clauses as a simple co-ordinative; thus عَزَّرُوهُ وَنَصَرُوهُ *they have helped him and assisted him,* لِيُنْذِرَكُمْ وَلِتَتَّقُوا *in order to warn you and that ye may take heed to yourselves,* سَحَرُوا أَعْيُنَ ٱلنَّاسِ وَٱسْتَرْهَبُوهُمْ *they bewitched men's eyes and terrified them,* غُلِبُوا هُنَالِكَ وَٱنْقَلَبُوا صَاغِرِينَ *they were overcome there and were rendered contemptible.* The particle فَ however sometimes unites single words as is noted in § 540, but more usually it connects two clauses showing either (*a*) that the latter is immediately subsequent to the former in time, or (*b*) that the clauses are linked internally as for instance by cause and effect: thus (*a*) صَوَّرَكُمْ فَأَحْسَنَ صُوَرَكُمْ *He fashioned you, and then He beautified your forms;* أَلْقَى عَصَاهُ فَإِذَا هِيَ ثُعْبَانٌ مُبِينٌ *he threw down his rod, and behold it became a serpent manifest;* اِخْتَارَهُمْ فَلَمَّا أَخَذَتْهُمُ ٱلرَّجْفَةُ قَالَ رَبِّ *he chose them, and when the convulsion seized them, he said, O my Lord;* (*b*) يُحْيِي وَيُمِيتُ فَآمِنُوا بِٱللّٰهِ وَرَسُولِهِ ٱلنَّبِيِّ ٱلْأُمِّيِّ ٱلَّذِي يُؤْمِنُ بِٱللّٰهِ وَكَلِمَاتِهِ وَٱتَّبِعُوهُ (*because*) *He gives life and causes to die, therefore believe God and His apostle, the illiterate prophet, who believes God and His words; also follow him.* When فَ means *because* it is

usual to employ فَإِنَّ, thus اِهْبِطُوا مِصْرًا فَإِنَّ لَكُمْ مَا سَأَلْتُمْ *go down into Egypt for (there) shall ye find what ye ask.* We have seen in §§ 415 *d*, 417 *c* and rem. *c*, that فَ may be used to separate an apodosis from its protasis: after the disjunctive particle أَمَّا (see § 367 *d*) فَ must always introduce the apodosis, thus أَمَّا مَنْ آمَنَ وَعَمِلَ صَالِحًا فَلَهُ جَزَاءً ٱلْحُسْنَى *as to whoso believes and does right, he shall have a most excellent reward.*

577. If a second subject be added to the concealed pronoun which serves as subject to the verb, we must employ a separate personal pronoun in repetition of the latter, thus قُلْنَا يَا آدَمُ ٱسْكُنْ أَنْتَ وَزَوْجُكَ ٱلْجَنَّةَ *We said, O Adam, dwell thou and thy wife in the garden*; but أُسْكُنَا وَزَوْجُكَ is permissible.

578. If after a pronominal suffix expressing the object a substantive be connected by وَ, we may employ a separate personal pronoun in repetition of the suffix, thus أَرْجِهِ هُوَ وَأَخَاهُ *put him off and his brother*; but this is not usual. Also we may write أَرْجِهِ وَأَرْجِ أَخَاهُ; or we may employ إِيَّا (see § 189 *a*) thus أَرْجِ أَخَاهُ وَإِيَّاهُ *put off his brother and him.*

579. We must repeat a preposition, if with its pronominal suffix a substantive is connected by وَ; thus اِغْفِرْ لِي وَلِأَخِي *pardon (the sin) to me and my brother.*

580. When preceded by وَ connecting two nouns, لَا represents all the antecedent negative sentence except that word for which the noun that follows لَا is substituted; thus لَا تَأْخُذُهُ سِنَةٌ وَلَا نَوْمٌ *drowsiness doth not seize Him nor sleep*: here ولا represents ولا تاخذه.

582. The copulative particles are sometimes used in Arabic in place of an English disjunctive or adversative; thus قَالُوا نُؤْمِنُ بِمَا أُنْزِلَ عَلَيْنَا وَيَكْفُرُونَ بِمَا وَرَآءَهُ وَهُوَ ٱلْحَقُّ *they say, We believe what has been sent down to us, and they ignore what (has come) after it, although it is the truth.* We have noted in § 540 the use of فَ between two verbs, the second of which modifies the first.

583. Mention has been made in § 444 *c*, rem. *c* 4, of جُمْلَةٌ حَالِيَّةٌ *a circumstantial clause,* which will commonly be found prefaced by وَاوُ ٱلْحَالِ, i.e. the copulative particle وَ, often meaning *whereas* or *seeing that.* Here وَ serves to connect two clauses the second of which describes the state or condition either of the subject or other part of the first clause, or else of a new subject.

(*a*) The circumstantial clause may be nominal (see § 513) as أَغَيْرَ ٱللّٰهِ أَبْغِيكُمْ إِلٰهًا وَهُوَ فَضَّلَكُمْ عَلَى ٱلْعَالَمِينَ *shall I seek for you a god other than God, whereas He has favoured you above all creatures*: here the second clause refers to الله, and is compound nominal (see § 519) having a finite verb for its predicate.

(*b*) The circumstantial clause may be verbal and affirmative, its verb being in imperfect indicative preceded by وَقَدْ. Without قَدْ we must not employ وَ, and by omission of both we obtain sentences like the examples in § 408 *d* where the second clause is حَالٌ مُقَدَّرٌ *ḥâl indicating the future*; or like those in § 408 *e* whose second clause is حَالٌ مُقَارِنٌ *a contemporaneous state.*

(*c*) The circumstantial clause may be verbal and negative, its verb being in imperfect indicative preceded by وَمَا, or in the jussive preceded by وَلَمْ; thus خَلَقْتُكَ مِنْ قَبْلُ وَلَمْ تَكُ شَيْئًا *I created thee beforehand when thou wast nothing.* If لَا be used, وَ is nearly always omitted, and not seldom in other cases.

(*d*) The circumstantial clause may be verbal and affirmative, its verb being in the perfect usually preceded by وَقَدْ; thus هُوَ عَلَيَّ هَيِّنٌ وَقَدْ خَلَقْتُكَ مِنْ قَبْلُ *it is easy for Me, seeing that I created thee heretofore.*

(*e*) The circumstantial clause may be verbal and negative, its verb being in the perfect preceded by وَمَا, or even by مَا alone: if لَيْسَ be employed it is preceded by وَ, thus لِمَ تَسْأَلُ عَمَّا فِي يَدَيَّ مِنْ أَمْوَالِهِمْ وَلَسْتَ بِوَارِثٍ لَهُمْ *why dost thou enquire concerning what of their property is in my (two) hands, seeing that thou art not heir to them?**

---

584. *Adversative, restrictive* and *exceptive* sentences call for notice; the commonest adversative particles being لَا and لٰكِنْ or لٰكِنَّ.

(*a*) We employ لَا (see § 362 *dd*) in opposition to a preceding affirmative proposition or command; thus قِيلَ لِمُوسَى كَلِيمُ ٱللّٰهِ لَا لِهٰرُونَ *Moses, not Aaron, was called the interlocutor of God.*

(*b*) We use لٰكِنْ and لٰكِنَّ (with or without وَ, see § 362 *ee*) in opposition most frequently to a preceding prohibition or

* This example is taken from line 5 on page 18 of *Chrestomathie élémentaire de l'Arabe littéral avec un glossaire* par Hartwig Derenbourg et Jean Spiro, Paris (Ernest Leroux) 1892; copies of which (second) edition I have placed in the Bodleian, Cambridge University Library, and the British Museum. See also the opening words of Corān ii. 270.

negative statement: لَنْ تَرَانِي وَلٰكِنِ ٱنْظُرْ إِلَى ٱلْجَبَلِ *thou shalt not see Me, but look toward the mountain*; لَيْسَ بِي ضَلَالَةٌ وَلٰكِنِّي رَسُولٌ *there is in me no error, but I am an apostle.*

585. We have mentioned إِنَّمَا at § 436, rem. *d*, this word being most commonly restrictive (see § 362 *n*). It is usually placed at the beginning of a proposition, and that portion of the proposition which it affects must stand at the end; thus إِنَّمَا طَآئِرُهُمْ عِنْدَ ٱللّٰهِ *their luck* (or fate) *is at the disposition of God only*; see § 517 for a restricted incohative.

586. Exception (ٱلِاسْتِثْنَاءُ) is of three kinds; ٱلْمُتَّصِلُ *the joined*, in which ٱلْمُسْتَثْنَى *the thing excepted* is similar in kind to the general term (ٱلْمُسْتَثْنَى مِنْهُ *that from which exception is made*) as لَا إِلٰهَ إِلَّا هُوَ *there is no god except He*; ٱلْمُنْقَطِعُ *the severed*, in which the thing excepted is different in kind from the general term, as مَا قَامَ ٱلْقَوْمُ إِلَّا حِمَارًا *the people did not stand up but an ass*; and ٱلْمُفَرَّغُ *the emptied*, where the general term is not expressed, as مَا تَنْقِمُ مِنَّا إِلَّا ٱلخ *thou dost not resent (any action) on our part except etc.*

(*a*) The commonest of exceptive particles is إِلَّا (see § 367 *f*) in employing which the following rules are observed.

(i) After an affirmative proposition containing the general term, a thing excepted must be in the accusative; thus سَجَدَ ٱلْمَلَائِكَةُ إِلَّا إِبْلِيسَ *the angels prostrated themselves except Eblis.*

(ii) After a negative proposition containing the general term, a thing excepted is best placed in same case with the general term; thus إِنْ هِيَ إِلَّا فِتْنَتُكَ *this is nothing but Thy temptation,* لَا إِلٰهَ إِلَّا ٱللّٰهُ *there is no god but God* (where إِلٰهَ is virtually nominative though grammatically accusative, see § 439).* The same holds with propositions implying a negative, which are usually interrogative (اِسْتِفْهَامٌ إِنْكَارِيٌّ *a negative interrogative*); thus وَمَنْ يَغْفِرُ ٱلْخَطِيئَاتِ إِلَّا ٱللّٰهُ *and who forgives sin except God?* The general term may be a preposition with its dependent, as مَا أَصَابَ مِنْ مُصِيبَةٍ إِلَّا آلخ *no mischance has befallen except etc.* مِنْ مُصِيبَةٍ being equivalent to مُصِيبَةٌ, and the thing excepted follows the general rule in respect of case. When the general term is not expressed, we must give to the thing excepted that case in which the general term should be; thus مَا لَنَا إِلَّا حِطَّةٌ *we have nothing to do but to unload* whence شَيْءٌ is eliminated, لَا يَقُولُونَ عَلَى ٱللّٰهِ إِلَّا ٱلْحَقَّ *they do not say (anything) concerning God except the truth.*

NOTE. Beside nouns, other expressions may follow the exceptive particle such as (i) an adverb, (ii) prepositional phrase, (iii) ḥâl, or (iv) clause known as maçdarîyah. Thus (i) مَا شَجَرَةٌ فِي الجَنَّةِ إِلَّا هُنَا *there is no tree in the garden except here*; (ii) إِلَّا بِإِذْنِ ٱللّٰهِ *except by God's permission*; (iii) إِلَّا نَكِدًا *except scantily*, see § 444 *c*, rem. *f*, Note; and (iv) إِلَّا أَنْ آلخ *except that* etc., see § 448 *c*.

---

* In these two examples the words following the particle of exception stand in the category of بَدَلُ ٱلْبَعْضِ مِنَ ٱلْكُلِّ, see Wright's Grammar, ii. § 139, rem. *b* 2 *b*.

587. We have treated *conditional and hypothetical* sentences in §§ 404 to 406, § 413 and § 417: it must now be explained that the apodosis of a conditional sentence commences with فَ (see § 366 *b*) when the conditional particle (إِنْ, إِذَا, or other) of the protasis cannot exercise any influence upon the apodosis, or is not required to do so.

(*a*) This happens when the apodosis is a nominal sentence; thus مَهْمَا تَأْتِنَا بِهِ مِنْ آيَةٍ فَمَا نَحْنُ لَكَ بِمُؤْمِنِينَ *whatever sign thou bringest us, we do not believe in thee*; مَنْ يُوقَ شُحَّ نَفْسِهِ فَأُولَآئِكَ هُمُ ٱلْمُفْلِحُونَ *whosoever is made to guard against his own covetousness, those are the prosperous.*

(*c*) If the apodosis be a verbal sentence expressing command, prohibition, or desire; thus إِنْ كُنْتَ جِئْتَ بِآيَةٍ فَأْتِ بِهَا *if thou hast brought a sign, produce it.*

(*d*) If the apodosis be a verbal sentence preceded by سَ, سَوْفَ, قَدْ, مَا, لَنْ, or لَيْسَ; thus إِنِ ٱسْتَقَرَّ مَكَانَهُ فَسَوْفَ تَرَانِي *if it stand firm in its place, hereafter thou shalt see Me.*

REM. There are cases when the use of فَ is optional.

588. The hypothetical particle لَوْ implies that what is supposed is, as a matter of fact, not true or at any rate is improbable (see § 404 *a*), whereas إِنْ simply indicates a condition.

590. The affirmative particle لَ (see § 361 *c*) may be prefixed to the apodosis of a hypothetical sentence, thus لَوْ شَآءَ رَبُّكَ لَجَعَلَ ٱلنَّاسَ أُمَّةً وَاحِدَةً *if thy Lord had willed, He would have made (all) mankind one people.*

591. Arabic poetry during the so-called classical period, from about 500 to 750 A.D., always takes the form of short poems, which rarely exceed the length of a hundred and twenty verses. Such poems are named *ḳaṣidaħs* (قَصِيدَةٌ, plur. قَصَائِدُ); whereas a mere fragment, consisting of only a few verses, is termed a *ḳiṭ'aħ* (قِطْعَةٌ, plur. قِطَعٌ, also مُقَطَّعَاتٌ).

REM. Rhyme without metre or measure does not constitute poetry.

592. Each verse or *bayt* (بَيْتٌ, plur. أَبْيَاتٌ) consists of two hemistichs.

593. Rhyme (قَافِيَةٌ) is of two kinds. When the verse ends with a consonant, the rhyme is called *fettered* (مُقَيَّدَةٌ); when it ends with a vowel, *loose* (مُطْلَقَةٌ). According to ancient rule, the two hemistichs of the first verse of a *ḳaṣidaħ* must rhyme with one another, and the same rhyme must be repeated at the end of every verse throughout the whole poem.

594. The essential part of the rhyme is the letter called *al rawi*, الرَّوِيُّ, which remains the same throughout the entire poem.

REM. The letters ا, و, and ي cannot be employed as *rawi* when they are long vowels and in some other cases.

595. The *loose* rhyme (see § 593) terminates in what is called الصِّلَةُ, the *annex* or *appendix* to the *rawi*. The *ṣilaħ* may be either one of the long vowels ـَا, ـِي, ـُو, or the letter ه preceded by one of the short vowels (ـَهْ, ـِهْ, ـُهْ).

Rem. *a.* The final vowel of a verse is always long, because it is regarded as being followed by the homogeneous letter of prolongation (see § 6), whether this latter be written or not. The vowel-letter ا is invariably expressed, but و and ي are often omitted, *e.g.* وَيَدِ for وَيَدِي *and my hand,* صَنَعُ for صَنَعُو or صَنَعُوا *they made.*

598. The last two *quiescent* (§ 9, rem. *a*) letters of a verse form the limits between which is comprised the rhyme. Hence the Arab grammarians distinguish five varieties of rhyme, according to the number of *moving* (§ 4, rem. *b*) letters which come between the two *quiescents.*

600. Every verse in Arabic poetry consists of a certain number of *feet*, and a certain collocation of feet constitutes a *metre* (بَحْرٌ, plural أَبْحُرٌ).

601. The metres are ordinarily reckoned to be sixteen in number.

Note. The following sections include only those metres of which examples occur in Wright's *Arabic Reading-Book.*

603. Of the iambic metres we shall mention the *rajaz*, *kâmil*, and *wâfir*.

604. It is a peculiarity of *rajaz* (اَلرَّجَزُ *the trembling*) that each hemistich usually forms, as it were, an independent verse and rhymes with the preceding one.

Trimeter acatalectic

⏒ – ⏑ – | ⏒ – ⏑ – | ⏒ – ⏑ –
⏓ ⏑ ⏑ – | ⏓ ⏑ ⏑ – | ⏓ ⏑ ⏑ –

Trimeter catalectic

⏒ – ⏑ – | ⏒ – ⏑ – | ⏒ – –
⏓ ⏑ ⏑ – | ⏓ ⏑ ⏑ – | ⏒ – –

606. The *kâmil* (اَلْكَامِلُ *the perfect*) is either dimeter or trimeter.

Trimeter acatalectic

⏖ – ⏑ – | ⏖ – ⏑ – | ⏖ – ⏑ – || ⏖ – ⏑ – | ⏖ – ⏑ – | ⏖ – ⏑ –

Trimeter catalectic

⏖ – ⏑ – | ⏖ – ⏑ – | ⏖ – ⏑ – || ⏖ – ⏑ – | ⏖ – ⏑ – | ⏖ – –

Dimeter acatalectic

⏖ – ⏑ – | ⏖ – ⏑ – || ⏖ – ⏑ – | ⏖ – ⏑ –

This last variety is sometimes lengthened by the addition of a syllable

⏖ – ⏑ – | ⏖ – ⏑ – || ⏖ – ⏑ – | ⏖ – ⏑ – | –

in which case it is said to be مُرَفَّلٌ *having a train.*

607. The basis of the *wâfir* (اَلْوَافِرُ *the exuberant*) is the same as that of the *kâmil*, but with the order of the component parts reversed, ⏑ – ⏖ –.

Trimeter

⏑ – ⏖ – | ⏑ – ⏖ – | ⏑ – – || ⏑ – ⏖ – | ⏑ – ⏖ – | ⏑ – –

609. Of the amphibrachic metres we shall mention the *mutakârib* and *ṭawîl.*

610. The basis of the *mutakârib* (اَلْمُتَقَارِبُ *the tripping*) is ⏑ – ⏑ (amphibrachys), for which may be substituted [illegible]

Tetrameter catalectic

⏑ – ⏑ | ⏑ [illegible]

611. The *ṭawíl* (اَلطَّوِيلُ *the long*) is one of the finest, as well as the most common, of the Arabic metres.

Acatalectic

⏑ – ⏒ | ⏑ – ⏓ – | ⏑ – ⏒ | ⏑ – ⏑ – ‖ ⏑ – ⏒ | ⏑ – ⏓ – | ⏑ – ⏒ | ⏑ – ⏑ –

The last foot of the second ḥemistich may be changed into ⏑ – – –.

Catalectic

⏑ – ⏒ | ⏑ – ⏓ – | ⏑ – ⏒ | ⏑ – ⏑ – ‖ ⏑ – ⏒ | ⏑ – ⏓ – | ⏑ – ⏒ | ⏑ – –

613. Of the anapaestic metres we shall mention the *basíṭ* and *munsariḥ*.

615. The *basíṭ* (اَلْبَسِيطُ *the outspread*) is a favourite metre with the older poets.

Tetrameter

⏒ – ⏑ – | ⏓ ⏑ – | ⏓ – ⏑ – | ⏑ ⏑ – ‖ ⏒ – ⏑ – | ⏓ ⏑ – | ⏓ – ⏑ – | ⏔ –

616. The *munsariḥ* (اَلْمُنْسَرِحُ *the flowing*) has the same base as the *basíṭ*, but the first ⏑ ⏑ – is reduced to a single long syllable.

Tetrameter

<table>
<tr><td>⏒ – ⏑ –
⏓ ⏑ ⏑ –</td><td>–</td><td>⏒ – ⏑ –</td><td>⏑ ⏑ –</td><td>‖</td><td>⏒ – ⏑ –
⏓ ⏑ ⏑ –</td><td>–</td><td>⏒ – ⏑ –</td><td>⏔ –</td></tr>
</table>

618. Of the ionic metres we shall mention the *ramal*, *madíd*, and *khafíf*.

619. The *ramal* (اَلرَّمَلُ *the running*) has for its base ⏑ ⏑ – – (ionicus a minore).

Trimeter catalectic

⏓ ⏑ – – | ⏓ ⏑ – – | ⏓ ⏑ – ‖ ⏓ ⏑ – – | ⏓ ⏑ – – | ⏓ ⏑ – –
⏓ ⏑ –

620. The *madíd* (ٱلْمَدِيدُ *the extended*) may be either acatalectic, as

⏓ ⏑ – – | ⏓ ⏑ – | ⏓ ⏑ – – ‖ ⏓ ⏑ – – | ⏓ ⏑ – | ⏓ ⏑ – –

or catalectic, as

⏓ ⏑ – – | ⏓ ⏑ – | ⏓ ⏑ – ‖ ⏓ ⏑ – – | ⏓ ⏑ – | ⏑ ⏑ –

621. The *khafíf* (ٱلْخَفِيفُ *the light* or *nimble*) is one of the more usual metres.

Trimeter acatalectic

⏓ ⏑ – – | ⏓ – ⏑ – | ⏓ ⏑ – – ‖ ⏓ ⏑ – – | ⏑ – ⏑ – | ⏓ ⏑ – –

Trimeter catalectic

⏓ ⏑ – – | ⏓ – ⏑ – | ⏓ ⏑ – – ‖ ⏓ ⏑ – – | ⏓ – ⏑ – | ⏓ ⏑ – –
⏓ ⏑ –

623. Something must now be said concerning the forms which the final syllables of words assume at the end of a verse.

624. Final short vowels are either dropped or retained as long (see § 595, rem. *a*), the tanwín of the noun disappearing at the same time; e.g. فَإِنَّ عُقُوقَ ٱلْوَالِدَاتِ كَبِيرْ *for verily disobedience to mothers is* (a) *great* (sin), for كَبِيرٌ; خَلِيلُكَ مِنْ مُرَادِ *thy friend of* (the tribe) *Murád*, for مُرَادٍ. In this case final fathah is always accompanied by an 'alif, as وَمَا يُغْنِي ٱلتَّمِيمَاتُ ٱلْحِمَامَا *and amulets do not avail against death*, for ٱلْحِمَامَ

625. The accusative termination اً generally becomes ـَا, though it occasionally disappears altogether.

626. The feminine terminations ـَةٌ, ـَةٍ, and ـَةً become ـَهْ, more rarely ـَتْ; likewise ـَةُ and ـَةَ, whether masculine or feminine.

627. Nouns ending in ـًى or ـًا simply drop the tanwîn; thus فَتًى *a youth* becomes فَتَى or فَتَا, and عَصًا *a staff* عَصَا. Those ending in ـٍ drop the tanwîn and either resume the third radical or not, at pleasure; e.g. قَاضٍ *a judge* may become either قَاضْ or قَاضِي.

628. The long vowels ـَا, ـِي, and ـُو usually remain unchanged.

Rem. *b.* The genitive and accusative suffixes of the first personal pronoun, ـِي and نِي, have several pausal forms, namely ـِيَهْ, ـِيَا, نِيَهْ, نِيَا.

Rem. *c.* In rhyme the long vowels ـِي and ـُو are often expressed merely by kasraĥ and ḍammaĥ.

629. When the penultimate letter of a word bears sukûn, the vowel of the final letter may be transferred to it in rhyme, e.g. اَلصَّدِرْ for اَلصَّدْرِ.

Rem. *a.* This transference (نَقْلٌ) is not allowed when it would give rise to a form which has no example in the language.

630. Indeclinable words ending in a vowel when used as

rhymes take a final ه, which is technically called هَاءُ ٱلْوَقْفِ *the hâ of pause* or هَاءُ ٱلسَّكْتِ *the hâ of silence*; thus كَيْفَ *how* becomes كَيْفَهْ. The same letter is added to some verbal and pronominal forms (see § 628, rem. *b*).

The concluding sections (232—253) of Wright's Grammar illustrate the principal poetic licenses which affect the form of words used in verse. This subject does not fall within the scope of an elementary work; moreover, the slight changes which custom permits are seldom of such a nature as to cause any difficulty to the student.